The Art of Prophesying

The Art of Prophesying

*New England Sermons
and the Shaping of Belief*

TERESA TOULOUSE

The University of Georgia Press
Athens and London

© 1987 by the University of Georgia Press
Athens, Georgia 30602
All rights reserved

Designed by Sandra Strother Hudson
Set in 10 on 13 Linotron 202 Plantin

The paper in this book meets the guidelines for
permanence and durability of the Committee on
Production Guidelines for Book Longevity of the
Council on Library Resources.

Printed in the United States of America

91 90 89 88 87   5 4 3 2 1

Library of Congress Cataloging in Publication Data

Toulouse, Teresa.
    The art of prophesying.

    Includes index.
    1. Preaching—New England—
History. 2. Clergy—New England. 3. New
England—Religious life and customs. 4. Cotton,
John, 1584-1652. 5. Colman, Benjamin,
1673-1747. 6. Channing, William Ellery,
1780-1842. 7. Emerson, Ralph Waldo, 1803-1882.
I. Title.
BV4208.U6T68 1987   251'.00974   86-7121
ISBN 0-8203-0892-7 (alk. paper)

This publication has been supported by the National Endowment for the Humanities, a federal agency which supports the study of such fields as history, philosophy, literature, and languages.

to my father
to the memory of my mother and Fr. Mike
and to Betsy, Dom, Mike, and Pat

Contents

Acknowledgments

IN the early 1970s, David Young and Lawrence Buell introduced me to the astonishing aesthetic and historical complications of form. From the inception of this study to its completion, Buell has continued to be an incisive and demanding reader of my work. Among my later teachers, Joel Porte and Warner Berthoff contributed substantially to my understanding of American texts. Alan Heimert taught me that Puritanism's most inner workings were social as well as personal. He initiated my exploration of a Puritan rhetoric of the "ear." Current and former colleagues at Tulane read my chapters and not only improved my style, but also honed my thinking. I particularly thank Michael Boardman, Purvis Boyette, Jim Catano, Earl Harbert, Michael Kreyling, Marvin Morillo, Les Perelman, Donald Pizer, J. L. Simmons, and Harold Weber. Maaja Stewart read the manuscript in all its states, giving me concrete encouragement when I needed it most. Two summer grants from the Tulane Committee on Research provided the time to write at especially critical moments. At the Newberry Library, John Aubrey and Paul Gehl helped me to grapple with interdisciplinary inquiry and Mary Beth Rose taught me rigor. I thank the Exxon Education Foundation for the support that enabled me to work at the Newberry. In this context, I also acknowledge the National Endowment for the Humanities, which awarded this study a publication subsidy. At dark periods in my writing and revising, earlier portions of the first two chapters of this book received the 1984 and 1985 Richard Beale Davis Prize from *Early American Literature*. I thank Everett Emerson and the Davis Prize judges for helping to renew my faith and my energy. I also thank *Early American Literature* for permission to reprint parts of these essays. I further acknowledge the Ralph Waldo Emerson

Memorial Association and the Houghton Library, Harvard University, for their permission to quote from an Emerson manuscript sermon. At this point, it is also fit to acknowledge the practical time and care expended by the librarians and staff of the Tulane University Library, the Newberry Library, the Houghton Library, and the Massachusetts Historical Society. I also thank Malcolm Call, Karen Orchard, and Debbie Winter of the University of Georgia Press. Rick Hermann made a difficult task far smoother.

The support of many good friends sustained me through the long writing of this study. For all their help, intellectual and otherwise, my thanks to Bill and Ann Craft, Andrew Delbanco, Denise Dorsey, Deborah Drattell, Eugenia Delamotte, Judy Ecklund, Barbara Ewell, Jerry Speir, Tricia Hill, John Klause, Dennis Marnon, Steve Nelson, Tim Pace, Mary Poovey, Richard Teichgraber, Alice Voros and Adele Wick. Throughout the course of my writing, Michael Zimmerman, philosopher and friend, taught me something about the meaning of free grace. The dedication attests to my first and greatest debt.

Introduction

THE TITLE of this study, *The Art of Prophesying*, suggests both a project and a problem for the four New England preachers who are its subject. Drawn from William Perkins's influential seventeenth-century preaching manual of the same name, the title demands its own explication. When it is "opened" in the manner of a Puritan approaching a scriptural text, the "art of prophesying" reveals a paradox. How can "prophesying," the inspired act of speaking forth the Spirit, be yoked to an "art," a contrived structure which, in the case of preaching, seems consciously directed towards teaching and persuading an audience? "Faith," says the Apostle, "comes through hearing." Yet to what degree is it the inspiration of the prophet that touches the ears and hearts of his listeners? And to what degree is it his manner, his "art" in presenting this faith, that is important? How can he ideally balance "prophesying" and "art"? Finally, if he stresses one mode of expressing the truth of faith over another, what does his choice indicate about his vision of his audience and its needs?

The project for each of the preachers considered here is to blend his art with his prophecy; the problem each confronts is finding the theory and developing the practice by which he could do so. In the process of so conceiving and so patterning the connections between the two terms, each man also, whether consciously or unconsciously, offers an image of the audience for whom he preaches. For both alone and in relation to each other, "art" and "prophesying" imply not only a speaker but his hearers as well. The purpose of the following study is to trace the interrelations among ideas of faith, their presentation, and their audiences, and to suggest possible cultural implications of these interrelations.

I

To set the stage for such a discussion, one must place it in the broader context of Protestant theories about scriptural interpretation. The question of the "true" connection between Spirit and external form lies at the heart of Protestant thought. Since the Reformation, Protestants of varying sects were clearly caught between worlds in their view of the biblical word. Protestantism became known as the religion of the Book, *sola Scriptura* its major dictum. Rather than relying on the church as the interpreter of Scripture, Calvin insisted on the self-authenticating nature of the Bible. If the Spirit was its own interpreter, it followed that the person touched by the Spirit, the individual elect soul, was now free of the church's interpretive mediation. The door to private interpretation had been opened: "Let it be interpreted then as an undeniable truth that they who have been inwardly taught by the Spirit feel an entire acquiescence in the Scripture, and that it is self-authenticating, carrying with it its own evidence, and ought not to be made the subject of demonstration and argument from reason."[1] Those who have been "inwardly taught," Calvin's statement implies, "acquiesce" to Scripture because the Spirit has touched them, not because Scripture's arguments have been rationally proved. Such interpretation, then, is linked not to one's "rational" abilities, but to the interpreter's experience of an intense spiritual awareness during which he or she becomes assured that God has granted not only forgiveness of sins but certitude of salvation. Such a person has been chosen by God. While these illuminating moments were to come and go, such people, from the instant of their first experience of grace in their lives, could consider themselves "visible saints" whose "inward acquiescence" to Scripture would somehow differ from the response of those who were not professed elect.[2]

But Calvin and his followers obviously had no desire that such individual experience of the Word should lead to antinomian disorder. They also believed that the Bible contains a clear, interpretable truth offered to humankind in general as well as a special spiritual knowledge available only to the elect. Anyone, even "those of the weakest capacity," can learn the historical and moral information offered by Scripture, "provided they are of a submissive and teachable disposition, and bring with them an earnest desire to be instructed." The Bible, for Calvin, thus contained a knowledge that has been called "objective and informational" as well as a knowledge reserved for the elect.[3] Acts of biblical interpretation have not only an individual, but also a social, dimension. The Bible offers an external moral knowledge interpretable and comprehensible even by those without an elect status.

This double vision of the Scripture—as a special and continual revelation to the chosen and as the source of moral law for everyone—was to have its effect not on theories of biblical interpretation alone, but also on notions of how scriptural truths were to be presented to an audience. For, as the seventeenth-century New England preacher John Cotton argued, the reading of Scripture was not the only part of God's worship; it must also include the "preaching, explaining and applying of the Word: the text being the same for Substance with the Exposition."[4] The preaching of the elect preacher, his explanation or "opening" of the Scripture, expressed in its own manner the divine text's very "substance." As such, however, the preacher's exegesis was subject to the same difficulties as the "text" it proposed to interpret. If Scripture somehow met the needs of both elect individuals and those who were unsure and even possibly reprobate, so must his preaching. In short, the preacher was faced with the task of bridging the gap between piety—that mysterious and overwhelming sense of ecstatic union with a transcendent Whole—and everyday concerns about moral judgment and moral conduct in the world.

The Antinomian Controversy in New England (1636–38) is only one famous example of a conflict that arose precisely over the relation that elect "piety" was or was not to bear to moral conduct. Anne Hutchinson and her brother-in-law John Wheelwright accused most of the ministers in the Boston community—with the exception of John Cotton—of putting too much weight on morality in their preaching. A corollary to their spoken accusation is the unspoken one: these preachers did not deal with the more spiritual needs of elect souls. Ministers such as Thomas Hooker, Thomas Shepard, and Peter Bulkeley were viewed as preaching a "covenant of works" rather than a "covenant of grace"; they were encouraging their people to believe that fulfilling certain moral conditions or following certain prescribed steps could either serve as an indication of their election or at least help "prepare" them to receive assurance if God had decided to grant it. But in establishing even possible conditions for election, the Antinomians argued, these ministers were relying on human reason, not on the mysterious workings of God's inscrutable will. Both Hutchinson and Cotton, at least initially, contested the rationalist leanings of those who came to be called "preparationists" on the orthodox grounds of High Calvinist doctrine, which very clearly argues that no human action, no "work," can serve as an efficient cause of election.

Midway through this controversy, however, Cotton began to recognize that Hutchinson's interpretation of the nature of piety and of the doctrine of election not only involved a repudiation of "works" but also approached a denial of the validity of Scripture.[5] Scripture, for Hutchinson, would be replaced by the Holy Spirit's direct revelation to the elect soul. She asserts at her trial that she has been taught by "an immediate voice," "by the voice of His own Spirit to my soul."[6] A horrified Cotton accuses her of having "no Scripture" to prove her claims, and warns the women of his church who had been influenced by her "to take heed that you receive nothynge for Truth which hath not the stamp of the Word of God from it."[7] In repudiating Scripture and the elect ministers who were its most fit expositors, Hutchinson has proved a "gangrene" and a "leprosie" both to the community and to many a "poore soule."[8] At this point, Cotton turns against his ardent follower and sanctions her expulsion from the community. By denying that the "letter" of the Word bears any relation to the Spirit, she has subverted the soul's ability to acquiesce to the Spirit's moving within Scripture and within elect preaching.

Three interrelated issues clustering around this controversy become problematic for preachers far beyond Cotton's generation. Most broadly, the conflict points up the difficulty of integrating the individual elect soul's beliefs with those of the community. How can the experience of inspired assurance, which is the value at the heart of Calvinist thinking, coexist comfortably with the community's needs for coherence, stability, and a social order based on a reading and hearing of the "letter" of Scripture? What is the least fragmenting relationship one can posit between the double desire for piety and a moral system? Finally, and most importantly for the study that follows, the Antinomian Controversy raises the issue not only of how Scripture is to be interpreted but also of how it is to be presented, preached to an audience in a form that acknowledges its status both as a code for moral belief and behavior and as the occasion for the continually deepening and transforming revelation of God's Spirit to the truly elect.

PERRY MILLER has traced both the nature and effects of the rationalistic and the pietistic strains in Puritan thinking about the Bible. He too was concerned with probing how the two strains could be integrated within Puritan notions of individual and community needs. He was also willing to admit that such notions are shaped in the forms of Puritan expression: "The manner incarnated the thought; it reflected the spirit of the thinkers: the technique as well as the content of the writings exhibited the combination of deep religious passion and severe intellectual discipline which is the supreme characteristic of Puritanism."[9] In spite of such an acknowledgement, however, Miller was unwilling to "discuss Puritan writings as part of literary history" or to evaluate them from any formal point of view. He preferred to focus on the Puritan concern with making logical propositions in a plain style which would touch the understanding of the entire community—and stopped there, arguing either that "aesthetics" were of no interest to the Puritans, given their task of forming a community, or that what aesthetic they possessed was a fairly threadbare derivation of European models. Later scholars have argued that in downplaying the role of aesthetics in Puritan life, Miller not only ignored the importance of the emotional side of Puritanism, its "stretched passion," but also discounted the historical and literary insights made available by studying the Puritans from this perspective.[10]

For example, although indebted to many of Miller's suggestions, scholars such as Charles Feidelson, Larzer Ziff, Norman Grabo, and Sacvan Bercovitch have not merely examined the intellectual content of Puritan writing, but have traced the ways in which their deep religious feelings became embodied in characteristic "symbolic forms."[11] A concern with the shaping of belief and the relationship this shaping bears to an audience has begun to supercede the search for a "true" interpretation of a text's "meanings."

While Feidelson, with his New Critical concerns, was not interested in analyzing the specific historical contexts in which the interest in typology took shape, he nonetheless opened a door to such study when he considered the Puritan roots of nineteenth-century theories of symbolism. Emerson and his contemporaries, he argued, used a method of viewing the relation of the outer to the spiritual world that was a secular version of the typology used by their ancestors.[12] Bercovitch, Ziff, and Grabo have been more historical in orientation, examining both the traditions out of which the Puritan aesthetic grew—the meditation tradition and theories of medieval and Renaissance scriptural exegesis, for example—and how these traditions took a similar or different, not necessarily threadbare, shape in

Puritan forms of expression. All three men argue that the knowledge derived from such study does not contribute merely to a theory about Puritan aesthetics; a study of symbolic forms can also add to an understanding of the ways in which a community structured its self-conception.

Like Feidelson, Bercovitch wishes to explore "the development of a distinctive symbolic mode"—the typological. Unlike Feidelson, however, he particularly relates this mode to a myth of America and the American character. Puritan writers, he argues, used their reading of the biblical types and the jeremiad (as the larger frame in which their "readings" were publicly displayed) to create and expand the myth of what they called the "One Man with one soul in one body."[13] This myth allowed its adherents to view individual and communal acts in light of a divinely ordained "mission" in which public and private characters and events were inextricably linked. More importantly, it also provided a means of understanding moments of personal or social crisis in light of a belief in the ultimate predestined victory of this mission. Typology for Bercovitch, then, is not of value only as an aesthetic mode of perception; its development, use, and transformation also have important social and cultural implications.

Larzer Ziff takes the question of understanding Puritan uses of particular forms in a direction other than the mythic. Arguing for the prevalence of an "antinomian" cast to Puritan thought in the seventeenth century, he explores how this theory is borne out in Puritan attitudes towards preaching and audience.[14] He compares sermons written by a royalist preacher, Andrew Wright, in both Anglican and Independent styles. According to Ziff, the Anglican preacher minutely (and often wittily) analyzes the individual words and syntax of his scriptural text. Once the meanings of the text have been displayed, the sermon is completed. The style and means of presenting this analysis differ in light of the preacher's awareness of his audience's capacities: different audiences require different kinds of sermons. Puritan sermons, written in a "plain" style, differ from such Anglican efforts "not because they are plain in the sense of having no conceits . . . but because in their steady movement from doctrine to reason to uses back to another . . . , a sense of the concrete behind the word emerges, a sense that the words themselves are artificial vehicles but that the truth they are intended to carry is absolute and independent of them."[15] The Puritan preacher, in short, does not concentrate on the meanings of individual words, but on attempting to impart the divine message imperfectly manifested through them. His sermon form, moreover, is never relative; all the members of any audience are directed towards the same elusive truths in the same manner. Ziff concludes that the "antinomian" impulse implied in this theory of the sermon and its listeners casts light on the sources of a unique American aesthetic that is specifically involved with the interrelation of piety, "plain" style, and allegory.

In the following discussion, I focus on issues laid out by Bercovitch and others—the relation of the individual to the community, of piety to morality, of faith to works—but examine them within the context sketched by Ziff: the structure of particular New England sermons and the audience whose needs are expressed and shaped in this structure. Like Bercovitch, I am concerned with the cultural implications behind the theory and use of certain religious modes of discourse, but my emphasis is more formal than explicitly mythic and symbolic. Like Ziff, I am interested in the structure of Puritan sermons, but my interest is less in a unified aesthetic impulse operative in these forms than in their possible disjunctions and discontinuities. I am concerned with the way in which sermon form can be used as a means not only of expressing, but also of shaping and possibly reconciling, interlinked religious and social assumptions.

Ziff, for example, postulates an antinomian impulse behind the Puritan form; I would suggest, rather, that such is only one of the impulses operating within it. William Perkins's *Arte of Prophesying* reveals that its author wished to develop a sermon structure that attempted to hold Spirit and Word together. He desired to combine a belief in Puritan piety, in inspiration by the Spirit, with a belief that the law must still be followed and that adhering to it involved voluntary, responsible human action by an entire community. In this case, rather than postulating one audience for the Puritan sermon, as Ziff does, I would argue that Perkins's stress on a mysterious, God-given assurance and an equally necessary moral behavior causes him to imply the existence of at least two kinds of listeners—the elect and those who for whatever reasons remain unassured. Perkins, a prominent Puritan theologian as well as a writer of sermon manuals, thus believed that even the Puritan preacher addressed a variety of needs within the sermon and had to structure it accordingly.

The major concern of this study is to explore how the structure of the New England Puritan sermon, and of sermons written in this loosely defined Puritan tradition, provides an important means of expressing and shaping assumptions about the interplay of belief and believers at particular historical moments in New England. By structure, I refer most broadly not only to arguments which occur or recur in sermons, but also to methods whereby these arguments are juxtaposed, to the particular language—ornate, plain, mixed—used within these varying juxtapositions, and to the kind of progressive movement or lack of it that occurs within the sermon as a whole.

Such a study rests on the belief that sermon structures do not merely frame the "content" of faith, but can also be used to reconstruct the preacher's sense of his role, his attitudes towards his listeners, and wider cultural assumptions underlying these attitudes. Thus, when I use the term "audience," I am, like Ziff, not necessarily referring to a preacher's "real" audience. While at points I certainly refer to the actual hearers of varying preachers, my emphasis falls on the image of their hearers that is revealed in their distinctive uses of the sermon.

To analyze these relationships, I employ several overlapping approaches. Although the order of consideration varies, each chapter explores an individual preacher's conception of faith and then, depending on its relative importance, the preaching model that each used to express this conception to an audience. A preacher's degree of commitment to set homiletic models usually determines the direction of my analysis, but I have also felt free to consider other, less direct influences on his notions of form. A further step, of course, involves examining how these models are used, changed, or dismissed within each preacher's specific practice. This analysis helps to clarify the question discussed directly and indirectly in each section: What image of audience emerges from the theories and practices whereby these preachers attempt to structure an "appropriate" conception of faith?

Obviously, the notion of what the form of a sermon should be and the relation that this form might bear to belief and to audience differ for each preacher. What is clear in each case explored here, however, is that ideas about what properly constituted "faith" led to reactions, sometimes blatant, sometimes very subtle, against one manner of presentation in favor of another and, in the process, came to privilege one conception of audience over another. The relations posited between Spirit and law, faith and works, piety and morality, or (in Cotton's and Hutchinson's terms) justification and sanctification not only reveal an image of this audience; in the process they also uncover attitudes about the relation of personal belief to the standards of the community. If the community's vision informs these texts—the ministers are, after all, its spokesmen—the sermon also provides a means not simply of expressing, but also of forming and controlling, this vision. The resulting interplay implicit in the sermon's structure may thus seem balanced, but the attitudes informing it often prove contradictory. The structure of sermons, then, reveals fluid rather than static balances; it manifests the attempts made to unify response against the doubts, uncertainties, and countervailing beliefs and desires that pull against and undermine these attempts. An examination of the structuring of sermons provides, in short, another means of gauging how a culture maintains a sense of its continuity as it incorporates into its patterns the fact of change.

Given the obvious limitations of a single book for exploring such a complex set of relations, I cannot offer an account of all the possible connections among religious controversies, preaching manuals, and the audiences of New England preachers from one century or one sect to the next. From a myriad of figures I have chosen four Boston ministers: John Cotton (1584–1652), Benjamin Colman (1673–1747), William Ellery Channing (1780–1842), and Ralph Waldo Emerson (1803–1882). Historically, each of these preachers emerges from the Puritan sermon tradition, with its rigorous intellectual concern for shaping both the rational and emotional aspects of religious experience. That American Congregationalism and the Unitarianism arising in reaction to it provided the seedbed for the mid-nineteenth century flowering of religious, literary, and social theory in New England by now needs no proof. Scholars have long argued the usefulness of this tradition to the literary and intellectual historian both because of the contained quality of its cultural assumptions and because of its immense national effects up to and beyond the Civil War.

I am drawn to these four figures, however, by more than the simple fact of their place in a broader configuration of New England culture. Whereas each of them has been studied as a so-called transitional figure whose thought expressed the movement from one conception of self and community to another, the significance of the manner in which each shaped this transition in his sermons has rarely been recognized. This neglect is surprising since each man, at some point in his career, became directly involved with the question of how the "proper" relation of religious feeling to moral conduct should be expressed in the sermon form. John Cotton's preaching, for example, embroiled him in the Antinomian Controversy, yet little analysis has been done of how his problematic beliefs and his image of his audience were shaped in his theories about preaching and in his sermonic practice. The sermons of Increase and Cotton Mather and Jonathan Edwards have received a good deal of critical attention; far less has been granted those of Benjamin Colman, the popular preacher of Brattle Street, who engaged in a controversy with Increase and Cotton Mather that was centrally concerned with the forms of church practice. William Ellery Channing has been studied for the philosophical and social importance of his sermons' content, but the underlying formal assumptions of his debates with the Trinitarians and their relation not only to his preaching practice, but also to his attitudes towards an audience, have never been adequately examined. Ralph Waldo Emerson, of course, began his public life as a minister. When he left the ministry, he was attacked as much for his manner of speaking as for the content of his addresses. But, again, outside of the limited consideration of one or two sermons, little sustained attention has been given to the notions of faith and audience that inform Emerson's use of the sermon. Without such an understanding, I would argue, we cannot fully account either for Emerson's developing formal theory or for his assumptions about the personal and communal dimensions of response.

If no extended commentary has been written about the significance of the sermon structure to these individual preachers, neither has any theory been advanced concerning the retention or transformation of the sermon structure over time. The point of this study is by no means to explain such tendencies by a theory of "influence." It is rather to argue that sermon structure played a central role in both expressing and shaping the needs of New England audiences and that changes in this structure did not occur in cultural isolation. If, for example, Benjamin Colman can be viewed as reacting to problems encountered in earlier sermons such as those of John Cotton, he can also be even more directly linked to a figure far later in time—William Ellery Channing. Both preachers, I argue, return to more "classical," less Calvinistic notions of sermon structure. The young Emerson, despite his apparent break with the Unitarians, not only reveals his debt to them in his preaching but also, by a curious turn of structure, manifests important similarities with John Cotton. Thus, while it is important to consider each figure in his own context, such consideration should not inhibit the desire to suggest their interrelations.

This said, however, the point must be reiterated that such suggestions must grow out of a close study of sermon structure; they must not be imposed from above. What makes each preacher interesting for my purposes is the extent to which his sermon structure can be used to examine the gradual transformations and tensions in his thought that made it transitional. I ask to what degree the very shaping of his sermons projects an attitude towards his own role and that of his audience that is somehow double, simultaneously looking back to earlier projections and forward to new ones. How did ministers who felt uncertain, especially about the relation of piety and morality (with its inextricable link to the issue of individual and communal rights), express their confusions and their attempts to reconcile or even repress them in the structure as well as the content of their sermons?

In the terms of this study, then, neither the assumption about a unified audience at which each of these preachers arrived nor their similar assumption that an ideal structure existed that could generate such an image proves as important as the shifting drama implicit in the movement from argument to argument and from image to image within the containing patterns of the sermon. Responses to the so-called movement towards secularization, the replacement of religious forms with the forms of literature, and, even more broadly, the movement from an initially unified idea of community to one which becomes increasingly fragmented are displayed in the very texture of these men's writings. Indeed, the central myths which can be derived from Puritan sources have perhaps been largely described. What is examined here is not these myths but the process of arriving at them, the ways in which the sermon form holds old assumptions and new desires together in one form, until an Emerson breaks through this form altogether, consciously chooses a new one, and in the process attempts to project a new audience and to shape a new series of assumptions about it.

As Stephen Greenblatt and Clifford Geertz have recently suggested, the purpose of a study like this one cannot be to uncover some final "explanation" of all these phenomena—these conceptions of faith, these theories and practices of preaching and audience, these relations of "art" to "prophecy."[16] What remains important is that over time, in New England, in very different situations, preachers believed the interrelations among faith and works, piety and morality, and individual and community to be intimately tied to their public presentation to an audience. I offer an exploratory interpretation, not a conclusive statement. I suggest that in our separate concerns for each one of these categories we have neglected the possibility of their conscious and unconscious interaction, that matters of belief and social attitudes should not be separated from questions of their presentation and actual structuring within the sermon form. I would further suggest that such an approach need not be limited to the sermon. Indeed, study of this genre suggests the need for a new exploration of its interplay with other genres such as the lyric and the romance. Finally, I would argue that such study cannot and must not remain purely descriptive. Questions about sermon structure and historical debates about its shaping of piety and morality for whatever audiences must be turned outward to the far broader issue, only implied in this study, of how a culture, for better or worse, provides a "set of control mechanisms—plans, recipes, rules, instructions—for the governing of behavior."[17]

1. John Cotton
and the Shaping of Election

S TUDIES OF John Cotton invariably turn to that incident at St. Marie's Church in Cambridge where he disappointed the students who had packed the church to hear this witty preacher, renowned for his metaphysical style. On this occasion Cotton simply and in unadorned fashion "opened" his scriptural text into a numbered series of doctrines, reasons, and uses. The students apparently pulled their hats down over their ears in disapprobation, but, notes Cotton's grandson, Cotton Mather with some smugness, the great John Preston attended that same sermon and was converted by it.[1]

Modern critics, faced with thousands of pages of Puritan sermons that seem to follow an endlessly repetitive pattern from firstly to fourthly, fifthly, and even beyond have their own difficulties understanding Cotton's popularity both in Boston, Lincolnshire, and in Boston, Massachusetts. Cotton's colleague John Wilson in the American Boston was reported to have exclaimed, "Mr. Cotton preaches with such authority, demonstration, and life that, methinks, when he preaches out of any prophet or apostle I hear not him; I hear that very prophet and apostle. Yea, I hear the Lord Jesus Christ speaking in my heart."[2] In 1633, after Cotton's arrival in New England, reports John Winthrop, more people joined the Boston church than in the previous three years. Evidently, the Lord gave "special testimony of his presence" in the Church of Boston after Cotton was called to office there; indeed, claims Winthrop, the "Lord gave wittness to the exercise of prophecy."[3] If Cotton precipitated a minor revival, he also, to

13

his own great confusion and consternation, precipitated the Antinomian Controversy.

Given their appraisal of Cotton's sermons, however, historians have found it difficult to account for Cotton's clear popularity. Listening to Cotton's scrupulously logical exegetical method and his careful opening of every facet of a text could hardly have been as exciting as listening to Thomas Hooker—that "Sonne of Thunder"—exhort, threaten, or cajole them within the "uses."[4] Cotton, in contrast, shows very little interest in applying the doctrines he so carefully opens. One study confesses, "Why we have no really practical works by John Cotton is difficult to explain."[5] If practical application is not at the center of Cotton's sermons, and if he follows his model so rigidly, the question seems to be, how could he be so popular? There is an obvious distance between Cotton's powerful effect on his listeners, some of whom followed him all the way to America, and his effect on the modern scholars who have found him not only difficult to explain but "disappointing," "lacking in surprise," and rigidly "methodical."[6]

While one could ascribe Cotton's effect to a historically unrecoverable personal magnetism, or argue that the reason we cannot understand his popularity is that so many of his sermons exist only in the form of sermon notes, such explanations miss the point as much as the criticism he has received. Cotton's sermons should be reconsidered in light of this tradition: the sermon model in which he was trained and how he used this structure to frame the relation of faith to works—the issue at the heart of the Antinomian Controversy. At the same time, Cotton's use and gradual transformation of the sermon model laid out by William Perkins also helps to clarify his view of his audience. Both Cotton's popularity and his problems arose not only as a result of the content of his sermons, but from the way he structured an audience within them. The difficulty of linking orthodox theological interpretations with particular forms of presentation does not begin with Cotton, however; the very manual in which he was trained betrays this dilemma.

JOHN COTTON was well acquainted with William Perkins's *Arte of Prophesying* (1592, trans. 1607), a major text for early seventeenth-century preachers.[7] Perkins—also a respected theologian—examines both explicitly and implicitly how the scriptural Word was to be interpreted and then structured to fulfill the needs of two different groups of listeners. The needs of the individual elect soul must be properly acknowledged, but the need for exhorting both elect and non-elect to moral responsibility (and, implicitly, to social order) must also be observed.

While this might seem straightforward enough, the *Arte* contains a number of not necessarily reconcilable ideas about the nature of scriptural interpretation and its presentation. Before addressing the question of how to preach or even how to interpret, Perkins considers the nature of the Word with which the preacher deals. Following Calvin very closely, he maintains that preaching must take as its field the Word and the Word alone. Nothing extraneous can be added to Scripture, and nothing, even of the most minimal nature, subtracted from it.[8] From this perspective, the duty of the preacher is simply to "open" for his audience the "one clear and naturall sense" of a scriptural text. Interpretation must not be pushed beyond whatever the "naturall sense" is construed to be. "Opening" Scripture, at this point, seems to have little or nothing to do with persuading. From a purely doctrinal standpoint, there is, for Perkins, no causal relation between the manner of preaching and the spiritual state of one's listeners. Only the Spirit moving through a preacher's words can effect a lasting spiritual transformation; words themselves, however logical, however beautiful, cannot. Viewed in this manner, preaching can never be considered an efficient cause of grace; it can savingly move only those whom the Spirit has already touched—the elect. Others may receive moral exhortation, temporary comfort, or even, Perkins grants, a temporary sense of graciousness; but they cannot receive the assurance and the certainty that Christ's righteousness has been imputed specifically to them.[9]

Clearly, however, Perkins feels a responsibility to this latter group. Far from acknowledging that he preaches only to those who are consciously assured of their election, Perkins maintains that his audience consists of "unbeleevers who are both ignorant and unteachable," those who are "teachable but yet ignorant," those who "have knowledge but are not as yet humbled," those who are humbled, those who believe in an external way, and those who "are fallen in faith or knowledge."[10] Given his interest in those who have not, perhaps cannot, and perhaps never will experience the sense of spiritual regeneration, Perkins belies his own initial comments about the preacher's proper attitude towards "opening" his text. Opening Scripture in order to teach the ignorant, the humble, and the fallen cannot merely involve awakening in the elect the sense of an election they already possess. Throughout the *Arte*, in fact, Perkins seems compelled to return to the idea that St. Paul urged preachers to "exhort" their congregations, but that such exhortation had little to do with the elects' discovery of their election: "The manner of perswading is on this wise: the Elect having the Spirit of God doe first discerne the voyce of Christ speaking in the Scriptures. Moreover, that voyce, which they doe discerne, they doe approove: and that which they doe approove, they doe beleeve. Lastly beleeving, they are (as it were) sealed with the seale of the Spirit. Ephe.1.13 'Wherein also after that ye beleeved, yee were sealed with the holy Spirit of promise.'"[11] Scripture itself, with very little exegesis on the part of anyone, might be presumed to be the way in which the elect could discern the fact of their "seale" by the Spirit. Other people, however, would appear to demand a definite and lively form of exegesis mixed with exhortation.

Perkins's *Arte* thus balances between views of Scripture's presentation that could, in practice, become contradictory. On the one hand, Perkins wishes to emphasize the role of the Spirit in the effectual hearing and preaching of the Word. On the other hand, he is concerned with listeners other than the professedly elect and thus with questions about how the preacher should "divide" the Word, interpret his divisions, and finally address them (in a particular persuasive form) to his listeners. In sum, if Perkins acknowledges the sole power of the Spirit to infuse spiritual knowledge within an already justified soul, he also recognizes the practical, pastoral responsibilities of the preacher to an entire community of listeners.

How then, keeping his two sorts of listeners in mind, does Perkins attempt to reconcile ways of interpreting Scripture to ways of presenting it within the sermon form? First, like other Calvinists, he appears to dismiss the method of interpretation laid out by medieval exegetes and the Fathers. The fourfold way, for Perkins, has been replaced by a method of reading Scripture that asserts the primacy of the "literall" sense: "There is one onelie sense, and the same is the literall. An allegorie is onely a certaine manner of uttering the same sense. The Anagoge and Tropologie are waies whereby the Sense may be applied."[12] Rather than relying on the analogizing imagination of the exegete, Perkins, as a good Calvinist, prefers to direct his hearers' attention back to the notion that the Bible is reflexive, offering its own interpretation of itself. Like Calvin (and Augustine), Perkins insists upon the overall consistency of the parts of the Bible and demands that any valid interpretation be based on the interaction of these parts rather than directing attention only to the "levels" of meaning present in one of them.

Accordingly, Perkins believes he and other Puritans have replaced the hierarchical interpretive method of Catholicism—in particular—with a type of interpretation that allows Scripture truly to speak for itself. The method he advocates for young "prophets" in his *Arte* involves placing a text in its context, which Perkins calls finding "the circumstances of the place propounded," and then "comparing the places together," or collating a text with similar texts found throughout Scripture. Finally, both as a preacher interpreted his text and as he presented it in a finished form within the sermon, he had always to conform his preaching to the "analogie of faith." In other words, any statement he made had to be contained in or implied by the Apostles' Creed as interpreted by Calvinist theologians such as Perkins himself.[13]

In order to locate this "literall" meaning, the preacher does not engage in a series of metaphoric speculations. Rather, he simply applies Perkins's three methods—circumstance, collation, and application—to the "analogie of faith." Perkins offers a brief example of this method in his analysis of 1 Cor. 24: "This is my bodie which is broken for you." Using collation, Perkins shows how the words of Paul's text "disagree" with another scriptural statement: "He ascended into heaven." They also disagree with the "analogie of faith" which would maintain that "the nature of a sacrament . . . ought to be a memoriall of the body of Christ absent." Given these textual clashes, Perkins argues that the preacher should search for a "new exposition." He himself finally concludes that "in this place the bread is a signe of my bodie by a Metonymie of the subject for the adjunct."[14] Christ's use of the term "bodie" in this particular circumstance must therefore be understood as figurative, not literal. Thus, while God's meaning is invariably "naturall" and plain, Scripture can often use tropes that the exegete must first determine to be figural by employing the three "waies" of interpretation. Once the "literall" meaning has been established, the process by which the preacher arrived at it can then be shaped within the sermon model.

Since Perkins, like Calvin, reads Scripture as a consistent whole, he clearly feels licensed to expand the possible meanings of any passage. In the following two cases, for example, he confidently enlarges the scope of Scripture's historical content and then generalizes about the broader, although still "literall," meanings resonant in particular commandments or laws:

> Things spoken as if they were already finished, if they be not as yet finished, they are to be understood as being begun and in the way to be fulfilled.
>
> Morall commandements or lawes under one sinne by name expressed doe signifie and mean all the sinnes of that kinde, their causes, occasions and allurements to them, and command the contrarie vertues.[15]

Such synecdochical readings of texts are justified by the exegete's knowledge of the entire Bible and by use of the three "waies" of interpretation. The "naturall" signification of texts is arrived at by the three most objective methods—methods, Perkins would claim, that allow Scripture to remain self-interpreting.

It could, of course, be argued that this way of understanding the Bible—as a whole in which each text is interrelated—conditions the methods of interpretation which Perkins suggests. In the *Arte,* he further refines such an assumption by telling divinity students to begin their study of the Bible for preaching purposes with Paul's Epistle to the Romans. Only after this epistle has been satisfactorily understood can the interpreter move on to the rest of the New Testament and finally to the Old. Given the content of this epistle, however, with its focus on justification, sanctification, and the nature of "true" faith, it is clear that Perkins's "literall" reading of Scripture will obviously lean towards the confirmation of an "analogie of faith" already gleaned from Paul's writings by Calvin and other Protestant theologians.

But there is still another strand closely interwoven with the issue of how theological assumptions help to color methods of interpretation. This strand involves the sermon form Perkins advocates to shape the results of his interpretive methods. When we turn to consider formal presentation, we also return to Perkins's view of his audience. Writing a text on preaching, Perkins very naturally becomes caught up not only in the doctrinal but in the rhetorical problem of preaching for an audience that consists of justified and unjustified hearers. He supplements his comments on proper methods of interpretation with remarks that acknowledge the need to persuade an audience in ways other than the simple collection of circumstances and similar texts:

> The foundation of Application is to know whether the place propounded be a sentence of the Law or of the Gospell. For the Law is thus farre forth effectuall as to declare unto us the disease of sinne, and by accident to exasperate and stirre it up; but it affords no remedie. Now the Gospell, as it teacheth what is to be done; so it hath also the efficacy of the Holy Ghost adjoyned with it, by whom we being regenerated, we have strength both to beleeve the gospell, and to performe those things which it commandeth. The Law therefore is the first in the order of teaching, and the Gospell second.[16]

This remark may initially appear doctrinal; the exegete must question whether the place propounded is of the Law or the Gospel; but, by the end of his remark, it has become clear that Perkins is not simply discussing doctrine; he is also detailing the most efficacious way of presenting Scripture to an audience. The Law can first be used to terrify an audience into a knowledge of their failings; the Gospel can then be used to comfort them. Thus, while preaching that explains a text's position within a larger whole and within its own context may be required, beneath all such explanation lies the consideration of how a text relates to the preacher's sense of how to move his audience. "Plain" explanation as the end of preaching clearly yields to exhortation in Perkins's *Arte*. A way of conceiving the what and how of Scripture gradually yields to a way of applying its dicta in a manner that encourages moral behavior in both the elect and the unprofessed.

While it is not the purpose of this discussion to offer an analysis of Perkins's theology, the doctrinal implications underlying the question of how to preach should be considered more fully. R. T. Kendall has shown that Perkins's soteriology in *The Golden Chaine* and other treatises wavers equally between his desire to acknowledge people's passivity in the reception of grace and his awareness of the doubts and confusions of those who desperately want some measure of active participation in determining the state of their souls: "This dilemma stems from Perkins's vacillation between Calvin and Beza, of which he does not seem to be aware: his efforts to define faith show him agonizing to retain Calvin's concept (faith as a persuasion, assurance, or apprehension) and that of Beza (applying or appropriating). . . . He wants simultaneously to define faith both ways and is torn between holding out hope to the weak one who has but the desire to believe and maintaining the undoubted opinion of Calvin that faith assures."[17] It was this dilemma, according to Kendall, that led Perkins to become more of a preparationist in his theology. The preparationists believed that a certain process could be followed "by which a man becomes willing to believe. This process is to be seen largely as a function of God's Law and is either that which may be included in the regeneration process, but prior to faith, or prior both to regeneration and faith."[18] In other words, the preparationists argued there were steps one could follow in order either to prepare oneself for the possibility of justification by a hidden God—or to indicate that one's regeneration had possibly already begun. The point to stress about preparationists in this particular context is that Perkins, too, regards regeneration as part of a process which occurs in steps, and that this belief leads him to an increasing interest in the voluntary nature of faith.

A similar confusion about whether to emphasize a strictly doctrinal notion of faith, or a faith defined more in terms of his believers' needs, also surfaces in Perkins's attitudes towards the ends of preaching. His struggle between his sense of his audience's incapacity before God and the need to give them some freer say in matters of their salvation takes shape in the very sermon form he advocates.

Perkins suggests a preaching form that consists of a logical movement from the divine text to its practical applications in the daily lives of his congregation. He describes four steps, proceeding from the reading of the scriptural text to its "uses" or "applications." The preacher is encouraged

1. To read the Text distinctly out of the canonicall Scripture.

2. To give the sense and understanding of it being read by the Scripture itself.

3. To collect a few and profitable points of doctrine out of the naturall sense.

4. To applie (if he have the gift) the doctrines rightly collected to the manners of men in a simple and plain speech.[19]

According to Perkins, this basic four-part sermon structure frames material that has already undergone the three acts of scriptural interpretation discussed above; that is, the model shapes an interpretation derived from collating texts, considering their "circumstances," and applying all findings to the "analogie of faith."

Given Perkins's theological ambivalences, however, it is clear that his sermon form manifests something other than the simple shaping of interpretive methods. Caught between his sense of a congregation's incapacity before God and his need to give them some voluntary responsibility in matters of their salvation, Perkins wishes the Spirit to speak through his words in a special way for the elect and at the same time desires to persuade his entire congregation to moral behavior. Interpretation at this point escapes the confines of a discussion of the "waies" of "opening" a text. The preacher, in effect, must reinterpret this interpretation in his manner of offering it to an audience. It is the sermon form that gives interpretation a persuasive shape, not a random listing of the circumstances in which a text occurs or its relation to similar texts or doctrines. The public manifestation of interpretation is inescapably shaped by the sermon model.

The progression from a text to doctrines to reasons and to uses (or applications) is the pattern Perkins assumes most clearly manifests God's intended meanings to a congregation. In the progression from description to explanation and application, Perkins also plays out his desire both to address the piety of the "saints" and to move his whole congregation to compliance with moral law.

Discussion of the "text" and its "reasons," for example, could involve the simple "opening" of the Word unornamented in any way by the preacher. The movement to the "uses," however, would include attention to how the text could be integrated into the daily belief and behavior of the congregation. The Perkins sermon form, in fact, encourages a movement towards this end. The "uses" consider the application of the text's doctrines and reasons to godly conduct within the present moment. Any interpretation that the preacher may do prior to organizing his sermon, then, is subsumed into this rhetorical process; his meaning unfolds consecutively within the sermon form. Process becomes the key term here. The listeners' understanding of God's intentions can, in the terms of the Perkins pattern, occur only gradually through time and end, with the "uses," in time.

Movement from a point in biblical time (the text) to a point in present time (the uses) means traversing a distance between two points. The Perkins sermon model, viewed in this broader sense, involves a preacher and listener in a nascent narrative that unfolds in the logical movement from the sacred text to its application in the temporal human world. Such a movement has implications, however, that Perkins himself failed to recognize.

To postulate such a movement takes attention from the scriptural text and places it on the end point—the uses with which the sermon concludes. Many preachers became particularly famous for their "applications" and "uses." In America as well as in England, for example, Thomas Hooker became well known as a great man "with a use." Hooker, it must be remembered, was also a proponent of the preparationist theology. Although Alfred Habegger has argued that Hooker broke down the Perkins form because of his excessive interest in the uses, it could also be argued that the form itself encourages this attention. Perkins's sermon form as well as his theology implies his own voluntarist leanings.

The sermon model manifests this emphasis. In its very progress from the text through the doctrines and to the uses, it enforces a conceptual movement in which the final stress falls on moral behavior in the human world. When Perkins speaks of the "unweaving" of even the most cryptic passages in Scripture, he therefore does so with the conviction that any text will eventually yield up a set of reasonable meanings applicable to moral uprightness. In Cotton Mather's analogy, the nut of the text can always be cracked and the nutmeat extracted.

Interest becomes focused where the preparationists were to focus their theology, on the necessary steps one could take towards the moment of assurance—granting, of course, that a hidden God had the final say about whether it was to be given or not. But such fine distinctions had a tendency to break down in the light of the preacher's need to encourage his entire audience to good conduct. The idea of the steps that could be taken to prepare oneself for a possible justification gradually became replaced by the notion that either such steps could help to earn salvation or were, in fact, an indication that one had already been justified (otherwise, he or she would not be able to fulfill the requisite steps). The Perkins sermon form, with its obvious "movement" towards the applications, attempted to adhere to an orthodox Calvinism that stressed the special status of the divine text in the hearts of the elect, while at the same time encouraging moral activity in the world. Given Perkins's emphasis on the varying needs of his different listeners, however, it seems clear that, practically speaking, the model suggests his leanings towards a non-elect rather than an elect audience. If theoretically he could retain a balance between these two groups, it remains to be seen how preachers trained in his method were to put it into practice.

EVEN A SIMPLE GLANCE through a sermon by John Cotton reveals that he uses both Perkins's interpretive method and the sermonic model of text-doctrine-reasons-uses. Cotton reports attending Perkins's terrifying sermons while he was in Cambridge even before he experienced his own moment of conversion at the hands of Richard Sibbes. Cotton's friend John Norton reports that when Cotton heard the bells ringing for Perkins's death, "he was secretly glad in his heart, that he should now be rid of him who had (as he said) laid siege to and beleaguer'd his heart."[20] In spite of such feelings, Cotton obviously was affected by Perkins, and the effect was not simply theological. We have already commented on Cotton's transformation almost overnight from an ornate style of preaching to the style of "plain" preaching recommended by Perkins. Such "plain" preaching, however, seen in the light of Cotton's ensuing problems in America, was to have consequences which neither Cotton nor his early biographers recognized.

As early as 1615, following what was becoming increasingly common practice in many reforming churches, Cotton split his congregation in Boston, Lincolnshire, into two groups—those who had professed their election, and those who had not. The "godly," including the preacher, apparently removed themselves from church when the more Romish rituals were being performed by Cotton's assistant. Clearly, a large portion of his audience came only to hear Cotton preach.[21] When Cotton came to America, in fact, a great many from the English congregation followed him, most notably Mistress Anne Hutchinson and her husband, William.

Once in New England, Cotton realized that even here two audiences could still exist. Even a seemingly "elect" audience could contain hypocrites possessed of a "temporary," not a "saving," faith. In a fallen world, audiences must inevitably be double: the wheat mixed with the tares, the sheep with the goats. Within a company of professed saints themselves, some could still be doubtful about or ignorant of their true spiritual state.

The preacher thus was still faced with the problem of how to preach to two audiences.[22] In America, as in England, the question of who these audiences were and how the preacher was to preach to them took on a distinct theological coloring only faintly suggested in Perkins's preaching manual. Before examining Cotton's distinctive use of the Perkins sermon form, then, we should recapitulate the well-known theological problems in which Cotton's preaching and his attitudes towards audience came to involve him.

English Puritans like Perkins and Cotton derived a flexible step-by-step movement towards salvation from the writings of St. Paul. While these steps are not necessarily sequential, the regenerate soul must, at some point, experience all of them. These steps have generally been termed election, calling, justification, sanctification, and glorification.[23] Election and glorification, it was largely agreed, took place outside of time—the one before birth and the other after death. In America, John Cotton's problems with a divided congregation and the hostility of his fellow ministers clearly arose over his definition and presentation of the relationship between justification and sanctification. The all-important question became "whether evidencing Justification by Sanctification be a building my Justification on my Sanctification or a going on in a Covenant of Works."[24]

Briefly, justification has been defined by religious historians as that step in the regeneration process which was thought to imply "an acquittal or declaration of righteousness."[25] Christ died freely for humankind, and the righteousness before God which he thereby gained he freely "imputed" to the elect. Christ's "imputed righteousness" gives elect souls the grace needed to have confidence—faith in their God's mercy to them. Justified individuals who perform moral actions therefore do so not out of a sense that they are thereby "earning" God's love—they already have it. Such acts only manifest their possession of the free gift of God's grace through Christ. Cotton speaks of the certainty of justification as an experience that makes everything in life appear new. Heavenly things

> are new, full of fresh and sweet variety of newnesse: to a new creature behold all things become new, 2 Cor,5,17. Not only within him, new mind, new judgment, new conscience, new heart, new affections, new joyes, feares, griefes, cares & desires &c new speeches, new life. But also without him, new company &c.

Yea, those things he busieth himself about they yeild him continually new matter to be refreshed withall: The favour of God, the blood of Christ, the fellowship of the Spirit, the more they are heard or seen, the more novelty they are to us; the Word the oftner read, still yieldeth as more (new) knowledge, new comfort &c.[26]

If justification refers to an acquittal from guilt and an assurance of mercy, sanctification refers to the process whereby the justified purge themselves from sin in order to grow gradually worthy to approach the God who has acquitted them. In those who have "the Word and Spirit dwelling in them, the dominion of the whole body of sin is destroyed, and the several lusts thereof are more and more weakened and mortified, and they are more and more quickened and strengthened in all saving graces to the practice of that holiness, without which no man shall see the Lord."[27] The internal "hallowing" of sanctification does not remain internal; it will manifest itself in "services" and "the practice of holiness."

The Antinomian Controversy in America arose over the way in which each of these terms was to be construed. Ideally, of course, there is a seamless connection between them: one's justification is made manifest in one's sanctification. Cotton, however, at some point, in England and certainly after his arrival in America, began to have doubts about this schema, particularly about the way that preparationists were defining it. Unlike the preparationists, Cotton argued that "there are no steps unto that Altar." That is, one could use preparatory steps neither as a means to union with Christ, nor as evidence of such union.[28] As the result of this belief, Cotton's sermons rarely place their stress on notions of "progressive . . . hallowing" but consider instead the moment of union with Christ or, often, the ultimate passivity of the longing, not the "prepared," soul.[29] To his fellow ministers in New England, such a belief seemed dangerously close not only to denying the need for sanctification, but to denying the "Word" of Scripture itself, which dictated the laws of moral action. Whereas Cotton, for example, is certainly within orthodox bounds when he claims that the "Spirit could offer greater light than the Word of itself is able to give," this position, if pushed to the extreme, could result in an antinomian insistence that the Spirit is totally separate from the Word.[30] Sanctification viewed as a progressive external manifestation of internal changes could, in fact, be totally distinguished from justification and thus from the real workings of the Spirit. Word and Spirit could be split, with the result, as Patricia Caldwell has recognized, that reading and hearing the Word could also be viewed as a "work" to be performed in order to earn grace and therefore to be avoided by the truly justified.[31]

Thomas Shepard, seeing this possibility, writes to Cotton some months before the real beginning of the controversy with Hutchinson and her followers, asking point-blank that Cotton reveal his ideas about the proper relationship between the Word and the Spirit. The underlying issue is the connection between sanctification and justification. Can revelation, asks Shepard, ever be "beyond and above the Word?"[32] In his reply, Cotton equivocates in the extreme: "The Word and Revelation of the Spirit, I suppose doe as much differ as letter and spirit, and therefore, though I consent to you that the Spirit is not separated from the Word, but in it, and ever according to it, yet above and beyond the letter of the word it reacheth forth comfort and Power to the soule, though not above the Sence and Intendement of the Word."[33] Cotton's obvious discomfort in this passage is highlighted when it is compared to a similar statement by Calvin: "For the Lord hath established a kind of mutual connection between the certainty of his word and of his Spirit; so that our minds are filled with a solid reverence for the word, when by the light of the Spirit we are enabled therein to behold the divine countenance; and, on the other hand, without the least fear of mistake, we gladly receive the Spirit, when we recognize him in his image, that is, in the word."[34] Calvin portrays a calm mutuality between Word and Spirit. Cotton, in contrast, virtually strains to hold them together. Cotton does not "gladly" see the Spirit in the Word's "image"; rather, the Spirit appears constantly in the process of escaping the Word—"according to it" yet somehow "above and beyond" it, giving not only a comfort, but a "power" transcending the "letter" of the Word.

Cotton implies two things in this statement. Those interested in the letter of the law, he acknowledges, can explain and analyze the denotative and legalistic elements of the Bible—the "sence" and "intendement" of the Word. For certain preachers, then, understanding Scripture would mean using Perkins's methods of scriptural interpretation—locating, collecting, and collating scriptural texts and then applying them to the predetermined analogy of faith—in order to apply their findings to moral behavior. Cotton, far more urgently than Perkins, appears to have worried that such systematizing might conceivably ignore the infusing presence of the Spirit as it moved through a preacher's words and stirred in the hearts of elect listeners. Reading the Bible as nothing but a legal system could reduce it to a mass of moral precepts through the use or application of which anyone could appear to manifest a sanctification that was evidence of a prior justification. In this reply to Shepard, Cotton calls for a way of understanding that acknowledges the "letter" of the law without losing a sense of the Bible as God's continually dynamic and new revelation of "comfort and Power" to his chosen ones.

Passages like this one clearly derive from Cotton's extreme ambivalence about the role sanctification should play in expressing the soul's justification by Christ. Cotton's attitudes towards sanctification seem to underlie his comments about the "sence" and "intendement" of the letter of the law. In spite of his ambivalence, however, Cotton does not want to let go of a concrete text, a verbal revelation. After all, he does finally condemn Anne Hutchinson for her belief that she can dispense with Scripture. Cotton is still faced, however, with the problem of how to preach in a manner that takes into account both his congregation's moral needs and the "spiritual" needs of the elect.

The dilemma is one, as we have seen, that also appears in Perkins and, to a degree, in Calvin himself. For Calvin, however, humankind's inability to see the true relation between election and the necessity for moral action is simply another testimony of its fallen state. God in his wisdom integrates ways of knowing that his creatures see as double. Yet Calvin, too, often speaks of the soul's knowledge of Christ in two ways. On the one hand, he views knowledge offered by the Scriptures as cognitive, in the sense that it communicates information about something "in the state of affairs about which it speaks." While Calvin insists that if a doctrine and a scriptural passage are at odds, Scripture should be followed, he will generally maintain that Scripture is eminently reasonable. It presents knowledge about itself that all people, using their God-given reason, can understand. On the other hand, speaking of the elect soul's knowledge of faith, Calvin strikes an entirely different note: "When we call it knowledge, we intend not such comprehension as men commonly have of those things which fall under the notice of their sense. For it is so superior, that the human mind must exceed or rise above itself, in order to attain to it. Nor does the mind which attains it comprehend what it perceives, but being persuaded of that which it cannot comprehend, it understands more by the certainty of this perception than it would comprehend of any human object by the exercise of its natural capacity."[35]

The assumption is that once the "knowledge of faith" has been passively received by the elect soul, all the information derived from the use of natural reason and the senses will suddenly be seen under the aspect of divine intention: the world, as Cotton put it, will be made "new," not because one has made it so, but because it has been revealed as such.

The battle over the role of sanctification in manifesting justification centers in the type of relationship posited between these two kinds of knowing. Sanctification—viewed as a series of external signs—is related to that biblical knowledge which is informational and can be rationally systematized into a code of behavior. All can perceive such a law and perform its dictates. On the other hand, under High Calvinist tenets, unless the believer has undergone the process of regeneration which only the knowledge of faith can bring, then performing any such external actions as a result of mere cognitive knowledge is fruitless. For the analyst of preaching, the point is not so much whether these ways of viewing religious knowledge affect scriptural interpretation; clearly they do. The issue is how these differing beliefs take shape in the very language and structures used in the presentation of belief to an audience presumed to possess mixed needs.

AN EXAMINATION of John Cotton's use of the form advocated by Perkins reveals that in spite of his apparent willingness to abide by its rules—in terms of both the collecting and collating of texts and of presenting them to the audience within the four-part structure—Cotton often employs Perkins's directives only to transform them. It also becomes evident that Cotton's theological assumptions about the relation of grace to works and, more specifically, of justification to sanctification, differ from those of Perkins. Cotton uses the Perkins model as the frame of his sermons— particularly as such sermons are addressed to non-elect as well as to elect listeners—but he also fragments the movement through the model (and thus fragments his hearers' apprehension of its continuity) in ways that clearly deny, impair, and sometimes finally destroy its interrelated structural and conceptual goals.

It has been argued that Cotton's overscrupulosity does not finally detract from the "logical" and "deductive" movement of his sermons.[36] I would assert, in contrast, that Cotton's excessive attention to his text, doctrines, and reasons not only creates a fragmentation of the pattern and of its movement, but that such fragmentation is precisely what makes his preaching unique and problematic.

A sermon from *God's Mercie Mix'd with His Justice*, a series published in 1641 but probably delivered in the 1620s, provides a point of departure for an exploration of Cotton's sermonic practices and the assumptions about the theological needs of different audiences expressed in it.[37] The text is from Rev. 3:20: "Behold I stand at the doore and knocke, if any man heare my voyce and open the doore, I will come into him, and will supp with him and he with me." Cotton breaks this text into three larger sections, each including its corresponding reason and use:

> That the heart of a man is the doore of the soule.
> The patience and bounty of God is great toward sinners, even admirable great in calling them home to himself.
> Such as do heare the voyce and knocks of Christ and doe open the doore of their hearts to him, hee will vouchsafe fellowship with them, feasting of them, and be feasted by them.[38]

Commentators on this sermon have noted its "logical" movement from section to section and how Cotton abides by Perkins's precepts, determining the meaning of the text within its "circumstances," collating it with similar texts, then presenting his findings in the "reasons" section of the sermon. Each reason for each sermon is next followed by a "use," which highlights the practical implications of the doctrine.[39] Habegger also calls attention to Cotton's small attempts to divert his hearers' attention from the numerical series of proofs for the doctrines by using a series of questions.

While such a pattern clearly forms the sermon's basic structure, this shared sense of its progress forward towards the applications of its doctrines seems problematic. I would like to examine the ways in which Cotton fragments the movement of the sermon towards the uses and then explore how his sense of his mixed audience seems closely involved with such fragmentation.

A very simple example of Cotton's tendency to impede conceptual

movement forward occurs in his opening of the word "behold" at the beginning of the sermon:

> In these words observe a note of attention and admiration in this word behold,
> for behold ever requires attention and often in Scripture, admiration, as ESA.
> 7.4 "Behold, a virgin shall conceive and beare a sonne," etc. 1. Behold. Attend
> to it, and consider and Behold it with admiration, so heer, Behold, consider it
> well, and stand and wonder that God should stand at the doore and knocke
> there and offer such conditions there, that if any man will open the doore, and
> he will enlarge his goodness and grace so farre to such, as that he wil come in
> and feast with them."[40]

Rather than fixing the meaning of the biblical address or linking it to any
argument he will make in the body of the sermon, Cotton's approach to
"opening" this biblical term is to broaden it out by referring to examples
of its usage elsewhere in the Bible. Although he may use collation to illustrate his opening, however, he obviously does not use it to move his argument. Rather, the technique reveals his pleasure in developing the different possibilities of meaning (and therefore of response) present in one
scriptural word. He clearly leaves a good deal to his listeners' capacities.
For example, the language of his primary text is not explained or interpreted in this initial "opening" but woven into this examination of the
text's first word. On a broader level, this technique of expanding possible
meanings continues throughout the entire sermon.

In the first doctrine, for example, Cotton uses references from the Acts
of the Apostles and the Psalms in order to discuss the idea that the heart is
the "doore" of the soul. Defining these doors, however, he curiously begins by telling his listeners what the doors are not: "They are not the
doores of a man's house, nor the gates of a city, for they wil bee consumed,
but these be everlasting doores, and such as into which the 'king of Glory
must enter,' and they must be inlarged, this is certainly meant of the heart
of man, and of the will of man which dwells in the heart."[41] He moves
attention from the scriptural text to everyday associations which are at
once offered and denied. Without any focused transition, Cotton then
turns to the psychological association of doors with the "hart"; not content
to evolve these associations, however, he next considers the "will" within
the heart. The result is confusing—no distinct analogy has been made; the
form itself does not progress. Instead, Cotton has offered a variety of possi-

ble connections, establishing no logical one-to-one correspondence between the word "door" and its most "literall" spiritual referent. Attention is therefore not focused forward towards the unraveling of an argument; it is suspended among varying possibilities and even nonpossibilities. As the sermon continues, the confusion does not diminish, but increases. The reasons following these unexplained comparisons introduce the very image which Cotton has just suggested his image is not—the heart as city gates. Abruptly, however, once he has settled upon this analogy, he upends it, too, and introduces a new passage from John 1:7–9: "I am the doore, by me if any man enter he shall be saved." The door here, of course, becomes Christ—not the individual heart, will, or soul. Cotton has also discarded simile as an explanatory device, turning instead to Scripture's own metaphor. In other words, his collation of the original text with a new text is not brought to bear on his discussion of the Christian's heart as door. He instead proceeds to launch into an extended digression on what it means to "have" Christ as an entrance: "Take Christ and you take salvation with him, you take heaven with you all the blessings of God at once, that if hee be opened unto you there is nothing denied you, of all the living treasures of the grace of God, have him, and you have a strong entrance into your owne salvation."[42] The reason ends with a quote from Proverbs which returns to the original analogy of individual soul/door: "My sonne give me thy heart." The final image presents God as a prince "lying" before the gates of a city.

The use following this convoluted reason is not an exhortation which makes a practical application of the doctrine. Cotton simply continues his attempt to encourage the soul to "open the heart." Within the use he presents varying examples of psychological states which still leave Christ "stand[ing] at the doore." Neither wisdom nor affections such as grief or joy will allow his entrance; neither paradoxically, do any "beginnings of grace." Cotton's dilemma is patent. He wants to encourage moral action, that is, the practical application of doctrine, but theologically he cannot assume that any human act can elicit God's grace. Just as Cotton holds off from completing his analogies, so does he refrain from clarifying what the soul can do to open the door. Feeling will not suffice; neither will the "beginnings of grace," yet the soul must freely give the heart. But only the elect soul can give the heart. At this delicate point, Cotton returns yet again to the image of Christ as prince. This time, however, the prince is at work within the city's walls, not outside. And confusion still persists about whether he has entered the heart because it has been "given" or taken.

From this sketch of the shape of the sermon from its first doctrine to its first use, it should become clear that Cotton is far less interested in following out a progressive, self-evident, deductive pattern than he is in exploring the varying ways of viewing the heart/door analogy offered by Scripture. While he uses scriptural images and even metaphor, however, he employs no metaphysical conceits. To the contrary, Cotton is not interested in developing a progressive image or series of related images that grow in logical and poetic density within the frame of a developing argument. Even while apparently using Perkins's three interpretive methods, he seems hardly interested in developing an "argument." His audience's attention has simply been moved towards meanings that remain half-activated, incomplete. Listeners are alternately directed from the literal to the figurative and from the active to the passive implications of a continually metamorphosing analogy. Cotton's disregard of logical and even metaphorical consistency again implies his willingness to leave final interpretation to his varying listeners. Thus, while at first glance this sermon has the apparent form of a straightforward and logical explication of a text that smoothly makes the transition from doctrine to reasons and uses, close analysis reveals that Cotton resists such movement.

The second doctrine is even more fragmented. Here Cotton considers the question of God's "patience and bounty" in dealing with sinners. Rather than proceeding to the reasons section in order to prove his doctrine, Cotton spends several pages simply "opening" his doctrine. This time, he desires to collate biblical uses of "standing" ("Behold I stand at the doore and knocke") that could be applicable to his particular text. Standing, he comments, refers to a "long season of grace," in some cases to three years, in others to "fourty years" or even longer: "The sonnes of God, the best of mankind are become flesh: yet his dayes shall be an hundred twenty yeares, he will stay for that generation before he bring the flood."[43] But "standing" has connotations other than the temporal; it also refers to God's state of mind towards mankind and thus becomes a figure for psychological as well as for temporal patience. God proves his patience by the fact that he "saith nothing"; he "doth usually threaten before hee strike." Even after threatening, he will "stay a good time" because "it comes into his mind, how shall I doe it, what would become of thee, if I should take this course with thee and so leave thee hopeless and helpless for after time." Finally, as he did in the cases of David and Paul, God may strike only lightly—and withdraw his blow after striking.[44]

But descriptively detailing God's historical and psychological patience throughout Scripture is only one part of this doctrine; God's "knocking" must also be considered. Cotton continues to "open" the doctrine by detailing the possible meanings of the "stroakes" whereby God knocks. He uses his word as a blow with a "loud Noyce." His judgments also knock; his Spirit itself knocks and even, at times, breaks through to the unwilling conscience. But suddenly, at the end of this progression, with no preparation, the image of God knocking at the heart metamorphoses into that of a woman chasing after Christ.[45] Again the argument does not progress; again Cotton lists differing possibilities for meaning, but does not assert the prominence of any one.

This examination of Cotton's opening of the first two doctrines shows how far he is from building what has been called a deductive "bridge" between his words and his audience. Examples of his method demonstrate his interest not in limiting the possibilities of a text, but in displaying a variety of possible logical, physical, psychological, and spiritual meanings for it. He is clearly suggesting the richness of God's revelation, not rigidly controlling its interpretation.

A sermon from Cotton's well-known series, *The Way of Life*, (1624, 1641) offers a more fully realized example of this fragmenting tendency that demonstrates how Cotton's notion of "logical" movement differs from Perkins's theory. His text is Zech. 12:10: "And I will poure upon the house of David and upon the Inhabitants of Jerusalem, the Spirit of Grace and of Supplication." Cotton derives from the text this doctrine: "In the days of the gospel, the Lord dispenseth a plentifull measure of grace, not onely upon Ministers, but upon all sorts of Christians."[46] Following Perkins in order to locate his doctrines, Cotton again uses collation, finding a similar text from John: "Out of his belly shall run streames of living water." He also turns to an account of a healing from the Acts of the Apostles. Once more, however, Cotton does not employ collation either to prove or to develop his argument. Similarity between texts is not used as the basis for determining God's "literall" intentions. Rather, Cotton appears more interested in the kinds of images these passages supply. In fact, before he even reaches the reasons for God's dispensations of grace, Cotton is already opening his doctrine by recourse to figurative language: "Running streames of the Spirit shall ever be flowing from a beleeving soule; he shall have a spring of grace in his soule, that shall ever be like a running river, cleansing his heart and way, and making him fruitful in all places, cooling and refreshing his own and other souls with the experience of God's favour to him in Christ."[47]

When he finally reaches the reasons for his doctrine, Cotton, instead of considering the doctrinal significance of these images, turns to the question of why such a "pouring out" is occurring in the present age. He thus leaves the images he has introduced to resonate in his hearers' imaginations without interpretation. In spite of this seeming avoidance, however, Cotton does imply how certain listeners in the current age can respond to Scripture. Using St. Paul, he argues that grace is flowing now because earlier people "could not clearly see the Lord Jesus nor the life nor the power of him in any Ordinance then dispenced; he meanes the vaile of Ceremonies and shadows, but now the vaile is taken away, and we all behold the glory of the Lord with open face, ver. 17,18. Shewing that by how much the more simply and plainly the Ordinances be dispenced, so much the more plainly do the people of God see Christ revealed in them, and ever where there is the less shadow, there is the more Substance."[48]

The passage provides a key to understanding Cotton's differences with Perkins because its evident paradoxes offer insight into why he fragmented the Perkins model. Despite his claims that "the vaile of Ceremonies and shadows" has been taken away, Cotton himself has been using figurative language throughout this sermon as the very "substance" of his argument. Such usage would seem to contradict his own assertion that the "ordinances"—preaching is an ordinance—are now "simply and plainly . . . dispensed." What is at issue in these apparent contradictions is Cotton's sense of the listeners for whom he preaches.

Those who are elect—"the people of God"—can conceivably read and hear the Word of God preached without "vaile" or "shadows." What appears to be figurative, "dark," or "cryptic" to non-elect listeners can for chosen hearers simply manifest God's "literall" meanings. Hence Cotton's interest in demonstrating the possibilities for meaning inherent in pieces of his text rather than in framing single interpretations that help to move a sermon's entire argument towards its uses or practical applications.

Cotton's apparently fragmented structure, then, in which figurative language appears where rational argument might be expected, does not show a simple inability or unwillingness to follow Perkins. It is the result of certain convictions about listeners who have been granted "eyes to see" and "ears to hear" the "literall" meanings of Scripture. Plain preaching, seen in these terms, would call for preaching that, rather than fixing a set meaning for the terms of a text, would either deviate from it as little as possible or offer multiple possibilities for its meanings.

The so-called "uses" of this particular sermon bear out this theory. In the first use, for example, Cotton chides Christians who refuse to recognize and act out their conversion; "rivers of grace" are all around, yet they remain in "barrennesse." Abruptly becoming more concrete, Cotton then argues that there are ways of determining whether one has been granted grace: listen to the "playn" word preached, abandon sin, and ask the Father to send the Holy Ghost.[49] In the second use, however, no such explicit listing of moral obligations appears. Rather, suddenly, joyously, Cotton expands upon all the figurative possibilities he can find in passages from John, Ezekiel, Hebrews, and the Acts. Perry Miller has aptly likened the following passage to an "ecstatic prose poem."[50]

For further encouragement hereunto, consider that place Ezech. 47.3,4,5. It shewes you the marvailous efficacy of the spirit of Grace in the dayes of the Gospel: First a Christian wades in the rivers of God his grace up to the ankles, with some good frame of spirit; yet but weakly, for a man hath strength in his ankle bones, Acts.3 and yet may have but feeble knees, Heb. 12.12. So farre as you walk in the waters, so far are you healed; why then in the next place, he must wade til he come to the knees, goe a thousand Cubits, a mile further, and get more strength to pray, and to walk on in your callings with more power and strength.

Secondly, but yet a man that wades but to the knees, his loynes are not drenched, for nothing is healed but what is in the water. Now the affections of a man are placed in his loynes, God tries the reines; a man may have many unruly affections, though he be padling in the wayes of grace; he may walk on in some eavennesse, and yet have many distempered passions, and may have just cause to complaine of the rottennesse of his heart in the sight of God: why then; thou hast waded but to the knees, and it is a mercy that thou art come so farre; but yet the loynes want healing, why, wade a mile further then; the grace of God yet comes too shallow in us, our passions are yet unmortified, so as we know not how to grieve in measure, our wrath is vehement and immoderate, you must therefore wade until the loynes bee girt with a golden girdle; wade an-end, and think all is not well until you be so deep, and by this you may take a scantling, what measure of grace is poured out upon you. And if thou hast gone so farre, that God hath in some measure healed thy affections, that thou canst be angry and sin not, &c. it is well, and this we must attain to. But suppose the loynes should be in a good measure healed, yet there is more goes to it then all this; and yet when a man is come thus farre, he may laugh at all temptations, and blesse God in all changes: But yet goe another thousand Cubits, and then you shall swimme; there is such a measure of grace in which a man may swimme as fish in the water, with all readinesse and dexterity, gliding an-end, as if he had water enough to swimme in; such a Christian doth not creep or walk, but he runs the wayes of Gods Commandements; what ever he is to doe or to suffer, he is ready for all, so every way drenched in grace, as let God turn him any way, he is never drawn dry.[51]

The gradual accumulation of images in this passage is directed at engaging an audience's emotional rather than its rational acquiescence. At the beginning, Cotton reminds listeners that these are "the rivers of God his grace"—that is, he initially posits a separation between the image and the concept to which it refers. As the passage continues, however, internal qualities and concepts become integrated with external sensory images by virtue of Cotton's very syntax.

The images, in other words, are no longer framed by the intended meaning; they are somehow bound up with it. Clearly the moving image of the wader/saint gives the passage its spiritual power. Note, for example, how Cotton blends "wading" and "walking" with ideas about "praying" and following one's "calling": "So farre as you walk in the waters, so far are you healed; why then in the next place, he must wade till he come to the knees, go a thousand Cubits, a mile further and get more strength to pray, and to walk on in your callings with more power and strength." In another part of the passage, the passions, seated in the "loynes," are unmortified unless the saint continues wading, at which point he will not only discover—externally—that "the loynes bee girt with a golden girdle," but find that he can even feel an anger which is no sin. Wading, walking, passions, righteous and unrighteous anger, "loynes," and golden girdles are all bound together in an image that, in the end, is not so much visual as psychological. The audience is presented with an image of what it feels like to be an elect "saint" rather than with a literal description of sainthood. They are not, in other words, asked to connect the images logically, but emotionally. These images are neither simply descriptive, nor argumentative; they are not used merely to exhort listeners to a specific belief or action. Cotton's language calls up a certain state in his hearers, but this state is never clearly defined by the preacher. As in other passages, so here. Because he concentrates so much on the images of his text, the use does not unfold as part of a logical argument. In the last period, for example, even the controlling image of wading is broken down. From swimming like a fish, the Christian suddenly "doth not creep or walk, but he runs the wayes of God's Commandements." Finally, without any attempt to discover connections among these activities—physical or spiritual—Cotton returns to the image of the "drenched" saint. He has clearly avoided ascribing any set interpretation to these images.

Furthermore, although the image of wading is taken directly from Ezekiel, Cotton does not use it for the same purposes. In the prophetic book, the wader/prophet is led to measure off the boundaries of the Promised Land.[52] Cotton presents no boundaries—there is only endless water in which to swim. Ezekiel's walker, moreover, never swims; he merely wades. Lastly, what seems purely external and historical in Ezekiel—the images are used to denote the founding of Israel—in Cotton becomes internal and atemporal. In a similar manner, the logical and temporal movement of the entire sermon form towards some external application of doctrine is momentarily superceded or, it seems, dismissed entirely. This use has no concrete application to moral conduct. The audience is left free to draw its own connections between the images and their possible meanings.

In the last use, Cotton draws back from the water imagery that has heretofore constituted both the subject matter and the recurrent structuring device of his sermon. He calls for a moral "uprightness [that] will draw you on to fruitfulnesse. Joh.15.2."[53] The focus of the sermon up to this point, however, has obviously not been on "fruits"—outer moral actions (sanctification)—but on bodying forth the experience of feeling one's "uprightness." Yet what this use suggests proves more orthodox and more in keeping with this image than it first appears. For the true Calvinist, there can be no outer fruitfulness unless uprightness already exists. Thus, only those already blessed, already justified, can even begin to wade, much less to "[run] the wayes of God's Commandments." Cotton has, in fact, already used more water imagery to color his audience's response to this rather flat application. His apparent nod to external morality (fruitfulness) is preceded by imagery now inextricably linked with the internal assurance of blessedness: "And then would the peace of our consciences and our estates have beene abundant, and our sanctification had beene like the waves of the sea, and every wave greater than the other, till there had been neither banke nor bottome, such a looking at Christ would have channeled us from one grace to another."[54]

Such a description of the peculiar movement of sections from these two sermons almost makes its own point. John Cotton does not examine each part of his text in a logical manner that leads unerringly to the next section; he concentrates instead on stopping the sermon's argumentative movement forward and showing, with few explanations or transitions, the possible affective resonances of fragments of his text. If the varying sections of the sermon are related, the connection becomes often not deductive, but emotional, encouraged not by argument, but by images. Connections are made through changing repetitions of imagery, connections that Cotton presumes certain listeners are left free to draw.

Cotton desires his hearers to become involved in the dynamic richness of God's revelation to his saints; he does not rigidly engender a static response by simply exhorting them to change their behavior in the light of a deductive program for change mirrored in the deductive patterns of a sermon. Perkins's rational sermon model has been fragmented, broken down, undermined. Perkins's interpretive strategies—circumstance, collation, and reference to the "analogie of faith"—have come to militate against the very structure in which Perkins intended to display them.

BOTH PERKINS'S METHODS of interpretation and his modes of presentation seem finally directed towards satisfying his own and his hearers' need to view God's ways as ultimately rational. The ways in which Perkins desires to frame interpretation and how this very frame comes to affect the act of interpretation itself already imply the rationalist leanings that scholars have encountered in his theological writings. This emphasis is manifested in a sermon model that by its progress from the text through the doctrines to the uses enforces a conceptual movement in which the final emphasis falls on moral behavior in the human world.

John Cotton's attitudes towards scriptural language, towards methods of interpretation, and towards the sermonic model laid out by Perkins differ significantly from Perkins's attitudes. Cotton's penchant for using images from Scripture as part of the substance of, not the ornaments for, his sermon is noteworthy. Norman Grabo and others have argued that many of these images are organic, referring to fountains, plants, growth, and nourishment.[55] They show Cotton's interest in the mysterious transformations and the growth of a spiritual state which the elect already paradoxically possess, rather than a desire to achieve a fixed mechanical assurance of a conversion arrived at through set steps. While Cotton is emphatic in his distrust of human imagery, both by example and in direct statement he manifests a belief in the power of scriptural language to provide the occasion for the elect's sense of a continually growing spiritual blessedness; justification is a "perennius actus," not a completed moment.

A later treatise, *The Singing of Psalms a Gospel Ordinance* (1646, 1647), for example, offers a defense of the use of scriptural ornamentation. Calling the singing of psalms an "ordinance," Cotton argues that "singing of a spiritual song prepareth to prophesy by Ministry'ing the Spirit. 2.King.3.15. 'Whilst the Minstreel played, the hand of the Lord (that is, his Spirit) came upon Elisha.' "[56] The preacher, in other words, needs to hear such singing before he preaches. He needs the "edification" the Psalms can bring. In the treatise's later pages, Cotton reveals a blunt belief that "godly" translators of the Bible are under obligation, then, not only to render the Bible's meanings, but its style, too:

> Now surely then it were a sacrilegious nicenesse to think it unlawfull lively to express all the artificiall elegancies of the Hebrew Text, so farre as we are able to imitate the same in a translation. Yea doubtelesse it were a part of due Faithfulnesse in a Translator, as to declare the whole Counsell of God, word for word; so to express lively every elegancy of the Holy Ghost (so much as the vulgar language can reach) so that the People of God may be kindly affected, as well with the manner as with the matter of the Holy Scriptures.[57]

In spite of Cotton's rigor in denouncing most ornamentation, by employing figurative language from Scripture, he himself has obviously opened a small door for the legitimate use of imagery that can stir the emotions of his audience. His attitude towards such language, as we have seen, also bears an obvious connection to the way Cotton will present it to his hearers. Within the context of a sermon structure that was designed to be logical and progressive, whether Cotton probes the varying contextual meanings of one word or attempts to evoke an experience of overwhelming grace, he has fragmented the forward movement of the sermon by introducing digressions which either tend towards metaphor or, in fact, are metaphorical. He constructs clearings for audience response that become possible only if the logically continuous movement of the sermon is impeded. Cotton's sense of fidelity to a text and to the capacities of an elect audience runs counter to the progressive structure he appears to use.

As we have noted, Cotton is less interested in the uses section of the sermon than he is in the expressive implications of doctrines and reasons. It is usually not his practice to reiterate his doctrine in terms of his uses, to plead for righteous behavior as the goal of his exegesis, or to threaten lack of godly behavior with divine punishment. Neither does Cotton, as does Hooker, set up a preparational schema in which scriptural texts are "opened" only to the extent that they help to provide justification for his system.[58] Rather, as the foregoing analyses demonstrate, Cotton's doctrines can shade off into barely distinguishable reasons. His uses, too, often prove closer to meditations on a text using the text's own language than they do to practical exhortation. His transformation of the language of Ezekiel is a case in point. In the selection from *The Way of Life*, even his final use, while appearing to follow the Perkins model of practical exhortation, is qualified by its position within the water imagery that shapes the other reasons and uses. Exhortation to behavior, then, is subordinated to suggesting the state of mind out of which (ideally) such behavior could originate.[59] Cotton's extended discussions of images begin to dictate his structure; the Perkins structure no longer frames or controls his images.

Cotton's attitude towards "opening" a text differs from that of *The Arte of Prophesying*. Maintaining that the "vaile" has been lifted for those who can truly hear God's Word, Cotton uses Perkins's interpretive methods and suggested model only to undercut them. He does so by subtly justifying the use of figurative language in preaching as long as it is derived from Scripture, by using circumstance and collation to locate related imagery as well as related ideas, and by using his findings to expand meaning rather than to narrow and focus it. Cotton even goes so far as to claim that the language he employs, when preached by an elect preacher and heard by elect hearers, is not, in fact, figurative at all. God's "literall" meanings are made manifest to his elect, even if they still appear figurative to the unassured and uncertain. "But now the vaile is taken away, and we all behold the glory of the Lord with open face."

Fragmenting his discourse, disrupting the sermon's progressive movement, and using scriptural language he claimed was "plain" as the very content of his digressions, John Cotton signified his belief in the power of Scripture—and, by extension, the power of elect preaching—to effect a complicated response in those already justified.[60] The preacher should not maladroitly translate Scripture, nor should he forbid the spoken and sung use of the Psalms for his own "edification" and that of his congregation. Above all, he should not limit the possible meanings of his text in order to reduce God's will to a single moral truth easily graspable by those eager to find assurance of their blessedness.

Cotton employs his "manner" as well as his "matter" neither simply to prove a theological point nor to encourage a sensuous delight detached from divine intentions. Instead, his particular means of presenting religious truth dramatize "the heart of an experience rather than its outward shape."[61] The phrase has elsewhere been applied to the lyric; here it seems equally applicable to Cotton's use of the sermon. Within a temporal structure, John Cotton is attempting to shape some sense of an experience not separate from the Word's "sence" and "intendement" but over and above the Word giving "power" and "comfort" to those always and already chosen. The direct experience of assurance may come and go in the saint's conscious mind, yet it is always there for the elect if they are open to it; most often, preachers would agree, the experience occurs while listening to the Word preached. Within a fragile, time-bound human structure, then, the divine and the eternal can unexpectedly break through.

Carried to an extreme, Cotton's reverence for God's will leads him very close to a denial even of the power of Scripture. In the tense days of the Antinomian Controversy, he felt constrained to distinguish the Spirit from the letter while still desperately attempting to hold them together: "Neither word nor work (being both of them creatures) are able to beget or confirm faith, unless the Spirit himself . . . breathe in both his own witness with them."[62] Scripture still has power, but only as the Spirit enfuses it with vitality. Words in themselves are not, can never be, the causal agents of salvation. In the end, no method of interpretation or presentation of meaning will guarantee a preacher's success or failure. Only if God has granted him grace can he speak truly to those who have "eyes to see" and "ears to hear."

Still, preaching is an "ordinance"; God has commanded his preachers to preach, in spite of the fact that he alone can make language fruitful in the soul. Thus, his preachers should continue to interpret divine texts. Texts have surfaces, after all, composed of words and sentences with denotative meanings. For the elect listener, however, this surface becomes transparent—the preacher's words merely provide a glimpse of Scripture's source in a Being who is always there for those whom he has given the ability to know him. For John Cotton, it is clear that the text does not, in the end, refer forward to mechanically extractable uses, but back to the mystery of a *Deus Absconditus*—the true Logos—whom language will never be entirely able to reach.

Cotton's subtle declension from Perkins indicates that there are two ways of viewing the movement of a text from its doctrines through its reasons to its applications. For elect and non-elect alike, the notion of "opening" a meaning that ends in the present moment demonstrates God's reasonableness in human terms and in human time. Reasons can be derived from doctrines, and practical uses derived from reasons. For the non-elect and the uncertain, in particular, this cumulative structure could at least be used to prove the need for outer morality—an attempt at "progressive hallowing"—even if it could not be used to assure one of justification. Cotton's continued adherence to Perkins's model indicates his realization that a congregation composed of saints, hypocrites, the unsure, and the unbelieving did, in fact, need such an outline. But in sermons like those discussed here—from *God's Mercie Mix'd with His Justice, The Way of Life, Christ the Fountain of Life*—and in sermons preached in America before the Antinomian Controversy, Cotton gradually shapes a response differing from a simple awareness of moral obligation. His sense of the Word's involvement in an elect soul's spiritual life proves far more complex than that of Perkins because John Cotton is finally more concerned with evoking the sense of God's ways at work in his elect than he is in encouraging a one-dimensional morality neatly detachable from God's Word.

Cotton thus paradoxically uses the prescribed Puritan sermon model only to attempt to transcend its moral as well as its rhetorical limitations. Through his use of fragments closely phrased in scriptural language, he not only introduces his own special awareness of the timeless presence of divinity in time; he also opens rather than constricts the power of the individual's response to the Spirit, a Spirit that moves alike through preacher, through Word, and through believer.

IN THE RESPONSE of Cotton's "real" Boston audience to his manner of preaching, it becomes clear how his theory and practical use of certain "forms" could redound in important ways on issues that initially seemed unrelated. If the Antinomian Controversy was in part about certain methods of preaching, it also concerned the conceptions of community projected by such preaching. The way in which Cotton transformed the Perkins model privileged one definition of community over another, and thus one audience's needs over another's. Cotton's preaching ideally shaped a free interpretive community of elect members which gathered together to worship and to hear the Word preached as an outward sign of a very individual, personal response to the Spirit. John Winthrop, Thomas Hooker, and Thomas Shepard believed that Cotton's manner of preaching was inimical to a different idea of community, one defined in terms of individual and group adherence to clearly delineated laws for belief and conduct. Cotton's serene belief in the transforming powers of justification precluded any fear of social disharmony; he does not posit dissension among those for whom the world is made "new." For most of the other ministers and many of the magistrates, however, acquiescing to his theology was one matter (although many of them did not), but putting it into social practice was another.[63]

Antinomians and "preparationists" alike, Kai Erikson has suggested, eventually needed to view each other as an "other" that was somehow dangerously deviant from the "true" interests of the Boston community.[64] Questioned by his fellow ministers, Cotton testily argued that he had been overread by both these groups: "By this I discern whence it comes to pass, that I am thought to speak so obscurely, for if men that hear me, do instead of my words take up words of their own and carry them to infer other conclusions that I am at; I do not wonder if they cannot well understand how that which I speake at one time, and that which they take me to speake at another can agree together."[65] According to Cotton, his words had been "taken up" and confused, not only by the Antinomians but by the other ministers. He himself intended only to awaken spiritual knowledge in his listeners, not to create social controversy. But what he had projected as the "appropriate" response of his ideal audience was now beyond his control. In the process of mutual recriminations, the shifting outlines of the Boston community became defined, and these outlines were not those envisioned by Cotton.[66]

In the end, the issue is not whether the danger of one group to another existed in reality, but that each wished to perceive it so. Cotton's and Hutchinson's more authentic Calvinism, with its emphasis on the importance of personal assurance, had somehow to be twisted into heresy, because placing such a stress on individual experience was considered problematic for a community that needed to project an orthodoxy and an order that could help it cohere. The concern of Wilson, Winthrop, Shepard, and Hooker for the unsure soul and for a more rationally defined community structure had likewise to be turned into a plot against the rights of the truly justified. As Perry Miller and Norman Pettit have demonstrated, the preparationists won the day in this battle, which was covertly as concerned with the verbal presentation of interpretation to an audience as it was with Puritan theology. In March 1637, the decree went out that no "strangers" (new emigrants) were to be allowed in the colony for more than three weeks without express permission from a magistrate. Those who possessed antinomian tendencies were, of course, denied entry to the colony. By March 1638, Hutchinson's trials were over and the "danger" had been dispelled. Cotton himself participated in her excommunication.

IN AN ESSAY addressing the historical and critical debate over the role played by "reason" or "emotion" in Puritan experience, Robert Middlekauf has argued that in order to understand the nature of either "faculty," one must not study them separately, but in relation: "Whatever else it is, the psychic process is not simply the sum of thinking and feeling; it is in some peculiar way their interaction. Men think within some emotional disposition and feel in a context that in part has been ordered by thought."[67] The structure of the Puritan sermon, initially laid out by William Perkins and used by John Cotton, forms precisely such a part of the "context" in which feeling is "ordered by thought." "Order" is the central term. The Perkins sermon model followed a pattern in which response to a scriptural text was carefully channeled from the text through the doctrines and the reasons towards practical applications to everyday belief and moral conduct. John Cotton used this form in a manner that resisted this implied intent, allowing feeling, and a scriptural language concomitant with such feeling, to begin to dominate and redefine the structure which was to frame it. He did so in the light of his perception of the needs of an elect as well as a non-elect audience, in the light, in short, of a different vision of the nature and definition of community.

But Cotton's attempt to express his conception of the "true" relation of faith to works by means of a sermon structure in which he addressed the needs of two kinds of listeners failed miserably. The magistrates, many of the other ministers, and prominent members of Cotton's own congregation demanded that there be but one clear way in which one unified audience—whether assured or unassured—could view the relation of grace to moral action.

2. Benjamin Colman
and the Shaping of Balance

To TURN FROM John Cotton in the mid–seventeenth century to Benjamin Colman at the century's close is not initially to discover major differences in doctrine. It is, however, to discover a transformation in attitudes towards how the standard sermon form can be employed, how the use of scriptural language is to be viewed, and what audience with what needs can be expressed and framed by a preacher's rhetorical strategies. If Boston's orthodoxy still seems well established, recent historians have charted fundamental changes in intellectual "tone" which will eventually come to challenge it.

The 1690s through the first two decades of the eighteenth century are marked by gradual yet important changes in the Harvard curriculum. The older emphases on scholastic logic and rhetoric, even if modified by Ramus and Talon, yield to an interest in—if not always a complete understanding of—the newer logic of Descartes. William Brattle, one of Colman's tutors at Harvard, compiled a logic based on Descartes that was circulated in manuscript before 1690.[1] It was not only the coming of the Anglican royal governors that more forcibly ensured some loosening of Congregational intolerance; as Norman Fiering has noted, such changes in curriculum had their own subtle effect on attitudes towards religious toleration. A good many of the students of the liberal tutors William Brattle and John Leverett were not simply becoming acquainted with Descartes; they were also reading the works of the Latitudinarian archbishop John Tillotson and imbibing his philosophical tolerance, if at the same time quietly rejecting his—for them—doctrinal inaccuracies.[2] But if an attrac-

46

tion for Tillotson betokened a distaste for religious factionalism, it also suggested that those who read him were interested in sources outside Scripture for proving the value of religion. The principles of religion could now be located both in nature and in human reason as well as in revelation. Although earlier Puritans had certainly allowed for such connections, all truths derived from other sources were still to be subordinated to Scripture.[3] But the Latitudinarians, in the words of an earlier rationalist divine, "bid John Calvin goodnight."[4] Scripture alone was no longer to determine the grounds by which other sources of knowledge were to be interpreted and applied. Moderate New Englanders, remaining doctrinal Calvinists, were also interested in finding grounds for religious beliefs to supplement Scripture's dictates.

Norman Fiering has clearly established the prevalence at Harvard College of Latitudinarian writings and those of their teachers, the Cambridge Platonists, before Benjamin Colman's trip to London in the mid-1690s. While in England, Colman himself came close to bragging about the "catholic" air of the "little" college in New England and the broad principles of religious tolerance which he had learned there.[5] Benjamin Colman's attraction to the great subjects of "the Age"—nature, reason, and humanity—was long ago established by Theodore Hornberger.[6] Fiering has now placed this attraction within the larger context of changes occurring at Harvard.

But it is not only Colman's interest in these topics as subject matter for his sermons that scholars have noted. Hand in hand with appreciation for Colman's support for religious toleration has gone recognition of the changes he wrought in colonial preaching. Perry Miller points out the "elegance" of his prose, arguing that very soon after Colman's return from England, not only did those of his own party—William Cooper and Ebenezer Pemberton, for example—begin to preach like him, but even his opponents among the Boston ministry learned their preaching techniques from Benjamin Colman.[7]

Yet while Colman's "gentleness," "ease," and naturalness are often mentioned, these categories have remained descriptive and abstract, offering no rationale for the particular rhetorical strategies used within his sermons. Attitudes towards the function of the sermon and the needs of an audience expressed within it have remained largely unexplored. Miller, as always, is suggestive: "To understand precisely the influence of Colman upon this provincial civilization, one must notice that while he points towards a freer and more rational theology, he also opens up a vein of rational emotionalism, of what may well be called a sentimentalized piety. Our labors, he said at the ordination of William Cooper in 1716, are of both head and heart, our pains require not only that we put our materials in to due frame, but that we bring 'lively affections with us in our work.' "[8]

While Miller then goes on to acknowledge Colman's part in developing a "natural" prose style, he does not develop the aesthetic, religious, and even the possible social implications of Colman's "rational emotionalism," his interest in a "due frame" for the "lively affections." Like his admired Latitudinarians, Colman was caught up in redefining religion's role and its ends in a manner that could both express and "frame" what he conceived of as his audience's new needs. Colman once commented with characteristic modesty that he had nothing new to offer to his congregation save in the way of "Style, Method, and Allusion."[9] However, the changes he introduced in the formal presentation of doctrine were, in fact, responses to the different desires of his congregation (as he saw them), changes that helped to alter the very "truths" he presented. To describe the way in which these differing needs were to press against and aid in the transformation of the sermon, the way in which Colman ultimately justified these changes (theoretically as well as in his rhetorical practice), and the way in which his sermon form came not only to express but to aid in controlling and focusing these needs is the burden of this chapter.

Seeking to express his audience's perceived desires for a piety and morality redefined within a changing intellectual context in a manner that would also appeal to their desire to consider themselves orthodox Calvinists, Colman expanded the Perkins model almost to the breaking point. Within this strained larger structure, he also developed two rhetorical strategies that seem designed to appeal to his listeners' rational and emotional needs (as distinguished from their strictly doctrinal expectations of preaching). While both Latitudinarian and Dissenting thinkers surely aided him in this task, his friends Isaac Watts and Elizabeth Rowe, both well-known Dissenting poets, helped Colman to justify his use of differing stylistic techniques in order to "move" the religious sentiments of his listeners.

In the process of so much conscious attention to matters of structural and stylistic presentation of religious belief and feeling, a focus on the sacredness of the biblical Word (central in the assumptions of the Perkins sermon model) quietly begins to disappear. Scripture's language for Colman becomes an ornament used to encourage a regard for ideas derived outside of Scripture. John Cotton's sermons attempted to hold together a conception of the Word of Scripture as the transparent medium through which the Word of the Spirit could speak to the elect and as a more opaque medium for teaching all listeners—elect and non-elect—about religious knowledge and religious duties. Even though Cotton seems often yearning to escape from the confines of human language, he himself believed he was preaching in a manner that held both these conceptions together. In Colman's sermons, in contrast, awe before the mysterious Word increasingly yields to an interest in the moral dictates of the legal Word or even to the usefulness of the Word as coloring for moral ideas derived from nature and human nature. As ideas such as "justification" or "sanctification" are slowly supplanted by notions of wisdom, rational self-interest, and common sense, attitudes towards the function of the Word as preached must change. The church must not only present and explicate Scripture's commands; it must convince and persuade church members and potential church members that these ideas are both reasonable and moving, while promising, furthermore, to have a beneficial effect on social conduct and social harmony. Clearly, as the uses of the sermon structure and biblical language are redefined, notions of piety and morality must also undergo subtle changes. Piety, once distinct from "works," gradually becomes limited to the controlled emotions a preacher can arouse through his preaching. Such emotions can attract people to the church and serve as the means by which they can be directed to appropriate behavior.

It is within the borders of Colman's sermons, in their juxtaposition of arguments, their movement, and their styles, that the need for a religion that appeals to feeling and moral behavior on new grounds is held in suspension with older appeals to doctrine. Colman does not resolve the tension that seems evident between the beliefs he is shaping and his means of shaping them. The church's sense of its function and its power (not to mention his own) seem momentarily dependent on how well he can maintain his balance.

"WE WANT," says John Leverett in the letter of request which the Brattle Street founders sent to Colman, "persons of your character."

"Broad" and "catholick" in his own leanings, a promoter of the "new learning" at Harvard, and Colman's former teacher, Leverett was well aware that an important part of the "Town" desired a new tone.[10] The *Brattle Street Manifesto* (1700) with its well-known attack on Congregational church polity and its ascription of its own polity to "tradition," "natural law," and "evangelical progress," also made the question of the "forms" in which religious ideas were to be presented an issue in Boston. Signifying their desire that church polity be altered, however, the members of this "progressive" church did not desire to repudiate their orthodoxy. It was up to Colman, their new preacher, freshly imported from contact with moderate Anglicans and Dissenters in England, to give shape to their need for both kinds of thinking. One of the first major questions Colman had to confront was how to integrate nonscriptural appeals to religion's reasonableness with appeals to Calvinist doctrine within the standard sermon form. One obvious way would be simply to introduce both kinds of thinking within the old frame. Doctrinally orthodox interpretations of scriptural texts could be juxtaposed to ideas found outside Scripture. In a sermon from *Practical Discourses on the Parable of the Ten Virgins*, one of Colman's first and most popular sermon series, he does just that. His text is from Matt. 25:2–4: "And five of them were wise and five were foolish. They that were foolish took their lamps and took no oil with them: But the wise took oil in their lamps."[11]

Let us consider the movement of the argument within the varying doctrines Colman offers and then analyze his juxtaposition of differing ideas within the frame of the sermon. After examining the patterning of Colman's first "observation," we can then consider the significance of the placement of this observation within the sermon's overall structure.

Colman begins in the prescribed manner, discussing the possible meanings of phrases from his text before "opening" it into doctrines. He explores, for example, the varying connotations of "oil" and "lamps." The meaning of the equal number of wise and foolish virgins offers him a momentary problem, however, because it seems to refer to an actual equality of sainted and reprobate people in the world. Such a reading, argues Colman, is against "Experience and ordinary Observation"; he quickly adds, however, that Scripture itself elsewhere discounts a literal interpretation of such equality, Christ himself revealing that "of the many who are called few are chosen."[12] Colman then comfortably concludes that it is the qualities—wise and foolish—which the preacher should stress, not the equal numbers. Colman, unlike Cotton, clearly feels no need to defend his "opening" in scriptural terms.

He then goes on to offer his "observations" (doctrines) on the text. The first, and by far the most important, "observation" of the sermon is stated thus: "Sincerity and holy living is the highest Wisdom of Man, Hypocrisy and Irreligion the greatest Folly."[13] Colman's "reasons" and "uses" for this assertion eventually encompass nearly half his sermon.

As one proceeds through Colman's opening of this first doctrine, his debt to Tillotson and Latitudinarian thinking in general becomes evident. Earlier, he has acknowledged his respect for Tillotson in the body of his text; the moderate Anglican is the "greatest model of Charity and moderation" which the age produced.[14] Colman's own opening of his text acknowledges, by implication, his attraction for this moderation. He does not pursue the reasons of his text by examining each word in light of its context and its usage elsewhere in Scripture, or by comparing each meaning thus derived to Calvinist doctrine and finally moving from his proofs to consider their application to daily conduct and belief. His reasons are derived from nonscriptural sources, yet given a scriptural legitimacy by the fact that they occur within the "reasons" section of the sermon structure.

Colman sets out to prove his "observation" by demonstrating how the religious person should be wise and prudent, how the "wise man" has the sense to "discern and choose the true Way and Means to compass our last End and Interest," and lastly how such a one realizes he must learn "diligently and industriously to improve and use the Means that conduce to our Ends and Happiness."[15] While the means he speaks of are ostensibly those offered by religion, Colman proves their validity not by showing that God has called for their use, but that the person who uses them is acting in accordance with "reason" and "common sense." Acting in a religious, i.e., a "wise," manner is thus also acting in one's own "best Interests."

During the course of these varying "proofs," piety and belief become subordinated to the personal usefulness of acting well. Manifesting proper conduct and using the proper means of being religious supplant simple piety and belief, just as the *Brattle Street Manifesto* had supplanted the old "profession of faith" with the minister's consideration of a church applicant's outer behavior.[16] Sin, in the context of this argument, becomes not a mark of depravity, but a sign of stupidity and ignorance. Sinners, in contrast to the wise men, are incapable of improving their "Advantages," unaware that "Truth is the proper Food and Nourishment of a rational mind." Nature as well as Scripture has indicated the means for achieving a "heavenly Prize," yet sinners are too stupid to use them.[17]

The sinner as hypocrite receives Colman's most scathing opprobrium. His aims, to deceive God and man, are "mean" and "little." Unwilling to see that his true advantage lays in planning for the "Future Day," he is "certainly a Fool." Because he fails to recognize how his own interest is served in learning the "wisdom" of religion, Colman's hypocrite seems finally damned by a God more disgusted with his folly than wrathful at his depravity.

In the "use" that follows these unorthodox "reasons" for acting in a manner commensurate with self-interest, Colman appeals not to the grief or fear which sinners should feel before a justly incensed God, but to the pride and the shame of his listeners: "Can we patiently bear this Charge of Folly, or like this Image of ourselves in the glass? Have we no resentment of the foul Imputation? Do we not value and stand upon this Priviledge and Dignity of our Nature, our Reason and Intellect? Remember this, and show yourselves Men, O ye Transgressor, (Isai 4.18) We forfeit that noble Name else, and may well be accounted despicably tame and stupid."[18] What is noteworthy about this "use" is that Colman speaks neither of depravity nor of mercy. He shames his hearers both for acting as if "destitute of common sense" and by referring to the "image" they present to the external world. Other men, not only God, will subject foolish men to "derision." Their actions receive external and social as well as internal and divine disapprobation.

The remarks about the stupidity of hypocrisy are followed by a discussion of what means exist to prove to this mocking world that one is truly wise. While turning away from hypocrisy and the sensual desires of the world may be one means, obviously once again the means Colman wishes to stress are those offered by the church—attendance at preaching, adherence to other church ordinances, private meditation and prayer, as well as good conduct. Learning these means, the congregation has learned to act to its own "advantage."

Colman's analysis of this extended "observation" ends with a comparison of a wise man to a canny merchant. Both have the sense to be "wise in the Execution and compassing of their project"; both show "Foresight and Cunning, they let slip no Opportunity"; and both are "ready upon every Advantage that offers to make the most of it." The truly wise man, however, is a merchant not of perishable earthly treasure, but of incorruptible wealth. For Colman's Brattle Street audience, largely composed of merchants, the simile must have seemed apt.

This description of the movement of Colman's arguments in this first section is offered in order to indicate broadly what he does not do, as well as what he does do. Unlike Cotton, Colman does not offer a doctrinal exegesis of a text in which the speaker's arguments and most particularly the movement of his arguments are inextricably linked to the boundaries established by that text. His argument proceeds less through numbered "reasons" than through a general comparison of wise and foolish behavior cast into the terms of self-interest and common sense. Significantly, however, the sermon does not stop here. Colman has opened only one of his "observations," and the formal constraints of the sermon demand that he analyze the rest. By the sermon's end, such a need to move through all the expected divisions of the sermon model will have provided Colman with a very useful, if mechanical, way of linking his so-called progressive thinking to orthodox doctrine.

In his next, shorter series of "observations," Colman puts far more emphasis on doctrine. He takes up the issue of hypocrisy in more depth, arguing that "among visible Professors there are many insincere and unsound," then moves to consider "that a profession without Grace in the Heart governing the Life is of no Value or Significancy." Colman finally concludes with the idea that "Wise and Holy Persons will be solicitous for the continual Supplies of the Spirit, for their growth in Grace and Perseverance in the Ways of God."[19]

Each of these discussions offers very strict doctrinal and scriptural "reasons" for the depraved person's inability to earn grace and for his or her consequent dependence on God's mercy for it. Each "use" stresses the need to trust the means God has offered as preconditions for discovering whether one possesses grace, not as the implied causes for a gracious condition. These means do not encourage grace in the soul; its reception is totally dependent on God's mercy. Almost imperceptibly, Colman has moved back to the realm of orthodox doctrine.

At the same time, however, when these apparently orthodox assertions are examined closely, they present curious inconsistencies. In the first, which deals with hypocrisy, the depraved and fraudulent hypocrite, initially attacked for his innately wicked nature, is then described as being the victim of external pressures—a "sensual education" and the "snares" of the world which help to account for his supposedly innate sinfulness.[20] Colman does not explain the interrelation of these seeming contradictions. He merely juxtaposes them. It is thus unclear whether avoiding such snares is being offered as a way of coming to possess a grace which, it is assumed, the truly elect already possess.

In the next "observation," Colman again begins with an orthodox discussion—the nature and necessity of "grace in the heart"—but then turns to a far fuller discussion of why this grace must be exemplified in outer practice. Quoting a passage from St. James, avoided or disputed by orthodox preachers of the first generation, Colman comments, "I will shew thee my faith by my works. This is Evidence to ourselves and to others: our Assurance and their Expectation depends therein."[21] His reasons for being gracious do not finally rest with inner certainty or piety, but on the outer effect which a Christian's works have on his or her neighbors. Good works become particularly necessary as indications of the faith because a profession without such works can lead others astray, moving them to "blaspheme and reject the Faith itself." Once again, doctrine seems qualified by a concern with the outer world. Works become important for their effects, not for what they indicate about an inner state.

The last observation initially seems to admit of little qualification. Using scriptural imagery of water, growth, and gardens of spice, Colman discusses the God-given ability to "persevere" in grace. In orthodox Calvinist terms, he asserts that none of this growth occurs as the result of human actions; only the electing Spirit can grant grace. What is curious here, however, is not so much the presence of a troublesome qualification of his argument, but how his initial emphasis on the need to "aspire" for God's grace yields to an almost enraptured discussion of the size of the reward the saint will receive for such aspiring. The fact that the very ability to yearn comes from God gradually fades from view. Colman is interested in the end, not the means: "The good Man craves Increase of Grace because so much shall the Brightness of his Crown and the Weight of his Reward be increased for ever. The more Grace the more Glory: so is the Reward proportioned and adjusted."[22] Such attention clearly puts emphasis on the desirability of grace, not on the fact that only the elect can aspire to it.

Grace seems less the already gracious cause of the ability to yearn for more grace than the reward of anyone (not simply the elect soul) who is desirous to attain the "Prize."

In his final "use," Colman notes how these "observations" can serve purposes of consolation, of reproof, and of exhortation to grow and aspire. The "use" adds nothing new to his discussion; it seems almost vestigial. The whole sermon has shown that "there is only wanting on our part raised Desires, Industry and Importunity and we should received good measure (of oil, of grace) pressed down and running over."[23] The idea of an innate, divinely given gracious disposition is uncomfortably wedded to the idea that "desire" and "industry" can win the wise and prudent man (molded in the image of the wise merchant) the heavenly "Crown."

This sermon from the *Virgins* clearly possesses a complicated dynamic. If it shows Colman's attempt to align his thinking with the best moderate English opinions about the wisdom of religion and the folly of unbelief, it also shows his desire to retain a still-Calvinist interpretation of his text. The structure of this sermon provides the way in which these different ways of thinking about religious belief and moral conduct come together. On a very broad level there is the juxtaposition of the long first section to the three which follow it. Colman offers no explanation for the connection between these sections; he simply puts them side by side. One could argue perhaps that beginning with the discussion of the religious meanings of wisdom and folly he seeks to moderate the Calvinist ideas that follow, or that, conversely, the orthodox notions considered in his second larger section (the last three observations) serve to qualify the more "progressive" ideas discussed in the first. The important point is that Colman himself does not offer the audience a logical or theological rationale for this juxtaposition; he simply uses it.

Looking more carefully at the Calvinist readings offered in his final observations, however, we have noted slight cracks even in them. This fact would lead one to suspect that the broader ideas of the first section subtly come to qualify the orthodox positions maintained in the second. They do so, however, not through direct statement but through juxtaposition. Comments on the hypocrite's innate inabilities are followed by remarks on the effects of a "sensual education" and exposure to the outer world. An analysis of grace yields to a discussion of the social significance of "works," and finally, the gracious ability to persevere in the search for more grace is juxtaposed to comments on the beauties of the heavenly reward. Orthodoxy is not denied in these varying proofs for Colman's observations; it is simply qualified by other emphases to which it is juxtaposed.

What Colman seeks is a means of attracting his listeners through the use of such moderate ideas, to offer them the image of a rational, yet spiritual, self-aggrandizement and self-approbation based on adherence to outer "norms" for conduct while at the same time assuring them that such an image and such actions are also consistent with Calvinist doctrine. If he does not or cannot prove this connection through sheer argument, he can suggest or even simply assume it at the level of structure.

The sermon form itself, not simply this broader, more abstract juxtaposition of two larger strands, also aids Colman in making tacit connections between notions which could prove theologically incompatible. Colman presents his audience with four "observations"; the conventions for the sermon model dictate that each be "opened" consecutively until the "uses" are reached. An audience's expectations of the sermon—at least formally—are met when this movement occurs. The interrelation of these differing doctrines need not be stated; it is implied by the ongoing movement through the prescribed sections of the sermon.

This is not to say that Colman's seeming abandonment of the boundaries of the text from Matthew (especially in his first "observation"); his reasons, so often derived from sources outside Scripture; and his uses, which have become almost vestigial because he has incorporated them throughout his text, do not undermine the sermon form which he uses. Clearly they do. In his first section, in fact, Colman's sermon threatens to become a self-contained discussion of "wisdom" and "folly" detachable from the rest of his sermon. The point here is that he does not detach this discussion; he remains concerned with linking his newer beliefs to an older orthodoxy, and the sermon form provides one means for doing so. The desires of Colman's audience for "progressive" religious ideas coupled with their need to adhere to a comforting orthodoxy and Colman's own need to preserve, on whatever contradictory terms, the church's role as definer and arbiter of belief and behavior, lead him to continue to use the old model and at the same time to participate in an expansion of it that hints not only at its fragmentation, but at its eventual abandonment.

THE *Brattle Street Manifesto* not only linked its varying changes in church polity to reason and nature; certain prposals were also made with the emotions of the congregation in mind. Colman's audience, it seems clear, sought to have its emotions moved as well as to have its orthodoxy aligned to "reasonable" ideas derived from nature and human nature. Proposals that met this desire included the preacher's right to read Scripture without offering any explication of it at all, and the practice, very close to this, of the recitation of "set forms" of prayer—such as the Lord's Prayer.[24] The assumption underlying both these practices appears to be that these forms provided legitimate means of moving feelings which did not necessarily have to be analyzed by the preacher.

Such proposals would have seemed anathema to many Dissenters. Increase Mather, in fact, attacked both "dumb" readings and "set forms" of prayer. The latter, in particular, he denounced as "syllabical Idolatry," closely related to the idol worship of the "Papists."[25] Among moderate Dissenters in England, however, it had become more common to discuss what lay at the base of these accusations: a distrust of the power of certain kinds of language to move the passions. Both Isaac Watts and Elizabeth Rowe, the one a prominent minister and poet, the other a well-known devotional poet, were concerned with establishing how such forms could be useful in moving hearers or readers to feelings which would bear fruit—not in enthusiastic or fanatical behavior, as was feared, but in virtuous, socially acceptable conduct. Their theories shed light both on Colman's own fragmented comments about the use of "ornaments" in his preaching and finally on formal strategies used in his preaching other than the broadly structural.

The discussion of Watts and Rowe which follows by no means asserts their direct influence on Colman. That he knew both of them well, corresponded with them on his return to Boston, and avidly collected their books has been securely established. He even wrote a notice of Rowe's death for a Boston newspaper.[26] But Colman picked up on notions they presented (which had become common in English Dissenting circles while he was in England) and used them in his own way for his own ends in America.

The contribution which Isaac Watts and Elizabeth Rowe made to Dissenting literature is brought out clearly in a review which Samuel Johnson, himself a good Anglican, wrote for *Miscellanies in Prose and Verse* (1756), edited by Elizabeth Harrison:

> The authors of the essays in prose seem generally to have imitated or tried to imitate the copiousness and luxuriance of Mrs. Rowe. This, however, is not all

their praise; they have labored to add to her brightness of imagery, her purity of sentiments. The poets have had Dr. Watts before their eyes; a writer who, if he stood not in the first class of genius, compensated that defect, by a ready application of his powers to the promotion of piety. The attempt to employ the ornaments of romance in the decorations of religion, was, I think, first made by Mr. Boyle's "Martyrdom of Theodora", but Boyle's philosophical studies did not allow him time for the cultivation of style; and the completion of the great design was reserved for Mrs. Rowe. Dr. Watts was one of the first who taught the Dissenters to write and speak like other men, by shewing that elegance might consist with piety.[27]

Johnson displays two ideas about piety here which are also pertinent to Colman. Johnson is interested in the fact that religious writers have borrowed certain techniques, the "ornaments" of romance, from secular writers. In Rowe's case, such ornaments seem to consist most generally of "copiousness," "luxuriance," and "brightness of imagery." Yet it is not Rowe's ornaments alone that mark her influence on other writers; Johnson also notes with approval her "purity of sentiment." The same connection is made, though more abstractly, between Watts's "elegance" and his "piety." If elegance "consist with piety," if ornaments consist with purer sentiments, then piety evidently should be given an appropriate shape.

For Johnson, religious feeling must obviously not be allowed to remain free-floating and indeterminate. He notes with approval that Watts, in particular, has "taught the Dissenters to write and speak like other men." Implicit is the criticism that the Dissenters at one point did not "speak like other men" and that this difference gave way to dispute, faction, and civil war. Rowe and Watts are not read by Samuel Johnson strictly as devotional writers, but as models for certain conventions in writing that could have positive social effects. Piety expressed in forms which all share and to which all respond joins rather than divides people.

Considered in Johnson's terms, Rowe becomes important for her belief that some forms of writing can help engender pious feelings and correspondingly pious actions. Watts notes that it was she who educated him to read French dramatists in order to apply their precepts and their style to discussion of the Bible. But she promoted such study for specific ends. As a Christian poet, Rowe was not interested in adding to techniques available for poetry unless they could play some part in encouraging moral conduct. In *The Athenian Oracle* (London, 1704), she queries "whether Songs on moral, Religious, or Divine Subjects, composed by Persons of Wit and Virtue, and set to both grave and pleasant Tunes, wou'd not by the Charms of Poetry, and Sweetness of Musick, make good Impressions of Modesty and Sobriety on the Young and Noble, make them really in love with Virtue and Goodness and prepare their Minds for the design'd Reformation."[28]

What is suggested here, of course, is that "moral, Religious, or Divine Subjects" are not themselves enough to move these upper-class hearers to virtue; the "charms" of poetry and the "sweetness" of music are needed if they are to make desirable "Impressions" on the "Young and Noble." Further, the impressions poetry and music can make are specifically related to outer conduct and social effects; in the order of effects, modesty and sobriety, definite forms of behavior, precede the more abstract "virtue" and "goodness."

There were those who would attack Rowe's work for its excessive attention to the "sentiments." As her biographer points out, Rowe's *Devout Exercises of the Heart*, edited by Watts and published after her death, "became a standard work for those more inspired by evangelical enthusiasm than by cold rationalism."[29] Watts himself, however, having supported a more emotional style in his own earlier writings, gently protests against some of her excesses in his preface, but urges readers to believe what Rowe herself had maintained—that passion must always be tempered by reason. If she speaks ardently, argues Watts, it is from true devotion, not from artificial sentiments. Furthermore, in spite of her moving language, Watts maintains "it should be remembered also there is nothing to be found here which rises above our ideas. Here are none of those absurd and incomprehensible phrases which spread a glaring confusion over the understanding; nothing that leads the reader into the region of those mystical shadows and darkness which abound in the Romish writers under the pretense of refined light and sublime ecstasy."[30] While she was certainly interested in expressing her feelings in an emotional form, Rowe by no means wished to darken the "understanding" or separate her style of writing from virtuous ends. What was important for Rowe, Watts suggests, is also important for him. The task for the Christian poet is not to decry the use of poetic forms—which Dissenting churches had heretofore done— but to apply poetry's forms to proper Christian subject matter and thereby to promote feelings which will flower in appropriate Christian behavior.

Watt's own *Horae Lyricae* first appeared in 1706. Rowe was said to have read it "with delight," and the second edition included her dedicatory poem to Watts. In his preface to these poems, Watts offers an apologia for a distinctly religious poetry. Seeking to justify the use of poetry by devout Dissenters, he begins by claiming that the Bible in its nature is "inspired Poetry" whose divine authorship could be proved by the very sublimity of its verse. His second argument for the use of poetry, however, qualifies these first comments by claiming not that the Bible is intrinsically poetic, but that it uses poetic ornaments to develop its sublime arguments. Poetry, in the end, becomes defined in terms of certain "ornaments."[31]

Watts's basic argument is that the forms of poetry can be useful in promulgating the religious sense within Christians. Since the Bible itself uses "higher figures" to enhance its arguments, surely it is possible for the Christian poet and minister to do so. Dissenters who have heretofore maligned the value of poetry or distrusted its effects have simply seen its techniques applied to the wrong subject matter. The Bible demonstrates how poetry can be properly used.[32]

Christian doctrine, argues Watts, is in desperate need of the ornaments which the poet alone can provide. False poetry applied to the wrong subject matter has subverted the mind's rational processes by arousing and inflaming dangerous passions. Touching the faculties in the proper manner is clearly not only a religious, but a social, necessity. Sermons have simply not had the same effect as poetry because "the same duty that might be despised in a sermon, when proposed to the reason, may here, perhaps seize the lower faculties with surprise, delight, and devotion at once, and thus by degrees draw the superior powers of the mind to piety."[33] Sermons, so concerned with explicating doctrine, have, in other words, not made use of techniques that could engender proper religious feelings. Both Watts and Rowe stress that the use of "a composition of virtue and delight" can successfully draw even the young and "well-bred" away from "vicious pleasures."

Both writers stress the beneficial social effects of poetic ornaments applied to religious subject matter. Neither wishes to engender disruptive mystical feelings; their poetry is meant to encourage sentiments which lead to appropriate conduct. Poetry is not to serve as a substitute for rational argument, but to better convince the reason. This is clearly a pietism with no radical social overtones. Watts showed initial enthusiasm for George Whitefield, but withdrew his support when the evangelical preacher began arousing the passions of the "lesser sort." Poetry is to "call back the dying piety of the nation to life and beauty," not to threaten the social order; it is to "confound the blasphemies of a profligate world ignorant of pious pleasures," not to start another civil war.[34]

While Benjamin Colman, unlike Cotton, writes no treatise justifying the use of figurative language in the sermon, there are comments scattered throughout his sermon series which closely resemble the remarks of Watts and Rowe. Like his friends, Colman is intent on proving the value to religion of using more emotional appeals in his sermons.

In his *Twenty Sacramental Discourses*, for example, Colman argues that "Lydia's tender heart breaking under the efficacy of the word or the jailor's rough heart breaking under it, did more set forth the doctrine of a crucified savior than all the preaching of a Paul or Appollos did at the time without like effects."[35] The remark proclaims the moving power of the Word, not the value of a dry explication of doctrine, even if such a doctrine is opened by St. Paul.

Colman also praises scriptural writers for their use of moving language. In *Souls Flying to Jesus Christ*, he commends Isaiah for his "elegant and Moving" use of metaphor.[36] Matthew, he notes, uses "sarcasm . . . the mocking Trope . . . a very excellent way to rebuke and convince, and therefore frequently used in Scripture."[37] Parables, too, are praised as effective means of utterance because they can "fix on the meaning while they take the Fancy." Since the Spirit is "imbodied," Colman argues, it can best be "worked upon" by impressions on our sense and more particularly by the eye and ear.[38] Here, of course, he justifies not only reading Scripture's tropes, but using them himself.

Like Watts and Rowe, however, Colman is not simply interested in the fact that these ornaments move the emotions, but that religious emotions encouraged through the proper forms have, in turn, an effect on virtuous conduct. In his early treatise, *The Government and Improvement of Mirth* (1706), Colman analyzes how religious mirth, which he refers to as both the source and result of "Poetry" and "Singing," will have positive effects on social interaction. A saintly mirth, properly engendered and properly expressed, "fits a man to work the better in his shope, to be a more pleasant Neighbor and a greater Comfort to his family." It makes him "serviceable to God's glory and acceptable in his Sight."[39] Desiring to raise emotions which can have valuable social effects, Colman, like Watts and Rowe, further suggests that urging a congregation to good conduct must consist neither in terrifying them by recourse to frightening doctrines, nor in simply and plainly explicating Scripture's moral meanings. The assumption is that knowledge of religious truth is not enough to move them to the sweeter, more sociable emotions encouraged through the use of newer forms of sermonic discourse.

The concern shared by these three writers for justifying poetic and stylistic techniques that can move the emotions to religious ends raises still another question about Colman's attitude towards Scripture. We have noted that in his larger structural use of the sermon form, exegesis of the scriptural text gradually gives way to consideration of ideas found outside Scripture. Here, in his more particular comments on ornamenting a discourse, it becomes apparent that Scripture is also losing its importance as the substance of doctrine. For Colman, it is not only gradually becoming a conceptual backup for beliefs located elsewhere; its language now serves to color such beliefs.

In his biography of Colman, Ebenezer Turrell, Colman's son-in-law, notes how the preacher "often made use of Scripture not for proof or Illustration, but for the sake of the inspired language."[40] Colman himself admits as much: "I have no colours that can at all show them to the life. Yet those that I have are the best, being what the Scripture supplies us with and I have as I cou'd skillfully mix'd and laid 'em on, both light and shade."[41]

The painting metaphor very directly reveals Colman's belief that Scripture can be used as a means of moving certain feelings as much as it can be used for doctrine. In its appeal to the affections, scriptural language can first attract listeners to the beauties of religion and then be used to persuade them of the beauties of moral conduct. A recent study has noted that while earlier Puritans would not have totally discounted the use of language appealing to the senses, using sensuous imagery solely for the pleasure it could arouse was a sinful act.[42] Sensuous imagery could be used typologically to "figure[d] forth, albeit imperfectly, the mind of its Creator."[43] More specifically, within the particular scriptural context of its usage, its doctrinal meaning could be explicated. The duty of the Christian, in other words, was not simply to feel the emotions which such language could help produce, but to interpret it in light of what Jonathan Edwards would call "the history of redemption."

In Colman's world, however, as doctrine gradually makes room for other sources of value, one of Scripture's uses has obviously become formal. "Dumb readings," "set prayers," and dramatic stories or parables used in sermons attract an audience to a preacher's message more than the plain, methodical "opening" of a text. The Word is no longer iconic, radiating with a special immanent meaning for those who have "ears to hear." As piety before the Word yields to a reasonable search for nature's intentions, Scripture's words have become distinct from the mysterious truths which they once so darkly "shadowed" forth. For Colman, moral conduct is the end to be served both by his sermon structure and his use of ornamental language. Piety as well as reason must be directed towards behavior.

The beliefs which Colman shared with Watts and Rowe about using "poetic" language to move the feelings help to explain why he initially supported both Jonathan Edwards and George Whitefield. If these preachers obviously touched their hearers' emotions, they were also filling the churches with pious new members who yearned for its moral guidance. At the same time that he praises them for their ability to move religious feelings, then, Colman also makes it clear that he believes these preachers raise such emotions to serve rational, virtuous ends. He portrays Whitefield as "a gentleman of good sense, strict veracity." His work is "countenanc'd" by "Scripture, Reason, and Observation."[44] Edwards's work is believable and to be accepted by other ministers because he is "free from an enthusiastick spirit."[45] While Colman thus feels free to support those who preach in a fashion which arouses his hearers' feelings, he, like Watts in defense of Rowe, obviously wants to dissociate his use of "moving" techniques from any intention of provoking an irrational response in his listeners. Again, like his friends, he wishes to move emotions in such a manner that they may be directed towards socially useful ends. Under advisement from Watts, Colman will, in fact, later back off from his support of Whitefield and the rabid James Davenport, erstwhile disciple of Edwards, because their preaching is becoming unduly affective.[46]

COLMAN uses the standard sermon form to juxtapose appeals to reason and to orthodoxy; Watts and Rowe, in turn, help us to understand Colman's more theoretical interest in applying the moving techniques of poetry within his sermons. It remains to be seen how Colman's overarching interest in appealing to "reason" and "emotion" is shaped in his stylistic practice. Excerpts from his *Ten Virgins* series and the later *Twenty Sacramental Discourses* show that early and late Colman adhered to what I call "rational" and "emotional" strategies.

Colman's own preaching practice follows the guidelines suggested in his comments on Whitefield and Edwards. His formal strategies carefully shape the appeal of religion to the emotions by framing affective passages with passages equally attractive to his hearers' reason. Unlike Cotton, Colman's word painting does not allow his audience a metaphoric participation in his subject matter, but carefully controls their response to it. Far from inciting his audience to any overwhelming personal or social change, the blend of reason and emotion in Colman's sermons seems intended to encourage his listeners to learn the decorous form of their own "sensibilities." Not for Colman the disruption of the self that Jonathan Edwards requires and believes language can help create. Colman's strategies offer a rationally controlled outlet for his hearers' religious emotions. He desires to shape his sermons in a manner that can attract an audience he views as desiring both the pleasures and the rational self-esteem involved in becoming, feeling, and acting "religious." He uses preaching strategies that he believes can dramatically attract this audience while at the same time persuading them of the beauty of external stability.

In a passage which demonstrates his use of rational form, Colman describes the proper marks of a person who possesses true wisdom and holiness:

> He prays and watches and strives against Sin, he follows after Holiness; this is his Pleasure, that his Burden. He bewails his past Sins, fears Temptations and Falls to come, depends on and cries for that Grace which is able to keep him, . . . is inquisitous after the signs of Grace in him; a critical Observer of the Evidence of it in his Life, infinitely Thankful for the least Measure he can discern, careful to improve it, rejoices in its increase, is solicitous and insatiable after more, and having attained the most, presses yet on toward the Mark of the Prize of our high Calling, laying himself always from first to last at the feet of the Crucified Jesus, whose Blood purifieth and whose Righteousness justifieth.[47]

The Augustan symmetry of the passage's opening strikes the reader/ hearer immediately. A good man both "strives" and "follows"; he possesses a "Pleasure" as well as a "Burden." This conscious balancing is repeated in the second sentence where Colman uses paratactical pairings of nouns and verbs: "Temptations and Falls," "depends on and cries for." The next sentence expands far more loosely into a series of predicate nominatives: the saint is "inquisitous," is "a critical Observer," is "infinitely Thankful," is "careful." Colman begins to use stronger verbs as the curious soul now "rejoices in" the increase of grace. The pattern is then suspended, awaiting the release of the strong verb "presses." The parallel structure at the end— "whose Blood purifieth and whose Righteousness justifieth"—formally and conceptually reestablishes the balance of the initial sentence. The parallelism is heightened by his use of *homoteuleuton*, similar sounding endings.

Colman's strategy involves setting a loose structure—the accreted predicates—against a balanced structure. The movement of the series of predicates builds an obvious tension that creates a need for the reassertion of the original balance. Internal noun/verb pairings and his parallelism provide a satisfaction that is tonal and structural as well as conceptual. The verbs move from "is" to "rejoices in" to "presses yet on," each increasingly more active until Colman draws back and reintroduces the soul's utter dependence on Christ's imputed righteousness. But for the most part it seems clear that Colman's interest in the passage is not doctrinal. The audience seems intended to respond not only to his subject matter, but to the manner in which he presents it. Neither concept nor style stresses personal inability or even awe. Rather, Colman's rhythmic breaking and rebuilding of balance gives a sense of a world formally contained, rounded, and understood.

His later writing, as an example from the *Discourses* demonstrates, shows Colman's continued reliance on this particular strategy:

> It is a good and comly thing for us always to remember with a becoming devotion, gratitude, and admiration, the early and continued care which a gracious providence has taken of us from the first hour of our being and existence. Every day we live we should be looking back on all the days that are past, and never let later mercies obliterate, but rather fix more on our memory those that were first received. And the more insensible we were of the goodness of a gracious God to us in the day of our conception, in our formation, birth and infancy, so much the more should we now bear the same in mind and adore our Maker and Preserver on the account thereof.[48]

Again, the use of classical balancing is evident: "good and comly," "early and continued," "being and existence," "Maker and Preserver." To persuade his audience that such remembrance is a "comly" as well as a "good" thing (and the two qualities seem linked), Colman felt it necessary to employ an almost mechanically balanced structure.

In the clause patterns used in the next section, he also carefully delimits response: "and never . . . but rather," and "the more . . . so much the more." His message could, of course, be easily restated: "Fix your heart on the mercies a good God has granted you from your birth to the present moment." The particular forms Colman chooses, however, indicate that he conceives of pulpit eloquence as more calculatedly rhetorical. He wants his audience to acquiesce to his subject only through the particular manner in which he presents it. Redundant in concept, this passage achieves its effect of harmonious order almost entirely through structure. In spite of the fact that Colman does write on orthodox subjects—he composed an entire sermon series on *The Incomprehensibleness of God*, in which he argues that reason alone can never probe the mysteries of his grace—passages like the above suggest his intense interest in humankind's own ordering capacities. The preacher's language hints at his audience's need for a harmonious world complemented not only by the subject matter, but by the verbal structures of their preacher.

The rational strategy is not Colman's only strategy. Other passages frame dramatic pictures rather than balanced abstractions. A close look at these pictures, however, reveals the essential similarity underlying their surface difference from the so-called rational passages. The following passage describes the Second Coming:

> As the sun rises in a glorious Attire of Light, so will he break forth from his heavenly Chamber. As at his Transfiguration, his Raiment was like his shining Countenance, white as the light. The splendor of his glorified Body will be dazling like the unapproachable Light. (John.17.5,Phil,e.c.Rev.i,13–16) "What streams of Glory shall his pierced Temple, his pierced Side, and Hands and Feet shoot forth?" Suppose on a radiant Cloud fashion'd and blazon'd with all the Skill of heaven into a great white Throne as if a thousand Suns were made into one vast Globe and on it the One outshining what he treads on, as Solomon's chariot of State did the Dust it pass'd over: "He made the Pillars thereof of Silver and the Bottom of Gold." So on a burning refulgent Cloud shall the King of Glory come, the most pompous show the world can ever see or Heaven afford.[49]

Christ, set at a distance from the audience, is "transfigured" by a light. His hearers are asked to "suppose" or imagine the cloud throne and the "pompous show" by which he will come. Edward Taylor or Jonathan Edwards would discuss the possible typological significance of the sensual images used or, less historically, their correspondence to some higher heavenly truth. Colman simply describes the scene: Christ's "Raiment," his "glorified Body," and his "great white Throne." Language from Scripture is blended with Colman's own "painting." The images do not seem intended to encourage an interpretive response—they simply describe the "show." Thus, while the language is sensuous, it is also static. Again, the biblical quotations and the preacher's own lush language create an impressive sense of the beauties of religion, but do not move an audience to exegetical inquiry.

An even more blatant example of Colman's "emotional" strategy appears equally designed to control his listeners' response. He uses *paralipsis*, saying he will not say what he then goes on to describe:

> I shall not go on to say, how the passions of the Damned will become so many furies in 'em, how pining Sorrow, confounding Shame, torturing Fear, Wracking Despair, fruitless Desires, black Envy, Hatred, Malice, and Revenge will, but turns, inrage and rend 'em. Nor know we how malicious and tyrannous Devils will insult and tear their Prey; as I have seen a hungry Tyger devour a Morsel of Meat with hideous grins and Snarls, and rolling Eyes and Flames: But least of all can we conceive what Agonies and Convulsions come of the Wrath of God, sent down and impress'd with Infinite Strength: This is the Weight that crushes and the Wheel that breaks all the Bones.[50]

Here, rather than demonstrating how the damned feel their "passions," Colman translates their pangs into allegorized "furies." He does not expand on the implications of his allegory, however, but turns instead to the simile of the "Tyger," apparently in order to give the picture more concreteness. The contrast with Edwards's spider is resonant. The similes are phrased in such a balanced manner that terrifying the audience can hardly have been the preacher's desire. The form carries as much weight as the meaning. Indeed, the audience experiences the language through the framework of Colman's denial of its adequacy. Phrases such as "nor know we how" and "but least of all can we conceive" allow Colman both to deny and then to present his own "imaginings" of the state of hell. Similes and disclaimers like *paralipsis* are both means of describing what hell is "like," not what it is. The language is vivid, but the structural devices Colman uses to portray his subject carefully guide his hearers' response to it.

The classical doubling of the "rational" passages is used once again: "inrage and rend," "malicious and tyrannous," "grins and Snarls," "Eyes and Flames," "sent down and impress'd." Once again the device slows down the pacing of the sentence and gives it a balanced shape in spite of the emotional thrust of the images. Finally, the parallel structure that frames the concluding biblical image—"Weight that crushes . . . Wheel that breaks"—brings the entire passage to a patterned close. Moved by the composition and the "colours," the listeners remain controlled by Colman's careful framing. They are not encouraged to speculate about spiritual truth. Rather, Colman's strategies consistently remind his hearers that these pictures occur outside of them. He does not use metaphors that could include his hearers as participants in an action. C. S. Lewis has called writing like this a "using" of the Word, not a "receiving" of it. Scripture's language is simply transformed into more language—words that describe but do not attempt to embody scriptural meanings.[51] Colman's audience views his "show" at a distance. In the end, both strategies demonstrate yet another means by which Colman tries to express and to focus desires for a religion that meets needs conceived as at once reasonable and emotional.

IN THIS DISCUSSION of Colman's different rhetorical theories and his sermonic practice, it becomes clear how his protestations that he had nothing new to add to preaching save changes in "style, method, and allusion" must obviously be qualified. Just as John Cotton transformed the Perkins form and developed his own loose theory for justifying the use of Scripture's figurative language in his preaching, so Benjamin Colman expands the sermon model almost to the breaking point and develops his own rationale for applying the "ornaments" of poetry to his preaching. In spite of these surface similarities, however, there are obvious differences.

Cotton fragments the Perkins model out of a need to express the immanence of the justifying Word within mere human language. His preaching seems shaped to provide the occasion wherein elect listeners could sense the Word within the words, but he by no means saw his preaching as that which caused this response in them. Also, in spite of his overweening desire to preach for elect listeners, Cotton realized how the sermon model was designed to present knowledge about Scripture and about the moral law to non-elect as well as elect listeners. In spite of his eventual failure to meet the needs of both types of listeners, he at least acknowledged that there were different listeners and that the needs of both must be met.

By Colman's time, however, the older sense of the complex ways in which the Spirit moves through the preacher has been supplanted by what was nascent in preparationist thinking even during Cotton's time. The preacher must no longer simply explicate his text, believing that it is up to the Spirit to touch the elect if he wished and that the preacher's duty is simply to present sound doctrine applicable to belief and daily conduct. Colman must also convince his listeners of religion's rationality (as compared to other sources of belief) and persuade them that it is in their own "self-interest" to learn religion's dictates and to follow the means for salvation provided by the Bible and the church. But he should not only convince them of religion's conceptual soundness; he must also move them to belief and proper behavior through his appeal to their emotions. Religion's beauties and terrors, described in figurative language derived from Scripture and from other "poetic" sources, help move an audience to acquiesce to its tenets and to respond to them morally.

When Colman disrupts the sermon form, then, he does it not in the interest of focusing more intensely and piously on the "doctrines" and "reasons" for his divine text. Colman's disjunctions occur because of the nature of the material which he wishes to introduce into the sermon model. He is not explicating a text in the Bible's terms (as he sees them); he is shaping the broader relations that certain religious ideas—grace and depravity, for example—should bear to secular notions of common sense and self-interest. He attempts to use the old model as a means of juxtaposing such notions to doctrinal Calvinist dictates. The conservative form of the sermon helps him to align ideas which logically could be seen as inconsistent. As we have noted, however, his introduction of such material within his overall structure and within the different sections of the sermon threatens to destroy it as a model for the interpretation and application of scriptural texts. For Colman, the sermon becomes a means of exploring "a general proposition arising out of the text, treated of under three or four aspects which lead naturally to a conclusion corresponding with the propositions."[52] This is, in fact, a description which W. F. Mitchell offers of Tillotson's sermons. Such a mode of discourse obviously takes attention from the text's central position in the sermon and places it on the "general propositions" which derive from it and which the speaker may treat of in sources and in language which is unbiblical. In Tillotson's hands, the sermon becomes the moral essay. While Colman is still drawn to the older form—in many sermons he rigorously opens his text and notes his observations, reasons, and uses—it is clear that he, too, is struggling with and participating in this change.

Colman's formal changes, like those of Cotton, show how a preacher's perception of an audience's needs can press against and transform the forms used to express those needs. They also suggest how these newer forms, in turn, could help not simply to express but also to channel an audience's desires in certain directions.

Calling Benjamin Colman home from England, the well-to-do Brattle Street founders revealed their wishes for someone who could support their desired changes in church polity and who could express a new image of them as believers. As Larzer Ziff has noted, many of Colman's merchant supporters, including his own brother John, were attempting to re-establish cultural, social, and particularly economic ties with England. Several of them had even married Anglicans and helped to support the building of an Anglican church in Boston. It was in their interest, not only intellectually, but practically, to become interested in a reasonable "toleration."[53] On the other hand, as Colman's rhetoric makes clear, unwilling to dissociate themselves from the beliefs of their Fathers, they argued that they were simply expanding the "forms" of their expression, not altering the beliefs themselves. Through apparently slight formal changes, the wish for rational and cultural progress, as they conceived it, as well as the need for "orthodoxy," could be met.

Desiring a more rational view of their religion, however, they did not want to relinquish the notion that religion should move the affections. Brattle Street did not support the use of "dumb" readings and "set forms" of prayer, nor did Thomas Brattle buy an organ for the church in order simply to laud reason; proper Christian feeling was not to be ignored in the new church. Had not Colman in his *Mirth* treatise assured them that spiritual song, Rowe's ideal of poetry combined with music, is "perhaps the best part of Worship: the best Affections of the Soul are in the best manner that can be carry'd toward the best Good"?[54] In no way, however, were the "affections" raised by such means to prove disruptive; they were simply to move those who experienced them to the "best Good."

Recent historians have shown how the early eighteenth century in Boston, far from being the stagnant period it was once assumed to be, was rocked by confrontations over economic innovations in banking and marketing not only among the different classes or between town and country groups but between varying upper-class factions themselves.[55] Many of Colman's congregation were involved in battles over paper versus hard money, and his brother John was at the center of a controversy over a land bank. There are reports that Colman, too, was reviled as the minister of such a group.

Clearly, Colman's congregation did not want him to raise emotions which could lead to any threat to its own status. In Colman's comments on mirth, for example, he stresses the soothing effect which holy mirth would have on a man's relationship with his neighbors. In 1743, Colman joined with other ministers to decry the anticlerical, socially disruptive preaching of Edwards's follower James Davenport. In no way did he wish his congregation to think him an enthusiast.

Brattle Street's adherence to a vision of rational progress coupled with orthodoxy and of religious "sentiment" comportable with appropriate behavior was based, then, not merely on a desire to emulate English norms. In the midst of these disturbances occurring around them (and which they were, to a large extent, helping to create), Colman's hearers desired an image of themselves and their world marked by a tolerance, moderation, and restraint that still had room for the expression of religious feelings. A different church polity and a different, more fashionable way of preaching were not intended to undermine an ideal of social order with themselves at its top, but to offer new frames whereby their experience could be focused, understood, and subtly justified.

It is in using the form of the sermon while at the same time breaking it down, in using Scripture while at the same time turning it to ornament, that Colman helps both to meet his congregation's desires and also to shape them. Religious doctrines are colored by their juxtaposition to ideas appealing to common sense and right reason, yet the purpose of this alignment is not in the end to explicate or explain these doctrines, but to prove how self-interest and self-approbation are involved in following religion's dictates. These dictates, moreover, have been redefined in ethical, not the-ological, terms. Colman makes the church's function into that of arbiter of a moral conduct that is to one's "best Advantage."

The same holds true for his "rational" and "emotional" stylistic strat-egies. Each is used to attract these listeners to the security of a religion that is at once reasonable and that allows for the controlled expression of pas-sion. Once again, as Rowe and Watts help to make clear, such strategies are designed to convince and persuade hearers to perform virtuous ac-tions, not to provoke them to "enthusiasm."

If Colman's varying formal strategies thus express his listeners' needs, as he perceived them, they also hint at how the church, in turn, redefined those needs in light of its own desires. For Colman, the church's function was no longer to serve as the pure "witness" of Scripture's truths. Neither was church membership to be determined by "public relations" of the grace-experience by prospective candidates. Brattle Street saw such rela-tions as scandalous, superstitious, and possibly damaging to the "love and credit" of those who did and those who did not make them. They were "mere formalities," and not even called for by Scripture.[56]

In *The Gospel Order Revived*, Colman and Brattle Street's reply to at-tacks by Increase and Cotton Mather, Colman queries if a church's pur-pose "be to reform Manners, if to maintain the Ministry and Worship, if to lay strict Bonds of Duty, if to bring men more effectively to submit to Discipline, why then are not the whole [congregation] brought in?"[57] For Colman, the church's function as an institution lay precisely in the degree to which men accepted its right to lay "Bonds of Duty" which would be applicable to the entire congregation, not simply to those who had pro-fessed their sense of election. "Election" has come to seem almost beside the point; it is once again the church's power to define and judge moral conduct that interests him. The desire for a religion which appeals to their "reason" and piety-as-sentiment is not only a need expressed by Colman's listeners; it becomes translated into the strategies by which he can draw them under the sway of church discipline and, in the process, prove the church's usefulness to them.

Thus, Colman's sermons come not only to meet his listeners' desires, but also to serve as ways in which the church's own ends could be met and subtly redefined. That Colman's manner of expressing his ideas was influ-ential is proved by his effect on the preaching style of ministers throughout the colony. If the tolerance and moderation framed in his preaching showed them, as Miller suggests, that "narrow controversialism" had become "bad form," his preaching strategies also showed them new and powerful ways of attracting church members and urging them to accept a church that increasingly defined norms not only for the conduct, but also for the feeling, and even for the taste—saints should respond to good poetry and music—of its congregants.[58]

In sum, the different structural and stylistic characteristics of Colman's sermons can be read in a number of interrelated ways. They serve the desire of his upper-class listeners to reshape their notions of religious beliefs without supposedly relinquishing their Calvinism. They serve the church's ends by providing means by which it can at once reassert and redefine its own role in expressing new conceptions of piety and morality. In the process of expressing and focusing these needs, however, these different formal strategies also help to break down the original structure in which ideas about the meaning of Scripture were examined. The four-part sermon model is gradually transformed into a structure built around moral "topics," moving away from the rigorous "opening" of a text into doctrines, reasons, and uses. Scripture's very language, furthermore, is no longer the ground and substance of these topics, but is coming instead to serve as an ornament for them.

What Colman and Brattle Street gained by the transformations in belief encouraged by such strategies seems clear. Colman structures a picture of a reasonable, ordered world that still has room for a measure of controlled emotional response. Morality is defined in terms of self-interest, and a piety once viewed as separate from morality is now subsumed into it. Religious belief and behavior are no longer grounded in a mysterious experience of divine grace working in the soul, a justification which manifests itself in sanctification. Such an intensely individual experience could lead to a dangerous enthusiasm and social fragmentation.

What finally becomes noteworthy about the drive of both Latitudinarians and Dissenters to make religion reasonable and emotionally appealing is their need to yoke belief so firmly to its appropriate outer effects. Religious feeling, especially, must be subjected to the scrutiny of external standards. By the mid-eighteenth century, argues Raymond Williams, the very general term "sensibility" itself has become essentially a "social generalization of certain personal qualities, or to put it another way, a personal appropriation of certain social qualities."[59] Proper feelings, Colman himself suggests time and again, are not the sole possession of the elect; they can be acquired by anyone who learns the appropriate means of expressing and possessing them. He offers his listeners examples of these external means in his sermons.

Seen in light of this massive externalization of belief and feeling in the interest of proper behavior, the significance of Colman's attempts to provide rational and emotional appeals to and forms for moral conduct must be reexamined. Colman has long been considered a moderate Calvinist who abandoned doctrinal rigidity, supported religious toleration, and searched out shared beliefs among all Protestants. Miller argues that such tolerant views gradually led him to "free" colonial prose and preaching for the expression of more "natural" feelings.[60] I am arguing that the rationale for his use and transformation of older forms and styles is far more complicated. If different forms were demanded to frame both the audience's and the preacher's needs, they at the same time provided ways in which personal beliefs and even feelings could be subordinated to the desire of an upper-class audience and its church to sustain and justify an interest in maintaining, if not the reality, at least the formal illusion of social harmony, hierarchy, and control.

3. William Ellery Channing and the Shaping of Unity

I take the New Testament in hand, and on what ground do I receive its truths as divine? I see nothing on its pages but the same letters in which other books are written. No miraculous voice from Heaven assures me that it is God's Word, nor does any mysterious voice within my soul command me to believe the supernatural works of Christ. How, then, shall I settle the question of the origin of this religion? I must examine it by the same rational faculties by which other subjects are tried. I must ask what are its evidences and I must lay them before reason, the only power by which evidence can be weighed.

—WILLIAM ELLERY CHANNING

W ITH CHANNING, the movement towards a religion whose principles must be grounded in nature and human nature as well as Scripture—which was tentatively advanced by Colman, and debated rigorously throughout the eighteenth century by rationalists and revivalists of all sects—comes to fruition. Indeed, Conrad Wright has argued, Arminian thinking of the kind increasingly linked to "rationalist" religion lurked as early as 1679 in the well-wrought justifications for the Halfway Covenant, became more and more evident throughout the 1730s, and provided an open and obvious threat to orthodoxy after the Great Awakening.[1] Congregationalism gradually split in three broad directions: those who remained Calvinist and "moderate" Calvinist according to lines traditionally established in New England; those who supported the reformulation of this Calvinism in the newer terms offered by Jonathan Edwards (and those who took this formulation in "enthusiast" directions Edwards himself never intended or supported); and finally those, most notably Jonathan Mayhew and Charles Chauncy, who, from earlier alignments with orthodoxy, moved gradually both before and during the Great Awakening to an Arminian position. Wright notes that although these preachers were not yet Unitarians, the framework for Unitarian thinking was established in Arminian debates with moderates, revivalists, and Hopkinsians in the fifty years after 1745 and eventually clarified and transformed in the hotly contested election of a liberal, Henry Ware, to the Hollis Chair of Divinity at Harvard in 1805.[2]

In the Unitarian Controversy of 1815, which starts as a series of interchanges between Unitarian William Ellery Channing and Trinitarian Samuel Worcester of Andover, what is implicit in Colman has therefore become explicit. Christianity is increasingly defined in terms of its ethical qualities, not in terms of doctrines which are grounded in a biblically based theology and which, according to Calvin, call for the two kinds of faith. The elect knowledge of faith, quite clearly for the Unitarians, has almost disappeared; neither a decidedly elect nor a decidedly unregenerate group exists. Grace redefined as a sense of acting according to one's own better nature is earnable by anyone who desires it. Faith should not be at all mysterious, argue the Unitarians, because such a notion could have and historically has had bad social effects. The second kind of religious knowledge, doctrinal and informational, must also be modified radically. Explaining Scripture for Unitarians does not mean explicating a text, but determining whether a general principle derived from the text and sharing in what was perceived as the "general spirit" of the entire Scripture (especially the New Testament) could be found analogous to insight gained from looking at nature and the constitution of the human mind. The text was thereby judged according to its correspondence with other truths and, finally, in terms of what effect belief in it could have on behavior.[3]

Moral behavior is the pivotal point. For Cotton, the mysterious grace infused by the Spirit was the essence of religious experience; conduct, though important, was secondary. Justifying faith preceded and was the ground of sanctification. Cotton's ideas of persuasion—of structure, of style, of the minister's role in the process—all hinged on keeping God's role in the conversion process at the forefront. In Colman, we saw a growing interest in different sorts of knowledge that was intimately connected to their usefulness in proving the value of religion to its adherents. Whereas Colman proved unable—conceptually or structurally—to pull these different ways of perceiving religious experience together, he was on the way towards emphasizing religion's role in persuading people to behave morally as the prime ground of faith. His varying structural and stylistic strategies mirror his effort to retain his orthodoxy while at the same time incorporating into it new attitudes about religion's connection to reason and to sentiment. The struggle for Channing became, in part, a struggle between speculative and practical knowledge. Even though his training in common sense philosophy led him to believe in the reality of the correspondences he found between nature and human nature, the important fact was not simply that correspondences or analogies existed, but what their effect on human behavior would be. Scripture, too, could not be judged valid simply because its tenets could be broken down into logical axioms; the issue was whether such axioms could be joined to those found elsewhere, and that, so blended, these composite truths could have positive effects on moral conduct. As Daniel Howe points out, "The Harvard Unitarians were confident they knew the truth, but they perceived a problem in achieving a proper relationship to that truth. Harvard moral philosophers did not need to ponder, 'What is justice?' They found reason and revelation reliable guides. What troubled them instead was the problem 'How can we make men just?'"[4] Channing emphasizes this point: "If it is only a theorem for the speculative intellect, an abstract science, without power to operate on the character, inapplicable to the conscience and life," then a doctrine is probably untrue.[5]

As perceptions of the nature and function of belief begin to change, a major shift in the orientation of preacher to audience occurs. The preacher's role is still important, but in a different way: he is no longer the explicator of a doctrine intimately connected to a scriptural text; he is no longer the passive instrument through which the voice of the Spirit calls to the regenerate. How far from Cotton and even Colman is Channing's comment at the beginning of his "Remarks on a National Literature": "We shall use the work prefixed to this article as ministers are sometimes said to use their texts. We shall make it a point to start from—not the subject of our remarks."[6] The scriptural text—the alpha and omega of the Perkins form—and the frequent occasion of the saints' recognition of their sainthood has become simply a topic. Scripture is no longer central; it is supplanted by the preacher's persuasion of his audience to moral conduct on grounds offered by three different, by now nearly equal, sources of knowledge—Scripture, nature, and human nature. Further, the "truth" of the interrelations among these three is not absolute; its validity must be proved on a practical level. The preacher, then, has several linked tasks. If he has to prove the correspondences among different modes of thinking—rational, moral, and religious—he has also to prove that such linkages call for certain forms of behavior as well as for belief. The Unitarian passion for searching out analogies reveals a key assumption: beliefs which can be so documented are innately more persuasive than others. But the preacher must not only demonstrate these truths, he must persuade his audience of their persuasiveness. Unitarian belief, just as that of Trinitarians, demanded its own appropriate mode of presentation.

Finding an effective form becomes of major importance for Unitarians because the very effectiveness of such a form helped to "prove" the truth of their doctrines. As we noted, Unitarian beliefs were composite beliefs derived from the analogizing exercise of the reason on Scripture, on human nature, and on nature. These beliefs do not derive from irrefutable texts; they are arguments that must be proved true and morally effective from sermon to sermon. Presentation thus becomes centrally important in this conception of belief. Breaking the old canon of what was "appropriate" religious subject matter by admitting new material, the Unitarians came increasingly to use their sermons not only to talk about religious truth, but to embody it.

This notion of belief, as intricately tied to the effects of its presentation, is validated not by the intrinsic nature of a truth, but by the response of an audience. The locus of truth has moved from a divine revelation to a search for "universal" principles whose universality is proved by the "common sense" of listeners responding to their presentation in the sermon. In the writings of the Common Sense school, studied with an almost scriptural fervor by Unitarians, both inner moral perception and inner apprehension of external reality depend for final verification on such "universal consent." Thus, while thinkers like Butler, Price, and Reid—all at one point enthusiastically read by Channing—postulate the existence of inner faculties (the conscience, the reason) to make what they called "original judgements," each man also believes the findings of these faculties must be corroborated in the communal world of actual experience. Approbation by a community and reliance on universal "common sense" are necessary to verify both intuition and action. What is individual in either rational or moral perception is thus subject to a hypothetical communal sharing of those perceptions.[7]

Emphasizing the audience as the validator of belief not only shows how Unitarians have moved from a scriptural to a rationalist, and even towards a psychological, approach to religious truth; it also indicates the essentially rhetorical nature of their conception of belief. Within this new context, William Ellery Channing deserves attention for the important part he played in linking the truth of belief to its reasonableness and to its emotional persuasiveness. If the "best" minds in his audience must be rationally convinced of religion's value, they must also be moved. On the other hand, if the enthusiasts, who could prove an equal problem, desired that their emotions be touched, they must also be convinced of religion's "rational" nature. Even more than Colman, and far more than Samuel Worcester, with whom he debated the issue, Channing realized the relation belief bore to the form of its presentation to an audience.

But Channing, Unitarian though he was, presents something of an anomaly, not because of his awareness of the relationship that the form of belief bears to its audience, but because his position about this relationship changes as his thought develops. As many have argued, Channing is both in the Unitarian circle and outside it, a fellow traveller of the Transcendentalists but, in the end, philosophically at odds with their (initial) denial of the importance of external experience. Like Colman, but without the comfortable context of traditional orthodoxy, Channing is a balancer, and the locus of his balancing, its nature and its rationale, can be found in his theory and practice of the sermon. In this chapter we shall reexamine his early debate with the Trinitarians in light of the link it creates between a theology and an audience's needs, explore the analogy between basic Unitarian premises and major eighteenth-century rhetorical assumptions, and suggest how Channing's developing ideas regarding the capacities of a unified audience (not one split along class lines) correspond to interlinked changes in his theology and in his preaching. It must be repeated that none of these changes mark him as a member of any distinct group; they demonstrate rather how his balanced allegiances led to his own particular way of expressing and focusing a sense of cultural change.

CHANNING'S DEBATE with the Trinitarians from 1815 onward centers not only in doctrinal disagreements, but also in the effects that preaching certain doctrines has on an audience. Responding to the charge in the

Trinitarian journal *The Panoplist* that Unitarians concealed their real beliefs by not discussing their views of the Trinity, Channing counters that the motive in omitting such debate from preaching was that it encouraged bad passions in the congregation. Pressed by the reviewer and later by Samuel Worcester of Andover in a series of charges and countercharges, however, Channing becomes more explicit about why this doctrine would help to cause bad feelings, and immediately the debate takes on a rhetorical as well as a theological cast.

Channing begins by arguing that the Trinity is a logical contradiction. How can there be three persons in one God who are—although distinct persons—not separate entities? If belief in such an absurdity is demanded by God, argues Channing, surely he would not phrase it in such "a mist of obscure phraseology"; surely he would have delivered it as plainly as possible to his people.[8] When the terms concerning the Trinity are broken down, the concept becomes nothing but a verbal construct, sounds without meaning, a fiction highly unfavorable to devotion, not simply because it is a logical absurdity, but also because it proves unfavorable to "devotion, by dividing and distracting the mind in its communion with God."[9] At the far end, Channing warns, a rigidly held belief couched in a meaningless phraseology will lead better minds to skepticism and even atheism, and lesser minds to the excesses of a socially destructive fanaticism and revivalism. Channing's audience, it quickly becomes apparent, is split not by virtue of any elect status, but according to capacities of mind.[10]

Channing's interest in beliefs that do not distract or divide the mind carries over into his varying discussions of the Second Person of the Trinity. The concept of a god-man is as absurd and dangerous in his eyes as the idea of a triune God: "For myself, when I attempt to bring it home, I have not a real being before me, not a soul which I can understand and sympathize with, but a vague, shifting image which gives nothing of the stability of knowledge."[11] There are two related problems with making Christ both human and divine. On the one hand, since it is intellectually more difficult to conceive of a God who is spiritual, the slothful human mind will turn away from Christ's real godliness, his sublime virtue, and turn instead to what is easier because instinctual: a passionate sympathy with him and a natural gratitude that he bore the sufferings of humankind. People will not see the lessons behind the life and the sufferings because they cannot abstract from the concrete. As a result of focusing on a materialized God, believers will begin, like Papists, to worship his image in Christ, and thus give up a reverence for his more spiritual attributes. The image of the god-man, warns Channing, helps in "suppressing and adulterating the pure thought of the divinity."[12] Human affections for Christ "may excite the mind more easily than a purely spiritual divinity; just as a tragedy, addressed to the eye and ear, will interest the multitude more than the contemplation of the most exalted character."[13] For Channing, emotions engendered instinctually can have no lasting effect. The mind—initially confused by the concept of a god-man—takes refuge in what is easiest and most transitory: fleeting human affections rather than deeply reasoned conceptions of a pure God uncontaminated by corporeality. Channing not very subtly implies that the Trinitarian emphasis on a corporeal divinity has formed a major part of revivalist rhetoric, in which the image of the bleeding, sweating Christ appears with predictable regularity. The notion of the god-man does not lead to an intellectual skepticism like that engendered by the Trinity, but to irrational excess unmarked by attention to an idea which would have a true and lasting effect: how a Christ who is less than God but more than man opened the possibility to all who followed his system (not those who attached themselves to his person) to become more godlike through the practice of Christian virtues.

Not content to debunk the Trinitarian notion of Godhead, Channing also turns his attack on the inconsistencies he locates in the doctrines of the Atonement and of Original Sin. Like the doctrine of the Trinity, he argues, these are not so much realities as verbal delusions. Both doctrines clash with the attributes which the reason—if properly applied to Scripture and nature—can locate in a benevolent, merciful, and just God. These doctrines offer an image of a cruel tyrant and a passive people and are thus not only irrational, inconsistent with God's known attributes, but immoral. Examined minutely and freed from their ambiguous language, however, both the idea of the Atonement and the doctrine of Original Sin vanish into air. They are fictions. Original Sin, with its psychological corollary, innate depravity, is particularly illusory. Inconsistent with the attributes of a just God, it can also be proved illogical on a more empirical level when compared to the real state of social relationships. If people were innately depraved, says Channing, not only would God be cruel, but the effect of real belief in this doctrine would destroy society. Everyone would distrust everyone else to such a degree that there could be no interdependency. Society is obviously not so destroyed; therefore even those who purport to hold such a belief do not. The Trinitarians have simply taken as "real" a verbal construction that disappears when subjected to empirical tests.[14]

Finally, the doctrine of "irresistible grace" focuses all Channing's previous ideas about inconsistency, illogic, and immorality on what constituted, for him, one horrible example. Channing reasons that God, as his world demonstrates, and as the minds which he has given people also show, must reason according to laws of cause and effect. Humans learn about themselves because they see verification in the outer world that causes and effects are linked and that means and ends cohere. Irresistible grace totally contravenes structures perceived in the mind and nature—with dangerous personal and social results:

> There is nothing more striking in the mind than the connection of its successive states. Our present knowledge, thoughts, feelings, characters, are the results of former impressions, passions and pursuits. . . . [To believe in irresistible grace] is to destroy all analogy between present and future, and to substitute for experience the wildest dreams of fancy. In truth, such a sudden revolution in the character as is here supposed, seems to destroy a man's identity. The individual thus transformed can hardly seem to himself, and others the same being. It is equivalent to the creation of a new soul.[15]

Unlike Cotton, for whom the experience of grace did make the whole world new and could even infuse a joyous sense of a new identity, Channing desperately fears loss of coherence and unity of the self. Irresistible grace affronts his need for cause and effect. It has an "immoral tendency" that would not only destroy stability of knowledge, but identity itself. For Channing, identity is based on a distinct separation, not a blurring of distinctions or sudden transformations.

Channing's arguments have obvious rhetorical implications. Trinitarian doctrine, for him, is by and large based on specious metaphors, not solid "truth." For Channing—a Lockean modified by the Scots Realists—"truth" is distinct from the artificially designated "sounds," the words by which people communicate. The difference between Unitarians and Trinitarians may, he argues, be simply a matter of such words, not of "realities." The Trinitarians have based truth on metaphors which divide, distort, and disturb the mind. Metaphors viewed as truth are not subject to

laws of cause and effect or to laws of analogy—i.e., the search for correspondences between Scripture and the world. Because they deny logical
criteria for gauging belief, the "piety" to which they give rise may in no
way be connected to moral action. Trinitarian doctrines, metaphoric mysteries, will lead to rigid sectarianism, possibly to a "passive luxuriance in
feelings," and, finally, not only to revivalist excess but to skepticism and
atheism on the part of the community's best minds.[16] In a rhetoric remi-
niscent of the American Revolution, Channing declares that the Trinitarians threaten "our dearest rights and liberties" and that the dissensions
they cause not only "topple" the "family altar" but also threaten the whole
society.[17]

To this dark picture, Channing juxtaposes the Unitarian system. The
issue he discusses is not what one is to believe, however, but what mode of
belief can result in the best moral behavior and offer also the best image of
human nature. Unitarianism provides the best "appeal" because "all its
doctrines and all its precepts have that species of Unity which is most
essential in a religion, that is, they all tend to one Object. They all agree in
a single aim or purpose, and that is to exalt the human character to a
height of virtue never known before."[18] Noticeably, the ideal of unity is
not tied merely to belief in threeness or oneness in the abstract, but to an
"aim"—achieving a "height of virtue." Such a conception does not divide
the mind by directing attention to three persons; it is, rather, directed
towards one God, the Father, whose perfection lies in the consistency and
unity of all his attributes, not in an absurd plurality of mysterious persons.

God's consistency engenders more than a logical pleasure. The doctrine,
argues Channing, is also most fitted to engender proper religious feeling:
"The more strict and absolute the unity of God, the more easily and intimately all the impressions and emotions of piety flow together, and are
condensed in one glowing thought, one glowing love."[19] The thought of
God's attributes is not separable from the love of them—as God is unified,
so may the human response to him be unified. It is not splintered by the
irrational, unfixed image of the Trinity.

A God who is unified in his faculties cannot be the cruel and inconsistent
tyrant of Trinitarian theology. Channing's God behaves according to his
nature as deduced from the laws of analogy and laws of cause and effects.
He governs "by giving excellent and equitable laws, and in conferring
such rewards and inflicting such punishments as are best fitted to secure

their Observance."[20] The mind perceiving such laws is free to act morally or immorally; it is not constrained by cruel limits placed by God on a nature he himself has created. Unity and consistency are therefore not absolute states. They depend on the validity of cause and effect reasoning. If starting with effects—whether ethical or moral—one can argue back to causes, one can argue consistency and from thence move to an underlying unity in which each cause and effect, each means and each end, is linked.

In order to view God as unified and acting in accordance with reason, Christ must be demystified. As a figure more human than godly, he inspires not by his mystery, confuses not by questions of his rank vis-à-vis the Father and the Spirit, but offers a plain and simple example of the possibilities all human beings possess to act virtuously. He is no longer an absurd metaphor, appealing to the instinct, bypassing the intellect—an amphibious god-man. Instead, he has become a clear exemplum, an analogy whose end, writ large, is to persuade humankind to a belief in his system that is inseparable from a belief in the necessity for virtuous action.

With God as unity, not inconsistency, and Christ as analogy, not mixed metaphor, religion is removed from the realm of mystery and connected to human reason. In accordance with his views on human freedom, Channing cannot have this unity or consistency dictated from above. This would put him back where he started—with a mysterious God who dictates to, rather than reasons with, his creatures. While God's unity is assumed by Unitarian thinkers, however, humankind must learn of it and constantly confirm it—freely—in the world of external experience. God does not inspire believers with an immediate knowledge of himself before which they lie passive, but improves them through their free efforts. Thus Unitarians, he concludes, unlike Trinitarians, appeal to people's active, vital, reasoning powers. Indeed, Unitarian beliefs activate these powers, allowing people to trace causes from effects, or effects back to their causes. Finding unity in one area, the ceaselessly analogizing mind, as Emerson will note, goes on to find more and more unities. Out of contradiction and confusion, the active mind reaches towards broad and general principles. Importantly, this search for unity is not only a rational, but also an aesthetic, drive. The reason "labors to bring together scattered truths, and to give them the strength and beauty of a vital order. Its end and delight is harmony. It is shocked by an inconsistency in belief, just as a fine ear is wounded by a discord."[21] According to Channing, Unitarianism is a better system than Trinitarianism for interlocking logical, moral, and even aesthetic levels. It clearly, simply, and plainly "calls forth reason and emotion to the perfection of human virtue." It is a system by which the mind is both convinced and persuaded to belief and to conduct, not tyrannized over by logical absurdities and confusing metaphors. It can at once convince and move the best minds as well as focus the emotions and direct the reason of lesser minds.

Channing's disagreement with the Trinitarians has resonances far more suggestive than a simple discussion of doctrine. These resonances inhere in the manner in which he conceives of the differences between the two sects. The debate centers in a series of opposing terms: unity versus mystery, harmony versus discord, consistency versus absurdity, and analogy versus metaphor. In each pairing, the Unitarian side emerges as more appealing to both the reason and the emotions, and, as such, more persuasive to virtuous behavior. Without consciously intending it, Channing has shifted from a vocabulary of theology to a vocabulary that increasingly resembles that of rhetoric. The validity of Unitarian doctrine seems to rest less in the substance of doctrines than in its practical power to move believers to perform virtuous actions. Implicitly, if not always explicitly, the truth of Unitarian beliefs is linked to its effects.

CHANNING'S CONCEPTION of belief as it appears in the debate with Worcester is strikingly analogous to criteria applied by eighteenth-century critics to the written and visual arts. Hugh Blair's *Lectures on Rhetoric and Belles Lettres*, the major rhetoric text used at Harvard in the late eighteenth century and throughout the nineteenth century, offers a theory about the ends and means of public discourse that Channing applies to Unitarian belief as well as to Unitarian preaching. For Channing comes unwittingly to conflate the value of Unitarian belief with the effects of its presentation.[22]

Blair begins by defining eloquence in terms similar to those that Channing will later employ in defending Unitarianism. For Blair, eloquence is not speaking well, as Quintilian would have it, but "the Art of speaking in such a manner as to attain the end for which we speak." The highest end is not pleasing or even teaching: "The flower of Eloquence chiefly appears when it is employed to influence Conduct and persuade to Action."[23] Preaching, a form of eloquence which Blair notes the ancients did not possess, currently presents one of the best fields for the orator's art, because it is directed towards moral ends. Summarizing the history of preaching, Blair praises the seventeenth-century Puritan sermon, not for its oversystematization of doctrines and reasons, but because of its awareness of the important persuasive role played by the uses or "applications." Modern philosophical preachers have forgotten that an audience must be moved through such application. Preaching is "not to illustrate some metaphysical truth," but to make men "better" by giving them "at once clear views and persuasive impressions of religious truth."[24]

Blair offers advice about how to gauge what arguments will have the double appeal to reason and to feeling that can result in virtuous conduct. He dismisses the notion of "opening" a text as the source of such arguments and suggests that to locate his topic a preacher first conceive a picture of the audience for whom he preaches. Imagining the hearers will give rise to ideas both about what topics and what method of presenting these topics will "move" them. For example, as a replacement for Scripture (which has become, as it was starting to become in Colman, more useful for "allusion" and for "illustration" than as subject), Blair encourages the close examination of a specific virtue or vice or an anatomy of a famous person's "character." These topics, he argues, are sure to engage almost any audience. Unlike the older exegetical method, such topics are not fragmented and do not engender the possibility of multiple meanings. To the contrary, argues Blair. The best discourses, whether in subject matter or in presentation, must be geared towards making "one main point."[25] If "unity" is not adhered to, the audience's attention could be lost: it could become distracted, confused, and thus no longer persuadable.

From a discussion of the "unity" of set topics, Blair moves to a consideration of how such unity is achieved. The minister must first separate the different parts of his discourse into "distinct" ideas. For Blair a mixture of ideas is abhorrent because, once again, it distracts and confuses the hearer. Once a topic has been broken down into such ideas, the manner in which they are organized becomes important. Blair notes that "in Division we must take care to follow the order of nature, beginning with the simplest point, such as could be most easily apprehended, and necessarily to be first discussed, and proceeding thence to those which are built upon the former, and which suppose them to be known."[26] Blair's argument relies on a belief in a "natural" order in discourse as well as in nature, which involves linking effects to causes or ends to means. This order, he believes, necessarily proves the most convincing and persuasive to listeners.

Moving from structure to style, Blair also considers the role of figurative language in a discourse. His attitudes towards tropes mirror his concern with patterning a discourse in such a way that distinctness of impression is not lost. Figures can add a measure of emotion to the "natural order" of arguments and thereby aid in making them persuasive. In no way, however, must the hearer be led to believe that tropes embody the substance of arguments.[27] Figures of thought and figures of words must only be used to clarify and not to embody arguments. Metaphor, for example, offers "the pleasure of two things seen under one aspect"; the mind is led to compare and contrast differences and similarities and to see how such distinctions contribute to an understanding of the argument. Understanding is the key. While all of Blair's injunctions indicate his interest in persuasion, they also highlight his concern that such persuasion, if colored by emotion, must still be ultimately directed to the hearer's reason.

Channing picks up and restates each of these tenets. He obeys the Scots rhetorician's injunction to use virtue, vice, and examinations of famous characters as the subjects of his discourse, writing not only on set topics such as self-denial, immortality, and sin, but also, famously, on the characters of Napoleon, Milton, Fenelon, and Christ. And he justifies his preaching in terms similar to Blair's by arguing that "Unity of impression should be an object to a minister. . . . His efforts should be systematic, not desultory, and governed, not by sudden impression, but by extensive plans."[28] This "systematic" approach to unity, furthermore, involves separating "from a subject all that is foreign to it" and placing "it in as clear a light as possible."[29] Like Blair, Channing expands his focus on "unity" and "consistency" by reference to the harmony involved in placing "distinct" ideas in a "natural" order. Channing stresses both the natural interconnectedness of the parts of a discourse and the "real" interconnectedness of objects, events, and beliefs in the mind and nature, commenting, "We should desire to have every idea connected in our minds, as its object is in nature, so that a clear view of it shall arise before us. Distinctness of conception is important. Wide views of beings and events should be desired; we should seek to see all things in their just extent, clearly. . . . All thoughts which they suggest should be connected in their natural order, be grasped at once so as to form a complete view."[30] For Channing, as for Blair, a discourse is additive; the distinct parts join together in a particular order to offer a composite image of a whole. The quality of any writing, be it an oration or a poem, can be judged in terms of how well its means are constructed to fit its ends.

The only point where Channing slightly diverges from Blair is in his attitude towards figurative language. Channing was extremely distrustful of tropes, and of metaphor in particular. With one very important exception, he uses them only rarely. As late as 1841, Mary Edrich notes, he continues to warn of the danger of theological systems based on metaphors. His distrust of the effects of doctrines based on metaphors such as those of the Trinity and of Christ as the god-man leads him to a general fear of any tropes other than the simple analogy.[31]

Discussion of metaphor as it is linked to belief leads back to the issue of the resemblance between the criteria Blair demands for successful discourse and Unitarian claims to be a better system than Trinitarianism. Unity; consistency of subject; clarity of idea and of style; attention to the connection of means to ends, of causes to effects; following the order of nature by leading the reader's mind step by step—all are criteria applicable to both Unitarian belief and Unitarian preaching. Thus, each theological tenet that Channing debates with Worcester takes on a rhetorical cast as well. Unitarianism seems eventually the better, because the more "eloquent," system. Universal consent to what is said and, more importantly, the effects to which such consent gives rise, will help to verify both the preacher's "truths" and his manner of expressing them.

Viewed in these terms, God himself becomes the consummate orator who displays his wisdom and worthiness of regard through the very methods by which he reveals himself: "A wise teacher discovers his wisdom in adapting himself to the capacities of his pupils, not in perplexing them with what is unintelligible, not in distressing them with apparent contradictions." As a "wise teacher, who knows the precise extent of our minds, and the best method of enlightening them, [God] will surpass all other teachers in bringing down truth to our apprehensions and in showing its loveliness and harmony."[32] Plainly, says Channing, it would be against human notions of the deity's consistency for God "to use an unintelligible phraseology to communicate what is above our capacities, to confuse and unsettle the intellect by appearances or contradictions."[33]

To persuade humankind of his own unity, harmony, and consistency, then, God must use methods of presentation commensurate with his qualities. But such an assertion could also imply that the methods he uses become themselves the factors which constitute these qualities. Viewed from this perspective, the substance of doctrines could become conflated with the modes whereby they are presented. Striving to dissociate themselves from what Channing called the "mere sounds" of Trinitarian doctrine, and to establish grounds for belief other than the irrationally metaphorical, Unitarians were nevertheless still bound by their own concern with the effects of belief on behavior. As a good Lockean, Channing could repudiate the artifice of language on the one hand, but acknowledge the external character of knowledge on the other. Such a concern with externals (particularly when their effects are at issue) could lead to a concern less with the substance of knowledge, however, than with the best modes of apprehending it. The issue could become one that involved not a repudiation of artifice, but an attempt to devise a hierarchy of artifice in which one mode of discourse can be judged better or worse than another. And this is precisely what happens in Channing's debate with Worcester and in his later comments as well. Trinitarian belief and Trinitarian expression are shown to be functions of one another. They are then compared to Unitarian belief and expression and found wanting. Unitarian discourse emerges as a "truer" discourse than that of the Trinitarians because it has better effects on its listeners.

Drawing back from Channing's specific case, we can note that in Unitarianism, as in neoclassical thought in general, interest in external modes of knowledge led back to an older concern with the relation of forms to action, and thus to a renewed interest in the older theories of rhetoric which were renewed and reformulated by Blair and his followers. For many writers as well as philosophers, the "new" thought became aligned to classical forms of discourse precisely because these forms were assumed to engender specific reactions in an audience. An emphasis on universal consent and moral effects came by a gradual process of conflation to aid both in justifying belief in certain truths and in justifying the manner in which they were presented.

Reverence for the biblical text lies at the center of John Cotton's preaching theory and practice. The preacher's explication is ideally "the same for Substance" with it. Elect listeners are moved by the Spirit moving through the Word preached, not by the sermon's outer form. Non-elect hearers learn from the context of the text, but neither their knowledge nor the form through which they receive it may be construed as the possible cause of their election. Benjamin Colman, in contrast, is involved in making the subtle shift (implicit in earlier preachers like Thomas Hooker) from a form that simply presents scriptural knowledge to a form actively engaged in moving an audience towards belief and action. As we have noted, Calvin himself would not have disagreed with this position; he believed in the two sorts of knowledge. He would, however, have argued that the knowledge of faith (possessed by the elect) remains far more important than a simple knowledge of doctrine or of moral responsibility. This second sort of knowledge should be conditioned by the spiritual gift of faith. For the Unitarians, however, the Scriptures on which Calvin's theory and the preaching of Cotton and, to a degree, of Colman were based had become problematic. Channing and other Unitarians spent endless pages explaining away the confusions of biblical metaphors, seeking to clarify their meanings in light of the historical circumstances of their composition and often thereby discarding them as inapplicable to current belief or conduct. They accepted only those texts which were found to correspond to the "unchanging" laws of reason and nature. As a result, the texts used in sermons were chosen less because they were scriptural than because they fit rational, moral, and aesthetic categories of the preacher's own choosing. There is no set text, aside from the imaginary one derived from locating Scripture's analogies with nature and human nature. The "text," in a sense, has become the preacher's creation. As Lawrence Buell notes, Emerson recognized the implications of such practice and was willing to claim that his own words had indeed become the new Scripture.[34] But the Unitarian preacher, given his belief in the external sources of knowledge (including Revelation, however truncated) and his belief that the "truth" of such sources must be verified by its effects on an audience, proved unwilling to make such an assertion. As a result of this recalcitrance, the value of the doctrines he preached did, in fact, become increasingly linked to how their presentation was experienced.

Admitting that such is the case, however, is not to argue, as some have done, that Unitarians simply had no doctrine and that they were thereby forced to become "artful" in their presentation. Rather, their art mirrors their sense of what doctrine is just as much as that of Cotton and Colman.[35]

They differ greatly, however, in the degree to which theories about art (such as Blair's) more consciously help to constitute their doctrines, not simply to "color" them. If, in Cotton, doctrine encourages a particular form of artistry, in Channing the reverse seems to be occurring. More and more, eighteenth-century notions of art's unity, consistency, and harmony come to affect doctrine. Such a reversal will have its own particular effect on a central concern of all these preachers—the relation of piety to morality. This issue, too, must be reformulated in terms of new assumptions about the interrelation of form and belief, and about the audience whose needs are both presumed and shaped not only in the theory but in the practical application of the theory to the sermon form.

IN HIS chapter on preaching, Blair notes of the sermon that "no sort of composition whatsoever is such a trial of skill as where the merit of it lies wholly in the execution."[36] How much more is this true in the case of the Unitarians for whom the execution has become so tied to the truths that it "executes." Initially, Channing seemed to think that a simple presentation of what he considered a unified, clear, and consistent truth would be enough to convince an audience. He admits to Worcester that "rather than enter the lists of controversy," Unitarians had chosen to be "less striking" preachers than Trinitarians.[37] At another point he warns that "that which is called pulpit eloquence is a mode of address calculated chiefly to warm the imagination and agitate the passions." Preaching of this kind seeks its "charm" in "brilliant ornament and striking delivery, and will finally fall into vagueness, affectation, puerility, mysteries and extravagance."[38] Unitarian preaching, just as Unitarian exegesis, must set itself apart from such practices.

Writing to a friend with Calvinist leanings, Channing suggests that Calvinist doctrine has had an effect even on the ways in which Calvinist believers structure their writing: "I see with sorrow that you are beginning to depart from the simple and affecting truths which you once cherished. . . . Perhaps I have mistaken your sentiments. Your letter is written in an obscure, mystical style, very different from what distinguishes your ordinary compositions. Your conceptions seem to me loose, unsettled, undefined; but, as far as they have form or substance, they are melancholy or forbidding."[39] Unsettled doctrine, it is clear, is mirrored in unsettled expression.

In spite of such strictures on the public and private expression of Calvinists, however, Channing begins to realize, before 1820, that liberal preaching is dull and, as such, ineffective. The preaching lacks the characteristics of the truths it presents, and if truths are implicitly based on effects and if this preaching fails to have such effects, the question must inevitably become how "true" are Unitarian truths. Clearly, the liberal mode of presentation must be revitalized. Considering the preaching of his fellows, Channing is led to query:

> Is it not the error of those who oppose the prevalent system of Orthodoxy, that they do not substitute interesting views for those which they would remove? They insist that Christ came to restore human nature, that moral good is his end. But do they present this end in its dignity and grandeur? Must we not strongly conceive and represent the glorious change which he came to bring in men and nations? . . . The world waits for a new exhibition of Christianity in all its sublime encouragements, its solemn warnings, its glorious assurances.[40]

In constructing this "new exhibition," Channing must militate between revivalist excess, that "whirlwind of sound," and the barren systematization of doctrine to which both Unitarians and Trinitarians are prone.[41] It is in the process of finding the best means of presenting Unitarian beliefs that Unitarianism itself becomes fully defined and its emphasis on the "effects" of doctrine becomes such a pronounced part of its theology. In this search, it is once again Blair who suggests not only the broad outlines necessary for defining a theory of discourse, but also the structure a "pulpit oration" should take.

Central to notions of preaching and of persuasive discourse in general is the assumption that appeals must be made to both the understanding and the passions. Cotton and Colman, in their different ways and with their different ends, used the Perkins text-doctrine-reasons-uses structure in which to make these appeals. Colman, however, manifested a far greater desire than Cotton to link such appeals to certain forms of discourse. In Channing, the need to shape such appeals within the old sermon model has disappeared and it has become acceptable church practice to persuade through the use of admittedly external forms. Accordingly, Channing turns from the older sermon form and uses the structure advocated by Hugh Blair—the demonstrative oration with its three- to six-part frame of introduction, proposition, narration (or explication), reason (or argument), the "pathetic" part, and the peroration. What is central to this form is the proof of a proposition through division into a "natural order." The introduction/proposition could be compared to the older method of stating a text and a doctrine. But now the text is treated like any general subject—for the starting point of an argument, not as the center of an explication of a text. The narration usually resembles the legal device of presenting the "facts" of a case. The most important section for Blair, the "foundation of eloquence," is that of the reason, or argument. The argument depends for its effects on its "disposition and arrangement" of "distinct" ideas. The pathetic part, which may or may not include the peroration, moves the audience to belief in and action on the arguments just disposed. The whole structure is geared towards making an "effect" through a variety of appeals. It provides, claims Blair, a particularly useful structure for the pulpit.[42]

Within this structure, Blair, unlike Perkins, allows for mixed appeals. That is, appeals to conduct, for example, are not to be separated from the argumentative section even though its general appeal should be to the understanding. The two sorts of appeal should be blended. Likewise, even though the pathetic part or the peroration are sections almost exclusively designated for emotional appeals, they, too, should draw in material that affects the understanding. The sections may be logically distinct, but they can have their best overall effect if they make use, at appropriate points, of material drawn from the other sections. Colman's tendency to blend emotion and reason in a manner not entirely in accordance with the Perkins model has now been justified, indeed, even encouraged, by Blair.

In a manner similar to his predecessors, Channing initially uses the Blair structure and then comes to emphasize elements within it that threaten to break it down. Yet he, too, cannot entirely divest himself of his model. Channing's use, development, modification, and final adherence to Blair's model can be seen by analyzing the broad organization of his sermons and, in particular, his use of "division" and the juxtaposition of arguments occurring within his divisions. In addition, the style used in each section is important in considering Channing's mode of expression and the presence or absence of figurative language in his sermons. Such an exploration not only reveals Channing's use of Blair, but also suggests how his changing sense of the interplay between belief and the needs and capacities of an audience remains intimately tied to his formal transformations.

Channing's adherence to and his modifications of Blair's model are strikingly exemplified by three sermons written at different points in his career: "Preaching Christ," from 1815, written around the time of the Unitarian Controversy; "Character of Christ," which from its style and structure dates from the mid-1820s; and the famous "Likeness to God," delivered in 1828. "Preaching Christ" and "Likeness to God" are both ordination sermons, whereas the middle sermon is more evangelical, not directed towards a specific occasion. The two ordination sermons serve to show where Channing's formal practice started and what it moved towards. The middle sermon suggests changes through which he passed on his way to "Likeness to God."

The text of "Preaching Christ" is Col. 1:28: "Whom we preach, warning every man, and teaching every man in all wisdom, that we may present every man perfect in Christ Jesus." After some preliminary placement of the text into its context, Channing announces the structure he will follow:

> I have thought that these words would guide us to many appropriate and useful reflections. They teach us what the Apostles preached, "We preach Christ." They teach us the end or object for which he thus preached; "That we may present every man perfect in Christ Jesus." Following the natural order, I shall first consider what is intended by preaching Christ. I shall then endeavor to illustrate or recommend the end or object for which Christ is to be preached; and I shall conclude with some remarks on the methods by which this end is to be accomplished.[43]

Except for the comment on following a "natural order," such could be the opening of a seventeenth-century sermon—what is said and for what end it is said. In the discussion that follows, however, Channing makes little or no use of Scripture as self-explicating. The "what" and "end" are not doctrinally substantiated by scriptural reasons; both they and the "methods" are determined by the direction the preacher wishes to take. This direction is not shaped by its correspondence to a text. Channing's approach is to ask a question, define his terms, and then answer it. In considering each subject—the what of preaching, its ends, and the method of preaching them—he mixes explanation with argument, closely and logically following Blair's suggestions.

In the opening section, for example, he asks, "What are we to understand by 'preaching Christ'?" He then notes how its meanings have been understood and offers his own definition: "Preaching Christ then, does not consist in making Christ perpetually the subject of a discourse, but in inculcating on his authority the religion which he taught" (W, 3:8). This definition lists the "truths" of Christ's religion. Channing then repeats, "Now whenever we teach on the authority of Jesus, any doctrine or precept included in this extensive system, we 'preach Christ.'"

Continuing this method of expansion through definition, Channing goes on to define what is meant by Christ in this text, arguing that the term refers to Christ's system, not his person. He follows with proofs from the Old Testament that "a religion was often called by the name of its teacher," offers an example from the New Testament, and finally concludes with the modern examples of Newton and Locke (W, 3:9).

At this point, having displayed arguments for his first proposition (and sermons can have several propositions), he pulls back to address the audience and to assure them of his own feeling for Christ as a person as well as a system:

> I hope I shall not be misunderstood in the remarks which I have now made. Do not imagine that I would exclude from the pulpit discourses on the excellence of Jesus Christ. The truths which relate to Jesus himself are among the most important which the Gospel reveals. The relations which Jesus Christ sustains to the world, are so important and so tender; the concern which he has expressed in human nature so strong and disinterested; the blessing of pardon and immortal life which he brings, so undeserved and unbounded; his character is such a union of moral beauty and grandeur; his example is at once so pure and so persuasive; the events of his life, his miracles, his sufferings, his resurrection and ascension, and his offices of intercessor and judge, are so strengthening to faith, hope, and charity, that his ministers should dwell on his name with affectionate veneration, and should delight to exhibit him to the gratitude, love, imitation and confidence of mankind. (W, 3:11)

After this passionate avowal in which he lauds and encourages his audience to love Christ's character, Channing suggests that this proves only a partial response: "But whilst the Christian minister is often to insist on the life, the character, the offices, and the benefit of Jesus Christ, let him not imagine that he is preaching Christ only when these are his themes."

He next turns to another rhetorical set piece, but this time rather than applying it to a subject he is not discussing—Christ's person—he applies it to his own argument, the vast extent of Christ's "system":

> It regards man in his diversified and ever-multiplying relations to his Creator and to his fellow creatures, to the present state and to all future ages. Its aim

is, to instruct and quicken us to cultivate an enlarged virtue; to cultivate our whole intellectual and moral nature. It collects and offers motives to piety from the past and the future, from heaven and hell, from nature and experience, from human example, and from the imitable excellences of God, from the world without and the world within us. (*W*, 3:11–12)

As in the preceding section, Channing retreats from the emotional cast of his observations to comment: "It is not intended by these remarks that all the instructions of Christ are of equal importance, and that all are to be urged with equal frequency and zeal." He is speaking of the Calvinist tendency to focus on too few doctrines and warns that no doctrine will have "proper influence, if swelled into disproportioned importance, or detached from the truths which ought to modify and restrain it" (*W*, 3:12).

Coming to the end of the section, Channing summarizes: "It has been the object of these remarks to show that preaching Christ does not imply that the offices and character of Christ are to be made perpetually the subjects of discourse" (*W*, 3:12). The result of such a focus, he concludes, is a mistaken notion of religion as consisting "in a fervid state of mind" that promotes a censorious spirit. He ends the section by warning his hearers—the ministers gathered for the ordination—not to encourage such a spirit in their congregations.

The next proposition follows the same pattern, asking the end for which Christ is to be preached and answering that "we should preach, that we may make men perfect Christians, perfect, not according to the standard of the world, but according to the law of Christ; perfect in heart and life, in solitude and society, in the great and in the common concerns of life. Here is the purpose of Christian preaching" (*W*, 3:14). He expands his question and answer by turning to yet another emotional set piece, detailing precisely what the gospel calls for in order to become "perfect":

With this spirit of martyrs, this hardness and intrepidity of soldiers of the cross, the Gospel calls us to unite the mildest and meekest virtues; a sympathy which melts over another's woes; a disinterestedness which finds pleasures in toils, and labors for others' good; a humility which loves to bless unseen, and forgets itself in the performance of noblest duties. To this perfection of social duty, the Gospel commands us to join a piety which refers every event to the providence of God and every action to his will; a love which counts no service hard, and a penitence which esteems no judgment severe; a gratitude which offers praise even in adversity; a holy trust unbroken by protracted suffering and a hope triumphant over death. In one word, it enjoins that loving and confiding in Jesus Christ, we make his spotless character, his heavenly life the model of our own. (*W*, 3:15)

As could be expected, Channing calls attention to what he has done: "I have dwelt on this end of preaching, because it is too often forgotten, and because a stronger conviction of it will give new force and elevation to our instructions." He follows his rational summary with another impassioned defense of his principle, this time of human beings' capacity for perfection, and he ends the section with another quiet attack on Calvinism: not only does it create bad "feelings" between people, but it is based on fear which debases the mind. To be truly effective, Christianity should, in contrast, encourage a sense of human dignity.

The third "place" concerns the "method" of accomplishing such an end as was called for in the introduction. Not surprisingly, Channing calls for this method to "be addressed at once to the understanding and the heart." He broadens this initial comment with a prolonged discussion of Unitarian exegetical method. This discussion focuses, however, not on touching the heart, but on the need to approach the Bible's language rationally. Channing warns that if Scripture is not so approached, the intelligent part of the community may "convert it into an instrument of policy, or seize a favorable moment for casting off its restraints and leveling its institutions with the dust." He follows this discussion with an almost reluctant section on the need to move the emotions.

The sermon ends with an extended exhortation to his hearers in which all his themes appear:

> Let him preach, not to amuse, but to convince and awaken; not to excite a momentary interest, but a deep and lasting seriousness; not to make his hearers think of the preacher, but of themselves. . . . Let him labor, by delineating with unaffected ardor the happiness of virtue, but setting forth religion in its most attractive forms, by displaying the paternal character of God and the love of Christ which was stronger than death, by unfolding the purity and blessedness of the heavenly world, by revealing to the soul its own greatness and by persuasion, by entreaty, by appeals to the best sentiments of human nature, by speaking from a heart convinced of immortality, let him labor, by these methods, to touch and to soften his hearers, to draw them to God and duty, to awaken gratitude and love, a sublime hope and a genuine desire of exalted goodness. (*W*, 3:22)

This peroration can serve as an example to make a general point about Channing's method within this sermon as a whole. In it he again makes use of an emotional strategy to include a blended content—everything which the Christian system asks a minister to be and to do. In the process of his exhortation, the reasonable propositions he has advanced throughout the sermon are made more "emotional." Such is the method he advocates in the last section—blending reason and affection. Such is the method he himself uses throughout the sermon.

Precisely how are Unitarian ends met in this particular sermon, and what seems to be its attitude towards the needs of an audience? The structure, it seems clear, attempts to embody certain aims. The "unity, consistency, and harmony" of his argument are born out in Channing's method of displaying them. Each idea is distinctly separated from the others; each is cast within the frame of a definition and answer structure. His concern for symmetry of structure in each proposition is particularly noteworthy: he begins with questions, briefly answers them, and then spends the rest of each section expanding his answer through the use of two modes: one rational, the other more emotional. The emotional mode is created not through the use of figures, but by anaphora, repetition, parallelism, and by a recourse to balanced doublets and triplets similar to those used by Colman. It differs from the rational mode more in its structure than in its content. Employing such structures, Channing in no way undermines the clarity of his rational propositions; he is simply asking for a more felt response to them.

Clearly, the audience's reactions are extremely tightly controlled by this structure. The subject matter, "preaching Christ," is broken into definitions, and any emotional response which is felt is experienced as a result of this method of approaching the subject. In other words, Channing leaves room for no more or less rational interpretation, no more or less feeling about interpretation than he himself offers. The sermon structurally exhausts (in its own terms) the properties of the subject by enacting the method he urges the preacher to use in the last section: juxtaposing appeals to reason with appeals to emotion. A curious note of fear emerges in Channing's comments about how the best minds in the community will turn away from an "unreasonable system" and, by extension, unreasonable preaching. He warns not only of the effects of rigid Calvinist belief on the community, but also of the need to shape the audience's response in a manner different from previous efforts. This manner is, of course, exemplified in the sermon just preached, in which reason and affection are both addressed but carefully controlled within a rational framework, not of the Perkins form, as in Colman, but in the shape of the demonstrative oration.

In the 1820s, around the time of his discourse on Milton's *De Doctrina* (1825), Channing's sense of what a sermon structure is to do and how it is to do it begins to alter. Claims he makes about the artist's adherence to inner, not outer, "rules" appear in comments from letters and sermons, but most importantly in a famous passage in which he discusses Milton's style:

> The best style is not that which puts the reader the most easily and in the shortest time in possession of a writer's thought; but that is the truest image of a great intellect which conveys fully and carries the farthest into other souls the conceptions and feelings of a profound and lofty spirit. To be universally intelligible is not the highest merit. A great mind cannot, without injurious constraint, shrink itself to the grasp of common passive readers. . . . A full mind will naturally overflow in long sentences, and, in the moment of inspiration, when thick-coming thought and images crowd upon it, will often pour them forth in a splendid confusion, dazzling to common readers, but kindling to congenial minds. (*W*, 1:21–22)

Milton's lack of clarity, his suggestiveness, gives his reader a feeling for the sublime possibilities of human nature; the poet does not rigidly define and limit human nature according to its "local" character, as Channing finds Samuel Johnson to do. But Channing also realizes that Milton can call forth a deep passion only in those who already have enough quality of mind to focus such passions in a proper direction. He takes great pains to point out that great minds are never rabid enthusiasts. At this point, Milton's techniques are attractive to Channing, but still too dangerous to use on "common" readers. Channing's growing attraction to the power of different techniques, expressed in the *De Doctrina* discourse, will, however, eventually come to change his sense of his audience's capacities. In "Demands of the Age on the Ministry" (1826), Channing is even willing to encourage the use of a rich diction and "imagery" where the preacher's own genius calls for them. Furthermore, in a letter to a friend, he admits that Unitarianism has suffered because of its connection to a "heart-withering" empiricism and could benefit from a knowledge of sources of imaginative power.[44] Poetry and the arts cannot necessarily create moral impressions, but as Colman, Watts, and Rowe recognized, their techniques can be used to further the cause of proper religious feeling.

These comments stand as a backdrop to what Channing attempts in "Character of Christ." The sermon still shows his use of Blair, but a use imaginatively richer than it was in "Preaching Christ," revealing his changing conception of how form should be used to persuade an audience to moral action by meeting their emotional as well as their rational needs. His text is from Matt. 17:5: "This is my beloved Son, in whom I am well pleased." The introduction itself marks a difference in method and intention from those in "Preaching Christ":

> The character of Christ may be studied for various purposes. It is singularly fitted to call forth the heart, to awaken love, admiration, and moral delight. As an example, it has no rival. As an evidence of his religion, perhaps it yields to no other proof; perhaps no other has so often conquered unbelief. It is chiefly to this last view of it, that I now ask your attention. The character of Christ is a strong confirmation of the truth of his religion. As such, I would place it before you. I shall not, however, think only of confirming your faith; the very illustration which I shall adduce for this purpose, will show the claims of Jesus to our reverence, obedience, imitation, and fervent love. (*W*, 4:7)

Turning to a "character" for his subject matter, Channing follows Blair's advice about using character as a more moving and thus more persuasive topic than doctrine. But he does not simply "place" the character of Christ before the audience; he announces his ends in doing so. Still, even though he uses the ends/proof-of-ends structure of the earlier sermon, he has moved away from its logical separation of Christ from his system. In this sermon Christ's system is emphatically a product of his character; thus its "proofs" must be entirely different. Channing tells his audience specifically what he wants to do: he will not lay out a method of approaching a subject which appeals to emotion without the use of images. He intends to "show" Christ's claims to a belief based on admiration as well as understanding.

In describing the means by which he will "prove" his case, he again sounds very much like Colman. Channing admits that Christ's character is not having its proper effect on people because his disciples are "leaving him to reveal himself by giving his actions and sayings without comment, explanation, or eulogy. You see in these narratives no varnishing, no high coloring, no attempts to make his actions striking, or to bring out the beauties" (*W*, 4:8). In other words, as Blair notes of most religious topics, this one, too, has grown habitual and therefore has been disregarded. The preacher must reawaken religious wonder and "almost . . . create a new sense in men, that they may learn in what a world of beauty and magnificence they live" (*W*, 4:9).

After this discussion of his ends and his method (although he does not call them such as he did directly in "Preaching Christ"), Channing offers his first proposition: "In this discourse I wish to show that the character of Christ, taken as a whole, is one which could not have entered the thought of man, could not have been imagined or feigned, that it bears every mark of genuineness and truth, that it ought therefore to be acknowledged as real and of divine origin" (*W*, 4:9). Following the proposition, one could expect proofs, but the proof Channing offers is far different from that of the earlier sermon. Channing now uses what he calls "views" to "color" the point he wishes to make. They form what Blair would call the narrative. In a manner similar to legal arguments, Channing must lay out the "circumstances," tell the story of the case. In line with his project to revivify the Gospel for his hearers, he must not only lay out these facts, however; he also must "color" them. To prove his initial proposition, then, Channing turns to a consideration of the Jewish people at the time of Christ: "Of all nations, the Jewish was the most strongly marked. The Jew hardly felt himself to belong to the human family. . . . His common dress, the phylactery on his brow or arm, the hem of his garment, his food, the ordinary circumstances of his life as well as his temple, his scriptures, his ablutions, all held him up to himself as a peculiar favorite of God, and all separated him from the rest of the world" (*W*, 4:9). After discussing the Jewish hatred of the Romans, their dreams of the messiah, and their clinging to the "mosaic institution," Channing appeals directly to the imagination of his audience: "You may judge of its [the Jewish religion's] power by the fact of its having been transmitted through so many ages amidst persecutions and suffering which would have subdued any Spirit but that of a Jew. You must bring these things to your mind. You must place yourself in the midst of this singular people" (*W*, 9:10).

Having set the scene in which Christ will appear, Channing introduces his major character, presenting the Jewish people "surrounding him with eager looks, and ready to drink in every word from his lips" (*W*, 4:11). The passage is structured as a series of comparisons between what the Jews desired and what, in contrast, Christ offered. What the Jews hear is, of course, disconcerting, for Christ continually notes that his kingdom is not of the world. He does not speak of the worldly victories of the chosen people. Completing this list, Channing sets himself apart from his "view" and announces: "Here I meet the annunciation of a character as august as it must have been startling." He does not analyze the picture just offered, but turns instead to another "view"—Christ healing the child of the Gentile centurion and praising his faith. The view presents another example of how Christ destroyed the myth of Jewish chosenness. As before, once the picture is completed, Channing turns to his hearers, asking if they do not find Christ's character "wholly inexplicable on human principles." The section concludes with a summary of the material just presented in which he notes how his "proofs" have demonstrated that neither Christ's character nor his purposes "fit" his Jewish context.

The sermon becomes increasingly analytical as Channing turns to answer "objections" to his portrait. To the two major objections—that Christ could have been feigning his role and that he was nothing more than an enthusiast—Channing responds by offering evidence to the contrary. Christ could not feign such a role, for surely his mask would have slipped; Christ is no "enthusiast," for his words and manner show his serenity, calmness, and rationality. Had he been an imposter or an enthusiast, moreover, his words could not have had their continuing effect. Channing offers these proofs not by simply listing them, but by appealing through direct questions to his audience's knowledge of the case and to their common sense:

> The charge of an extravagant, self-deluding enthusiasm is the last to be fastened on Jesus. Where can we find traces of it in his history? Do we detect them in the calm authority of his precepts; in the mild, practical, and beneficent spirit of his religion; in the unlabored simplicity of the language with which he unfolds his high powers, and the sublime truths of religion; or in the good sense, the knowledge of human nature, which he always discovers in his estimate and treatment of the different classes of men with whom he acted? Do we find this enthusiasm in the singular fact, that . . . he never indulged his own imagination, or stimulated that of his disciples, by giving vivid pictures, or any minute description of that unseen state? (W, 4:17)

At the end of his series of questions, he asks in lawyerlike fashion: "Now, how stands the case with Jesus?" But he does not go on to answer this question in the expected manner, i.e., rational interpretation of the evidence. Instead, he directly appeals to his hearers' intuition, arguing that Christ's truth should be seen not only in his concrete words and actions but must be sensed "by reading the Gospels with a wakeful mind and heart. It does not lie on their surface, and it is stronger for lying beneath it."

After each "objection" and "answer," Channing concludes with a summary beginning with a rational account of the "facts" as they now stand and ending with an emotional response to those facts. Increasingly, he reverts to a language of "I," "you," and "we," encouraging participation rather than distance from his subject. He notes, for instance, "I began with observing how our long familiarity with Jesus blunts our minds to his singular excellence. We have probably often read of the character which he claimed, without a thought of its extraordinary nature" (*W*, 4:19). At the end of the section, Channing powerfully summarizes his picture of Christ's nature:

> I confess, when I can escape the deadening power of habit, and can receive the full import of such passages as the following,—"Come unto me, all ye that labor and are heavy laden, and I will give you rest,"—"I am come to seek and to save that which was lost,"—"He that confesseth me before men, him will I confess before my Father in Heaven,"—"Whosoever shall be ashamed of me before men, of him shall the Son of Man be ashamed when he cometh in the glory of the Father with the holy angels"—"In my Father's house are many mansions; I go to prepare a place for you:"—I say, when I can succeed in realizing the import of such passages, I feel myself listening to a being, such as never before or never since spoke in human language. I am awed by the consciousness of greatness which these simple words express; and when I connect this greatness with the proofs of Christ's miracles . . . I am compelled to exclaim with the centurion, "Truly, this was the Son of God." (*W*, 4:20)

The second section of the sermon follows a similar pattern, only this time Channing does not offer an historical example, but a "supposed" one appealing more directly to the experience of his congregation. In fact, this whole view is cast in the language of supposition. He asks them to suppose that they had never heard of Christ's history but were told that such a man had lived and acted: "How would you represent him to your minds? Would you not suppose, that with this peculiar character, he adopted some peculiar mode of life, expressive of his superiority to and separation from all other men?" He follows with an extended list of what his congregation, not the Jews, might "rationally" expect of such a figure and then, just as he did in the first section, overturns their expectations. Jesus fulfills none of their suppositions. His sense of his own greatness does not demand the special reverence they suppose; it demands instead the sympathy towards others he himself has shown. Channing concludes with several examples of this sympathy towards all people of all classes, then argues as before, "I maintain that this is a character wholly remote from human conception. To imagine it to be the production of imposture or enthusiasm, shows a strange unsoundness of mind. . . . [I]t bears no mark of human invention. It was real. It belonged to and it manifested the beloved Son of God" (*W*, 4:26–27).

Noting that he should conclude at this point, he remarks that he has not yet done. He must locate the "principle" at the base of all his "views": "Do you ask what this deep principle was? I answer it was his conviction of the greatness of the human soul." Rather than continuing his consideration of Christ's character, Channing introduces an argument obviously of great interest to his own theology—the fact of the soul's greatness—but one which fits very awkwardly into the context of the argument he has constructed. Instead of proving this assertion with "views," as he has done throughout the sermon, Channing simply states it. After this brief interlude, he repeats, "Here I pause and indeed, I know not what can be added to heighten the wonder, reverence, and love which are due to Jesus" (*W*, 4:28). Then, as in "Preaching Christ," he ends with a moving peroration in which all his themes are brought together.

In "Character of Christ," Channing still uses the Blair structure—proposition, narrative, argument, and peroration—but these components are now directed towards exploring the traits and effects of a character rather than an abstract proposition. As Blair suggests, employing such a subject can simply be more effective in rousing an audience out of its lethargy regarding religious subject matter. Whereas Channing still employs the expected structure, appealing to his hearers' opinions of the "case" after every example, the point of the sermon seems clearly less to convince them than to move them, to engage them in an emotional, not simply a rational, participation in his subject matter.

The internal frame of the sermon is that of "views," historical and imaginary, which are offered and then commented upon in a frame of objections and responses to objections. Channing's method of answering these objections often seems equally as "moving" as the views themselves. He "proves" his points through the use of extended series of rhetorical questions directed to his audience's response. In other words, unlike "Preaching Christ" where the structure of the sermon itself seemed to limit his hearers' participation, "Character of Christ" continually and directly appeals to this response. However, in spite of the fact that Channing allows them more participation in the sermon and begins to allow the "views" he presents to them and the rhetorical questions he asks respecting these "views" to become the sermon's true substance, he is still in tight control of their response. After each view, he stands back and notes its persuasiveness before even entering into the objections and answers. He is not willing, in other words, simply to encourage a response; he must still tell them what their response should be. Describing his own reaction, turning to objections/answers, and concluding with a summation of the encapsulated "meaning" of each view constitute his means of shaping the audience's emotional reactions to his subject. While Channing thus offers more freedom, he is concurrently experimenting with different means of focusing this "free" response.

If "Preaching Christ" manifested Channing's belief that rational truths should be presented in a rationally structured manner, "Character of Christ" shows his growing belief that his presentation of this subject must demonstrate qualities that make belief "moving" as well as those which "prove" it rational. Channing continues to follow Blair, but his emphases are changing. Channing's transformation of his mode of presentation furthermore indicates a gradual shift in the focus of his theology; he is becoming more concerned with how internal truths manifest themselves externally, rather than with appying external rules to belief and behavior, however rational. At the same time, this transformation also suggests a shift in his sense of the needs and capacities of his audience. However much he still controls his hearers, he uses a subject matter and a manner of presentation increasingly geared to emotional response.

Channing's greatest experiment with the possibilities and limitations of the Blair form occurs in his most famous sermon, "Likeness to God," preached at the ordination of F. A. Farley in 1828. This sermon is important for those aspects of its structuring as well as its ideas that make it seem close to Transcendentalism, but it is equally important to note that Chan-

ning does not entirely relinquish his use of Blair within it. Like Cotton and
Colman, Channing participates in the simultaneous retention and repudiation of his model, a balancing act that not only involves questions of form,
but also the question of that form's relation to his theology and to his
conception of the audience for whom he preaches.

The introduction to "Likeness to God" sounds like that of "Preaching
Christ," but with an important disclaimer:

> To promote true religion is the purpose of the Christian ministry. For this it
> was ordained. On the present occasion, therefore, when a new teacher is to be
> given to the church, a discourse on the nature of true religion will not be
> inappropriate. I do not mean, that I shall attempt, in the limits to which I am
> now confined, to set before you all its properties, signs, and operations; for in
> so doing I should burden your memories with divisions and vague generalities,
> as uninteresting as they would be unprofitable. My purpose is, to select one
> view of the subject, which seems to me of primary dignity and importance;
> and I select this, because it is greatly neglected, and because I attribute to this
> neglect much of the inefficacy, and many of the corruptions, of religion. (*W*,
> 3:227)

Channing still follows Blair in his decision to preach about one "topic,"
but unlike "Preaching Christ," where he attempts to "unfold" the subject
in its completeness, "Likeness to God" dismisses the notion of creating
burdensome "divisions" in order to explain this topic.

His text is from Eph. 5:1: "Be ye therefore followers of God, as dear
children":

> The doctrine which I propose to illustrate is derived from these words and is
> incorporated with the whole New Testament. I affirm, and would maintain
> that true religion consists in proposing, as our great end, a growing likeness to
> the Supreme Being. Its noblest influence consists in making us more and more
> partakers of the Divinity. For this it is to be preached. Religious instruction
> should aim chiefly to turn men's aspirations and efforts to that perfection of
> the soul, which constitutes it a bright image of God. Such is the topic to be
> discussed. (*W*, 3:228)

He follows this doctrine with a lengthy observation, not a proof, which
will recur as a major theme of the sermon: likeness to God "has its foundation in the original and essential capacities of the mind." Unlike earlier
sermons, however, this one does not go on to propose this notion as his

theme; instead, Channing begins the narration/argumentation section of the sermon. While this introduction of the idea of the mind's innate capacities thus prepares listeners for his later discussion in the body of the sermon, at this point he only suggests it. He does not clearly distinguish an order of topics and carefully chart the transitions between them. For the moment, he leaves an idea to resonate in his hearers' minds without qualification.

The arguments that follow Channing's "observation" are likewise not numbered or differentiated from one another. He places the concept within different contexts and allows its meanings to expand more by juxtaposition than by argument. His first "proof," for example, maintains, "It is only in proportion to this likeness, that we can enjoy either God or the universe. The Gentiles saw the need for such likeness, the pure of heart see it, and it is a fact of daily experience." These facts having been introduced, the proof begins a crescendo into an emotional mode similar to that used in "Preaching Christ":

> How quickly, by what an instinct, do accordant minds recognize one another! . . . God becomes a real being to us, in proportion as his own nature is unfolded within us. To a man who is growing in the likeness of God, faith begins even here to change into vision. He carries within himself a proof of a Deity who can only be understood by experience. He more than believes, he feels the Divine presence and gradually rises to an intercourse with his Maker, to which it is not irreverent to apply the name of friendship and intimacy. The Apostle John intended to express this truth, when he tells us, that he, in whom a principle of divine charity or benevolence has become a habit and life, "dwells in God and God in him." (*W*, 3:229)

Upon completing this movement—assertion followed by emotional restatement—Channing turns without transition to his second proof. The connection between the two is again not clarified, only suggested. Using the same general structure, he first asserts, "It is plain, too, that likeness to God is the true and only preparation for the enjoyment of the universe." Then, as before, but this time with more immediacy, he returns to his "emotional" mode, using anaphora, rhythmic repetition, and the inclusive "we" to encourage his hearers to feel as well as to understand his argument: "In proportion as we approach and resemble the mind of God, we are brought into harmony with the creation; for, in that proportion, we possess the principles from which the universe sprang; we carry within ourselves the perfections of which its beauty, magnificence, order, benevolent adaptations, and boundless purposes, are the results and manifestations" (*W*, 3:230).

Even though—by Cotton's or Colman's standards—this crescendo-like movement is slight, Channing still feels it necessary to draw back at its end and comment on it, just as he did after each one of the "views" offered in "Character of Christ." He notes, "It is possible that the brevity of these hints may expose to the charge of mysticism, what seems to me the calmest and clearest truth" (*W*, 3:230). Instead of recapitulating what this "clarity" is, however, he turns to what is rare for him—the use of images: "For the creation is a birth and shining forth of the Divine Mind, a work through which his spirit breathes . . . We discern more and more of God in every thing, from the frail flower to the ever-lasting stars. Even in evil, that dark cloud which hangs over the creation we discern rays of light and hope, and gradually come to see, in suffering and temptations, proofs and instruments of the sublimest purposes of wisdom and love" (*W*, 3:230). Channing uses doublets comparable to those of Colman: "birth and shining forth," "light and hope," "suffering and temptations," "proofs and instruments," "wisdom and love." As in Colman, this classical doubling gives a sense of control to the passage. Yet there is a slight but important difference. Channing employs this structure in the creation of an image far more suggestive—the creation as "birth" and "shining forth" of the divine Mind—than Colman's static pictures or his own relatively simple "views." Furthermore, he does not explore this image, but moves on, leaving its interpretation to his listeners. Then, as if aware of the dangers involved in so doing, he draws back, much as he has done in the other two sermons, and summarizes his first series of proofs: "I have offered these very imperfect views, that I may show the great importance of the doctrine I am solicitous to enforce" (*W*, 3:230).

When examined closely, however, the similarity of this summary to those of the other sermons becomes superficial. Instead of following the summary with a baldly stated transition and then considering his next "proof," this "proof" is already contained in the summary: "I would show that the highest and happiest office of religion is, to bring the mind into growing accordance with God; and that by the tendency of religious systems to this end, their truth and worth are to be tried" (*W*, 3:231).

Up to this point it is evident that Channing still employs an argument/summary structure used elsewhere, but it is also evident that these arguments are growing less focused on religion's rationality and more on its emotional power. As a result, he increasingly disregards the clear-cut distinctions and "natural order" advocated by Blair. While Blair does allow for a blend of reason and emotion within the different sections of the oration, Channing's focus on emotion within his narration and argument threatens to supplant their original functions: to persuade the understanding.

In the sermon's next section, for example, he begins by comparing the Unitarian mode of scriptural exegesis to that of the Trinitarians, then turns to a discussion of Christianity as a system that calls for his form of interpretation. But, after a long series of New Testament texts centering on how perfection of the self is central to Christianity, Channing breaks away from his purported subject and launches into a discussion of how nature and reason confirm his ideas about "likeness." Turning from the assertion/proof mode he has been practicing, Channing has changed his rhetorical approach as well as his ostensible subject. He no longer uses scriptural proofs, but falls into the question/answer pattern used in "Preaching Christ": "Whence come the conceptions which we include under that august name [God]? Whence do we derive our knowledge of the attributes and perfections which constitute the Supreme Being? I answer, we derive them from our own souls" (*W*, 3:233). The questions gradually lead him into a more emotional mode that culminates in his uncharacteristic use of still another image: "The Infinite Light would be forever hidden from us, did not kindred rays dawn and brighten within us." The image reintroduces the theme suggested so long before in the introduction: that "likeness" can only be understood by minds with the capacity to recognize it. At this point the question/answer pattern once again reasserts itself, but it is cast entirely in an emotional, not a rational, mode: "And are these attributes revealed to us through the principles and convictions of our own souls? Do we understand through sympathy God's perception of the right, the good, the holy, the just? Then with what propriety is it said that in his own image he made man!" (*W*, 3:235).

Question/answer is succeeded by another standard pattern used in argumentation: objection/response. Beginning once again in the rational mode of address suggested by Blair, Channing notes two major objections to his theory about "likeness": God must be seen in the outer, not the inner, universe, and God differs utterly from humankind because his attributes are infinite. But Channing's responses to these objections again demonstrate his transformation of the techniques he has used earlier. Throughout this section his intensity is mounting, and he continually apologizes to the audience for speaking "strongly" and "obscurely." He asserts that while God's attributes may be infinite, humankind shares in them; one has only to look at love and moral duty as well as the external forms of nature's sublimity and human art. As he continues this argument, Channing's prose begins to pulse with repetitions and anaphora until, as before, he neglects the objection/response pattern altogether, falls into the rhythms of an emotional mode, and finally breaks into an extended series of images:

> The truth is, that the union between the Creator and creature surpasses all other bonds in strength and intimacy. He penetrates all things, and delights to irradiate all with his glory. Nature, in all its lowest and inanimate forms, is pervaded by his power; and, when quickened by the mysterious property of life, how wonderfully does it show forth perfections of its Author! How much of God may be seen in the structure of a single leaf, which though so frail as to tremble in every wind, yet holds connexions and living communications with the earth, the air, the clouds, and the distant sun, and through these sympathies with the universe, is itself a revelation of an omnipotent mind! God delights to diffuse himself everywhere. Through his energy, unconscious matter clothes itself with proportions, powers, and beauties, which reflect his wisdom and love. . . . [T]hat the soul, if true to itself and its Maker, will be filled with God, and will manifest him, more than the sun, I cannot doubt. Who can doubt it, that believes and understands the doctrine of human immortality? (W, 3:238)

Once again, Channing does not comment on these images, but instead considers his final "proof" of likeness: the fact that God is a parent, a "Father." Retreating from the intensity of the passage preceding it, Channing casts this section in the question/answer rational pattern. Continuing in the rational mode, he next offers the "use" of his doctrines: "The greatest use which I would make of the principles laid down in this discourse is to derive from them just and clear views of the nature of religion. What then, is religion?" The direct question is followed by a series of interwoven questions and repetitions. He opens the section, for instance, by noting that "the connection of this near and ennobling relation of God to the soul, and of his great purposes towards it, belongs to the very essence of true religion; and true religion manifests itself chiefly and most conspicuously in desires, hopes, and efforts corresponding to this truth." After a series of more questions, he then repeats, "True religion is known by these high aspirations, hopes, and efforts."

But this attempt to return to a more rational framing of the sermon is abandoned as the restraint of the old question/answer format once more gives way to a metaphor which is again left to resonate without explication: "To honor him [God], is to become what we praise. It is to approach God as an inexhaustible Fountain of light, power, and purity. It is to feel the quickening and transforming energy of his perfections. It is to thirst for the growth and invigoration of the divine principles within us. It is to seek the very spirit of God" (W, 3:241–42).

After a brief consideration of how these views are opposed to Calvinism's debasing views of human nature, Channing turns very directly to the audience: "You cannot, my hearers, think too highly of the majesty of God. But let not this majesty sever him from you. Remember that his greatness is the infinity of attributes which yourselves possess" (W, 3:242). He summarizes each of these attributes—intelligence, power, goodness, and so forth—each time explicitly reminding the audience that these are qualities which "you" share.

Then, as if aware that his imagery and direct address may move his hearers in directions he does not intend, Channing begins his famous qualification of his argument and, in so doing, returns to his more rational mode of address: "To complete my views of the topic, I beg to add an important caution." All the feelings of likeness which he has encouraged his hearers to feel are not to be directed to "enthusiasm" and misguided religious fervor: "Let none infer from this language that I place religion in unnatural effort, in straining after excitements which do not belong to the present state, or in anything separate from the clear and simple duties of life" (W, 3:243). He must balance between too much enthusiasm and too much rationalism.

As he begins to consider new and final objections to his argument, however, Channing does not remain in the rational mode. Countering the objections that such views are illusory, he exclaims, "What! Is it only in dreams that beauty and loveliness have beamed on me from the human countenance, that I have heard tones of kindness which have thrilled through my heart, that I have found sympathy in suffering, and a sacred joy in friendship? Are all the great and good men of past ages only dreams? Are such names as Moses, Socrates, Paul, Alfred, Milton, only the fictions of my disturbed slumber? . . . O! no. I do not dream when I speak of the divine capacities of human nature" (W, 3:246–47). In another response to an objection, to be considered separately, Channing confronts those who would argue that his views are not fit for the pulpit, nor for "common minds." Here, once again, he falls into the imagery by now associated with the emotional mode:

> I see God accomplishing his noblest purposes by what may be called refined means. All the great agents of nature, attraction, heat, and the principle of life, are refined, spiritual, invisible, acting gently, silently, imperceptibly; and yet brute matter feels their power, and is transformed by them into surpassing beauty. The electric fluid, unseen, unfelt, and everywhere diffused, is infinitely more efficient, and ministers to infinitely nobler productions, than when it breaks forth in thunder. (W, 3:248–49)

In his anticlimactic ending remarks, Channing admits that he has not touched on all possible ways of viewing human nature, and that a free being sins as well as acts virtuously. Yet he argues that even among convicts in prison he has found that his higher views of human nature best "promote a generous virtue." Calvinism, in short, can produce neither the response which Unitarian appeals to people's higher natures can produce nor, it seems (by extension), the response which Unitarian rhetorical structures can also encourage.

Near the end of the peroration, Channing unconsciously draws attention to this conflation of rhetoric, belief, and response: "That he [the Unitarian preacher] will rival in sudden and outward effects what is wrought by the preachers of a low and terrifying theology, I do not expect and desire" (W, 3:254). The theology, it is clear, walks hand in hand with its method of presentation. According to Channing, the Unitarian preacher must realize that his matter and his manner will have effects far deeper and longer lasting than those of the Calvinist: "His function is the sublimest under heaven; and his reward will be, a growing power of spreading truth, virtue, moral strength, love, and happiness, without limit and without end" (W, 3:255). These comments are couched within the framework of an extremely moving peroration in which he urges Farley and all ministers to worship their own souls.

"Likeness to God" attempts to use a proof-based logical structure—the "demonstrative oration"—in which unity, consistency, and harmony are products of the framework in which arguments are adduced. However, Channing's very theme, this likeness, threatens to break down the argumentative movement of this form towards what Blair called its "one main point." In the midst of proofs, answers to questions, and responses to objections occur impassioned declamations of feeling about the subject matter rather than reasoned analysis of its meaning and its application to conduct. Channing's older mode of presenting emotion uses rhythm and repetition; in this sermon he also increasingly turns to the use of images and extended imagery. Blair allowed for the presence of appeals to emotion, couched both in figures and in rhythmic prose, within the different sections of the oration, but these appeals were intended only to color appeals to reason, not to supplant them. The "natural order" of the address and the distinguishing of separate ideas was not to be disrupted. In "Likeness to God," to the contrary, the movement of different ideas progressing in clear distinction towards a unified conclusion remains far from evident. While each proof begins in a more or less rational manner and usually employs either a question/answer pattern or a response/objection pattern, again and again Channing falls into an emotional mode that both expands and threatens his "proof." Each proof expands into a brief rhapsody, a way of feeling, not simply understanding, the likeness theme. Indeed, in spite of its adherence to Blair's outer structure, it is the repetition in the sermon's different sections of this theme that often seems to give the sermon its consistency.

In its structure as well as its content, then, "Likeness to God" begins to manifest a changed sense of what unity, consistency, and harmony are. Rather than being qualities which are perceived as external to the self, the self (viewed in its godlike aspect) is found to be that which irradiates all things with these qualities. The qualities Channing has sought to impose from without are now found to be diffused from within. Unity, consistency, and harmony inhere within all things and among all things, from the soul to the frail leaf. Channing is clearly no longer thinking in terms of distinction so much as he is of identification. All things partake in God's likeness. Unity is not a function of adding up disparate phenomena to arrive at a composite picture of the whole; each apparently separate thing is becoming in itself a manifestation of one vast unity. As Channing moves close to thinking in terms of identity rather than likeness, it seems evident from the style and structure of this sermon that not only his ideas about the sermon form are changing, but that his idea of his audience has also been transformed.

Indeed, the sermon consciously draws attention to this change:

> It is said that men cannot understand the views which seem to me so precious. This objection I am anxious to repel, for the common intellect has been grievously kept down and wronged through the belief of its incapacity. The pulpit would do more good, were not the mass of men looked upon and treated as children. Happily for the race, the time is passing away in which intellect was thought the monopoly of a few, and the majority were given over to hopeless ignorance. . . . The multitude, you say, want capacity to receive great truths relating to their spiritual nature? But what, let me ask you, is the Christian religion? A spiritual system, intended to turn men's minds upon themselves. . . . What are the Christian virtues which men are exhorted to love and seek? I answer pure and high determinations of the mind. That refinement of thought, which I am told, transcends the common intellect, belongs to the very essence of Christianity. (*W*, 3:249–50)

Unlike the *De Doctrina* discourse, where Milton's views and his mode of presenting them were "dazzling" to "common minds," "Likeness to God" emphasizes the capacity of all minds to comprehend subtle truths. It does so by drawing attention to the relation of Christianity to the minds for which it is intended. Christianity is somehow fitted to those who receive it; it exemplifies the perfect correspondence between a system and its adherents. Christian virtues, for example, correspond to those "pure and high determinations of the mind," that "refinement of thought" possessed by Christians. The system assumes its audience, just as the audience's capacities assume (and justify?) the system.

Channing is moving away from the notion that Unitarian Christianity consists of external ideas presented to the mind in order to cause certain predictable reactions. In "Likeness to God," Channing recognizes how the mind itself creates systems; it is not simply affected by them. Viewed in these terms, hearers respond to a sermon not because of rational points rationally proved by external evidence and made convincing by equally rational rhetorical strategies. Rather, listeners respond because they are in intuitive accord with a sermon's propositions: its truths are less functions of external experience or external forms of presentation than of the internal correspondences strongly felt in emotional patterns of discourse, particularly in imagery. The images used throughout the sermon—electricity, diffusion, penetration, heat, light, fountains, springs, and so forth—suggest an intimate sharing, a participation in an illumination that occurs from within, not from without. The audience is offered neither wholly rational views (or structures) nor external views that can more emotionally move them to proper conduct. Instead, they are moved by rhythms and images suggesting the presence of an inner life expressing itself through them. Presented with such images (and the increasingly rhapsodic structures that usually precede them), hearers are led to sense harmony and consistency not because their preacher has logically or emotionally connected ends to means and causes to effects; such an audience is moved by its own capacity to share in the inner connections and relations implicit in their preacher's mere juxtapositions and analogies.

While these different techniques threaten the Blair form and project an audience moved to belief and action by intuition and feeling as well as by reason, however, it must be emphatically repeated that in the midst of his transformations of Blair's form, Channing also insists on retaining it. Viewed in the light of this retention, Channing's disclaimer near the end of "Likeness to God" must be taken seriously: "Let none infer from this language that I place religion in unnatural effort, in straining after excitements which do not belong to the present state, or in anything separate from the clear and simple duties of life" (*W*, 3:243). At each point where his structure and language may suggest a turn away from moral action in favor of religious feeling, Channing, as we have noted, pulls back to a rational mode. Whereas he does not repudiate the emotions he has engendered, he still attempts to place them within a broader rational framework.

Even as he threatens it, Channing retains a structure of argument based largely on objections and responses, questions and answers—a structure calling for a rational outer response by a community of listeners. But, at the same time, within this rational superstructure, he makes increasingly metaphoric appeals to inner feeling, to a participation grounded in individual, though shared, intuition. What is remarkable about this great sermon is Channing's evident desire to fall neither completely into rhapsody nor into an imposed rationalism. If he seems to approach the latter mode, it is invariably followed by a crescendo into the former. When he does employ the rhapsodic mode, he will generally end by framing its images

within the rhythms of balance and control. Channing clearly wants to retain both modes and to assume a "unified" audience as needing both and
capable of responding to both. Far more than Colman, Channing views his
retention of his model not as an attempt to acknowledge responses that
could prove at base opposed—the rational and the emotional—but as an
effort to encourage a sense of community large enough to include both
outer restraints and duties and individual feeling.

Channing's apparent deviation from the theological and rhetorical premises underlying "Preaching Christ" and his formal experiments in the
"Character of Christ" and "Likeness to God" need to be understood in this
context. Channing's emphasis, unlike that of many Transcendentalists, is
not on sudden transformations, but on inclusion. The changes in his
preaching that suggest changes in his theology and his view of his audience
must not be viewed as an entire repudiation and abandonment either of his
earlier thought or of his earlier adherence to Blair's form. They are the result
of expansion and development, not exclusion.

CHANNING'S BELIEF in a process of inclusion that would modify his
manner of preaching and broaden his notion of his audience was not shared
by his "real" listeners. As Andrew Delbanco has recently noted, Channing's
position in the 1830s was marked by a growing distance from his upper-class
conservative congregation in Federal Street, whose attraction for his
preaching became qualified by their discomfort with what he preached.[45]
Educated Unitarians in general had been led by their ministers to consider
themselves the rational flowering of New England's political, social, and
aesthetic possibilities. While "Likeness to God" as inspiration was permissible, as social reality it was unthinkable. As historians have shown, the
commercial ties to the slave interests ran deep among many Boston Unitarians. In fact, Channing's congregation refused their famous minister the
right to preach a funeral sermon in their church for an Abolitionist friend,
Charles Follen. But Channing fared no better with the Abolitionists, who
felt his stand on slavery was inadequate—rhetorically moving, but practically ineffective. In spite of his book on slavery (1834), Channing refused
them his full-scale commitment. If his congregation represented a social
hierarchy gone rotten at the core, the Abolitionists represented the possibility of social revolution coupled with its own form of moral despotism.
Neither position was acceptable to Channing. As Delbanco notes, Chan-

ning to the end of his life retained his need for outer structure and an order based on externally shared human experience.[46] This need, whether called Old Federalist or Augustan in its impulse, coexisted in Channing's thought with his increasing trust in the inner capacities of the individual mind. Yet as his discourse on Napoleon demonstrates conceptually, and as "Likeness to God" demonstrates structurally, Channing could not accept individual intuition, feeling, or perception as the sole ground of belief or of community. He desires an interplay between outer structures and inner capacities, a system based, in the solid Federalist terms of the eighteenth century, on checks and balances.

As shaped in Channing's thought, such a system was increasingly less grounded in revelation (save by analogy), and based more on a developing belief in an interplay between the power of the mind and the external world. As we move from "Preaching Christ" through "Character of Christ" to "Likeness to God," this intense interest in the interrelation of external "forms" to internal abilities does not abruptly change; it is transformed very gradually. The later sermons have less to do with defining these connections than they do with attempting to provide an experience of them. Yet, even though the proportions of the balance between the outer and inner worlds is shifting, Channing's emphasis on the necessity for their balance is never relinquished. Channing was criticized by his contemporaries and has continued to be criticized by modern scholars for his failure to take fixed positions. I am instead arguing that in structure, in content, and in the audience whose needs are projected in their interplay, Channing's later preaching reveals an inclusive and complex vision of communal balance and individual freedom.

Emerson, as we shall see in the next chapter, was unwilling either conceptually or formally to retain Channing's earnest balance. Channing's intricate view of community, implicit in the very structure of "Likeness to God," was translated into social action on behalf not only of slaves, but of the working classes in the 1830s. Young Emerson's emphasis on the self-forming capacities of individuals—of their divinity, not their likeness to divinity—called neither for the balance nor, initially, for the sense of social obligation implicit in Channing. Emerson's sense of the individual's relation and responsibility to the larger social world comes to differ as inevitably as his attitudes towards the sermon form.

4. Emerson, Coleridge, and the Shaping of Self-Evidence: Theory

IN 1832, at age twenty-eight, Ralph Waldo Emerson stepped down from his post at Boston's prestigious Second Church. Although he was to preach sporadically until 1839, he never again held a professional position as a minister. Differences between the young preacher and his congregation over the nature and function of the Lord's Supper were the ostensible reason for the break, but these differences had a long history in Emerson's journals of the period and in other sermons. From the very beginning of his preaching career, Emerson was wrestling with the relation of "forms" to religious experience. Trained by liberal Unitarians, including Channing himself, and sharing many of their assumptions, Emerson nonetheless had become increasingly dissatisfied with the Unitarian inability—or unwillingness—to carry out the implications of their thought. As Lawrence Buell and David Robinson have argued, what has been termed his rupture with his mentors is less an emphatic break (especially at the beginning) than it was an unfolding of principles already present in much Unitarian preaching.[1]

Comments from his journal for 1834 manifest Emerson's attempt to differentiate himself from his teachers. In a series of tight aphoristic fragments, he voices his dissatisfaction with the "formal" religions and calls for a new approach to "self-evident" truth. In spite of their randomness, these sententiae demonstrate Emerson's struggle with as well as his repetition and assimilation of major issues explored throughout this study:

118

Unitarianism & all the rest are judged by the standing or falling of their
professors. I refuse that test to this. It is true. I see this to be true though I see
it condemns my life and no man liveth by it. They are truth itself, they are the
measure of truth & can no more be affected by my falling away or all men's
denial than the law of gravity is changed by my acting as if it were not. Yet is it
dangerous! It is very far from a system of negatives; it lowly, earnestly sees &
declares how its laws advance their reign forevermore into the Infinitude on all
sides of us. Jesus was a setter up more than a puller down. Socrates was also.
Both were spiritualists. . . .

Spiritual Religion has no other evidence than its own intrinsic probability. It
is probable because the Mind is so constituted as that they appear likely so to
be.

It never scolds. It simply describes the laws of moral nature as the naturalist
does physical laws and shows the surprizing beauties and terrors of human
life. . . .

It is opposed to Calvinism in this respect that all spiritual truths are self
evident, but the doctrines of C. are not, & are not pretended to be by their
understanding defenders. Mystery.

This is the only live religion. All others are dead or formal. This cannot be
but in the new conviction of the mind. Others may.

This produces instant & infinite abuses. It is a two-edged sword because it
condemns forms but supplies a better law only to the living. . . . The popular
religion is an excellent constable, the true religion is God himself to the
believer & maketh him a perfect lover of the whole world; but it is only a cloak
of licentiousness to the rest. It would dismiss all bad preachers & do great
harm to society by taking off restraints.

Spiritual Religion is one that cannot be harmed by the vices of its
defenders.[2]

In his belief that "spiritual religion" is distinct from forms—here
viewed not only as ritual, but as the moral dictates of the "constable"
religions and the "bad" preaching by which they are promulgated—Emerson sounds like John Cotton. Yet while Calvinists like Cotton may have
possessed a more compelling belief in the power of the invisible than did
Unitarians, their acquiescence to outdated, mystery-ridden biblical doctrines made them problematic for the still-Unitarian Emerson. Moderate
Calvinists like Colman offered a perspective more congenial in some respects. Striving to align religious truth with natural harmony and reasonable self-interest, Colman helped to set the stage for the Arminian and

eventual Unitarian focus on rational religion. At the same time, he also drew attention to the relativity of the "forms" by which religious truth was presented to an audience. Both the "forms" of ritual and the "forms" of preaching should accord with the shared "manners of men on the earth." Whereas Emerson did not consciously share Colman's attitudes towards the social usefulness of these forms for arousing, controlling, and focusing belief and sentiment, he and the Unitarians from whom he sprang believed that Spirit must be found in sources other than the biblical "letter" and that means must be found in which to make the new ideas derived from these sources commensurate with an audience's needs.

But Emerson began to find even the Unitarian approach to the relation of Spirit to letter philosophically and methodologically unsatisfactory: "Unitarianism and all the rest are judged by the standing or falling of their professors." Unitarianism grounded its truth value on "standing or falling"—external moral effects. Whether Unitarians admitted it or not, it owed its appeal to the "proofs" offered by outer forms and was thus just as much a "constable" religion as the Trinitarianism it accused. Indeed, it was far less consistent than its opponents. On the one hand, Unitarians believed in miracles and retained those scriptural tenets that they deemed "rational." On the other hand, according to Emerson, Unitarians depended far too much on "rational" information offered by the senses to "prove" the value of religion. Depending on externals, whether scriptural or natural, Unitarians overlooked the fact that "true" religion must be "self-evident."

By grounding its principles in common sense philosophy, Unitarianism did in fact emphasize the power of a rational moral sense (if properly trained) to make appropriate judgments. It was therefore not solely dependent on external forms—scriptural or natural. Just as the reason could organize, classify, and put the data offered by the senses in some type of hierarchy, so could the moral sense organize, classify, and judge the data offered in the moral realm.[3] In his desire to distinguish himself from the Unitarians, however, Emerson came to downplay these possible similarities with his own thought. The key point for Emerson was that whether they dealt with empirical or moral "materials," the Unitarians still derived them from an outer, not an inner, world. The moral sense, like the reason, made its judgments largely on what were rational, not intuitive, grounds. Inner morality, like inner reason, was thus only the mirror of a static external harmony and design. Despite the existence of inner faculties, then, their operation depended on their being activated from the outside. The point here is not to discount the fact of Unitarian pietism (recent studies have stressed that piety forms an integral part of much Unitarian thought), but to argue that Emerson shaped his theory of a self-evidence that is at base affective as well as rational, and his theory of a form that is vital rather than imposed, in distinction to his perceptions of Unitarian "reason," Unitarian morality, and Unitarian concepts of form—whether ritualistic or verbal.[4] The contrast was not totally illusory. The Unitarian emphasis on the moral "effects" of Unitarianism could and did conceptually and formally implicate them in Emerson's charge. Their ideas of "unity," "self-evidence," and "harmony" were "true" not simply because they were mirrored in—or more correctly, mirrors of—nature, but because they were assumed to have positive effects on moral behavior. For Emerson, the Unitarians were indeed in danger of becoming yet another "constable" religion; they were simply replacing Scripture with "reason" and "nature" as their justification for imposing moral norms from the outside.

In the midst of his implicit and explicit debunking of the grounds on which other religions have based their truths, the young Emerson developed his own flexible definition of a truly "spiritual religion" which he contrasted to both "rational" and "revealed" religions. In the terms of the quotation, this new religion sets up "true" laws rather than simply knocking down false ones; its laws are developing rather than static; it is intrinsically, not extrinsically, self-evident to its believers, i.e., does not demand external verifications but is true "because the Mind is so constituted as that they appear likely so to be." The faculties of "reason" and the "moral sense" do not constitute this Mind. For Emerson, the one term, Mind, suggests an integrated, self-organizing Whole, not a series of separate mechanical faculties.

If Emerson sounds very much like Channing here, he shows none of the Unitarian's care to balance a belief in this inner Mind with an awareness of the need for externally imposed forms. He seems instead to be groping for an entirely new conception of form in which Mind or Spirit may inform a form, but is in no way caused or constrained by it. Emerson also seems aware that a concept of response is inseparable from these formal changes. Once again expanding on a Channing-like insight, Emerson pushes his idea about response in a direction of which Channing was wary. The passage speaks of two kinds of response to the "Spirit." Some perceivers, trapped in the formal assumptions of the constable religions, will be unable to hear the Spirit speaking through a form. They will see (or hear) only another form. Blinded by their own adherence to external forms, they may see/hear this new form as a "cloak of licentiousness," irreligious, immoral, and socially dangerous. Others, however, "true" believers, are capable of experiencing these external manifestations of Spirit as expressions of "God himself." Emerson's emphasis here falls neither on form, nor on response, but on their interaction. He does not thereby negate his contention that "spiritual religion" is not formal; rather, he is developing a new sense of how the Mind/Spirit speaks through forms to the hearts of true believers.

In his obliqueness, not his evasiveness, Emerson resembles Cotton responding to Shepard: "And therefore though I consent to you that the Spirit is not separated from the Word, but in it, and ever according to it, yet above and beyond the letter of the word it reacheth forth comfort and Power to the soule, though not above the Sence and Intendement of the Word."[5] Furthermore, Emerson faces a similar dilemma. This dilemma is encapsulated in the penultimate lines of the quotation: "It [spiritual religion] would dismiss all bad preachers and do great harm to society by taking off all restraints." At the same time that the passage acknowledges a problem with preaching, it noticeably does not deny the validity or the necessity of preaching. It is bad preaching, not all preaching, which must go. But the function of preaching would have to be immeasurably changed. If preaching ceased to serve external morality and functioned to remove outer restraints, it could, as Emerson notes, half earnestly, half tongue-in-cheek, "do great harm to society." One can imagine Benjamin Colman's and even Channing's horror at this perception of the preacher's role. Emerson, however, could argue that such fears were ungrounded. For Emerson used the idea of spiritual religion, formulated not only in his early journals or essays but in sermons written between 1826 and 1836, to explore the concept of a self-reliance, that is, a Spirit-reliance which in turn involves a total self-abandonment to the designs of the universal will. To knock down outer moral forms in favor of a reliance on the whole Mind's ability to gauge self-evident truths is to end up with a vision that is ultimately shared, ultimately communal, not fragmented and anarchical. In Emerson's later terms, derived from Coleridge and Carlyle, the conscious mind, the "understanding"—that part of the mind which takes in, classifies, divides, and arranges sensuous information—simply becomes the frame through which the Reason, also variously known as the universal Mind, the Oversoul, the daemon, passes on its way towards expression. This root assumption about the relation of inner belief to its outer forms, in yet another shape, lies at the base of Emerson's theory of compensation. What is in a person necessarily will push itself out; by his or her fruits, indeed, shall we know them—not because fruits in any way cause them to be what they are, but because fruits are, in fact, an expression of what they are. By the rules of compensation, even if one attempts to hide the inner reality by carefully shaping and manipulating its outer expression, this inner reality will inevitably be revealed and appropriately rewarded or punished. In Emerson's early thought, compensation is usually an extrinsic process of reward or punishment: judgment of actions will occur on Judgment Day. Later he will maintain that the reward or punishment will occur internally in the moment of the action itself. Both "doctrines," of self-reliance and of compensation, are involved with what on a very broad level we have been calling the relation of Spirit to letter, the relation of inner, universal, spiritual truth to its outer manifestations.[6]

As did the preachers before him, Emerson believed in the power and necessity of preaching as the middle term linking the world of Spirit and the world of letter, which he, however, defined not only as verbal revelation, but also as the "language" of nature. Like Cotton, he distrusted any reliance on form, and like Colman he saw the historical relativity of form; yet, like Channing, although from a changing perspective, he acknowledged the necessity for form. The issue for him, as he moved from the late 1820s through to the early 1830s and became the lecturer/essayist rather than the minister, was to find a proper theory for relating Spirit to letter and a way in which this theory could be not only explained but embodied in his own preaching. Finally, the manner in which his theory and practice coincided was also to reveal his conception of the needs of an audience and the role it came to play in "justifying" both his theory and his preaching.

If "spiritual religion" is not to be divorced from the preached word, the nature of eloquence must be redefined. Emerson did not forget his ministerial predecessors' concern with the relation of the hearing of the preached word to spiritual insight. His fascination with Edward Everett and Daniel Webster, even if it faded, stemmed from an assumption irremediably Protestant: "Faith cometh through hearing." Like John Cotton, however, Emerson did not credit the preacher with causing such faith. Indeed, he makes it explicit that the act of preaching is a two-way street: the preacher may speak the Spirit in his words, but it requires the Spirit in an audience to complete his act. He does not direct his sermon to himself alone, but to an audience presumed capable of response. Analyzing Emerson's aesthetic theory, Vivian Hopkins long ago recognized the contribution that the observer made to the "meaning" of an artwork:

> "Sensibility" and "perception" have the same meaning for the observer as for the creative artist . . . not merely a transference of images from retina to brain, but the interpretation of those objects by the receptive mind. In this higher power of the observer's/hearer's "sensibility" lies the "realizing" of the artifact, by which the observer's enjoyment is no mere addition to created beauty, but the very means of bringing it to life. It is this kind of sense impression that Emerson has in mind when he says a book may be everything or nothing according to the human eye that sees it.[7]

What Hopkins did not explore was the degree to which Emerson's belief in the importance of the listener/observer remained, at its deepest level, more religious than it was aesthetic. Emerson was concerned with his audience because he came out of a tradition that maintained a preacher's words had no meaning unless the Spirit spoke through them to the hearts of his listeners. If "Faith cometh through hearing," salvation itself depended on a mutual act of communication and reception. To say that the audience "responds" to the preacher's words, in Emerson's terms, is not to suggest that for him the sermon had become simply a mass of rhetorical techniques calculatedly imposed on listeners in order to achieve certain moral effects. The "elect" for the Calvinist Cotton and all people for the Transcendentalist Emerson were capable of a "spiritual" as distinguished from a strictly "moral" response to preaching. But again, their response was not to his form, but to the Spirit speaking through his words and in themselves.

The spoken word was essential to Emerson. The critical attention given to his metaphors of vision has neglected the attention which the young preacher gave to hearing. As Michael Colacurcio has noted (but curiously in reference to George Ripley rather than Emerson), the notion of "faith" for Transcendentalists was very much tied up not simply with seeing correspondences, as Hopkins suggests, but with hearing a communication.[8]

The Spirit "speaks," makes itself heard through the medium of the external word, but the hearing is of two kinds. The external word simply helps to activate (not to cause) the inner hearing of the inner Word. Listeners may respond initially only to external words by an external hearing, but all who truly desire to do so are capable of hearing "through" external words to the Spirit's voice. If Emerson (and the Romantics in general) wanted to see with an inner eye, Colacurcio argues that the Transcendentalists in particular wanted to hear with an inner ear. Listening, then, as well as sight, proves essential to the experience of revelation or becoming "transparent."

Whereas the young and older Emerson read the correspondential theories of Sampson Reed, Emanuel Swedenborg, and Guillaume Oegger, a related but different formal dimension to his writing emerges if we consider it in terms of hearing rather than seeing. Reading Emerson from this perspective, for example, leads to questions about the shaping of an entire discourse or the juxtaposition of its varying symbols in larger conceptual and experiential patterns, rather than limiting inquiry to a series of symbols whose meanings are interpreted in possible isolation from their context. Hearing involves a communication between preacher and an audience; it is an experience that moves through time and which is not as concerned with individual parts as it is with a total moving form. Thus, although Emerson may in fact have periodically asked his listeners to isolate his symbols, these symbols should also clearly be considered in relation to one another and to the whole structure of interrelations, the composition, in which they occur.

Finally, a stress on hearing does not simply contribute to the shaping of a discourse; without an audience's response, the preacher's act is incomplete. The self-evidence of "spiritual religion," to return to the opening quotation, involves far more than a visionary experience felt by an individual soul; self-evidence also centrally includes a speaker actively evoking the Spirit within a moving structure before a listening audience. Emerson came increasingly to view this response as no longer external to the sermon, but as an integral part of its shape.

THE STRUGGLE undertaken by the young Emerson as he began to develop a new sense of the interrelation of faith to its forms and to its audience is clearly revealed in a sermon of 1831. Emerson's distrust of outer forms combined with his need to appear a good Unitarian (and thus to allow external form some place in the life of faith) came to a head five years before the so-called Miracles Controversy broke out between George Ripley and Andrews Norton, and two years before his own declarations in "The Lord's Supper." In Emerson's sermon "Miracles," the issue of how external signs are related to internal, self-evident faith has already become a major one. Emerson manifests his division about the problem not only in the false starts and stops that appear in the manuscript, but also in the structuring of the argument that finally emerges.

Like Cotton and Colman, each of whom broke down the Perkins form, Emerson transfigures the Unitarian form of argument by using a Channing-like framework but introducing statements which undermine its function. It is perhaps because of this expected frame, however, that Emerson received no adverse comments on the sermon. The structure once again could provide both a means of revealing and concealing its own breakdown. Doing so, it could also project an audience whose needs were straining against, but not completely repudiating, assumptions inherent in this structure. At the end of the sermon, Emerson simply quotes a long passage from Coleridge's *Friend* in which he attempts to integrate the mix of "rationalist" and "inner" proofs he has offered in the body of the sermon, but which seems more to expose than to synthesize their differences. At this point, the young preacher has found neither the argument, nor the means of presenting the argument, for the necessary relationship between that inner voice of faith and outer signs, whether the latter be miracles, the Bible, natural phenomena, or the forms of preaching itself.

The following sketch of the sermon's erratic and inconsistent movement through its arguments serves as an example of Emerson's general dilemma at this time in his career. It further suggests, however, that although his undigested reading in Coleridge failed to resolve the contradictions of this particular sermon, it could offer him conceptual and formal means of reconciling them.

Emerson begins the sermon in a way we have learned to expect from Channing, with a short, clear introduction that lays out the issue he will analyze. His is to be a "plain account of the reasons which make the miracles recorded in the New Testament credible." To prove this assertion, he notes, involves his showing "that in some circumstances it is not unreasonable to expect a miracle and that such circumstances existed in the age of Jesus Christ."[9]

His first consideration is "that a miracle is the only means by which God can make a communication to men that shall be known to be from God" (*YES*, p. 120). The mind must recognize such a peculiarity as a miracle; otherwise none has occurred. Emerson avows here, as he will throughout his life, that God's inner speaking is miraculous, and that to deny the possibility of hearing a divine voice is to deny the possibility of there being any divine communication at all. But this assertion, important as it is, in no way corresponds to the plan of argument he has just laid out. Emerson makes no mention of the "circumstances" under which such a speaking occurs; it is an inner, not an outer, action, and clearly such a circumstance cannot be prepared for, if indeed "circumstance" is even the proper word.

The second consideration attempts to alleviate this confusion by speaking very definitely of the need for certain outer miraculous activities. In the best Unitarian fashion, Emerson notes that the mind has been fitted to respond to the external world; if a feeling of lack exists in the mind that external nature cannot satisfy, then surely God will supply this lack. Truth and religion demand it. "For the increasing processes of events without any interruption or any sign of intelligence beyond what the infinite beauty of the whole furnishes, without a hand outstretched, without a word, spoken in heaven or on earth, makes man doubt the existence of a cause that is never shown to his senses" (*YES*, p. 121). God's own order helps to conceal his hand in it. The problematic quality of this consideration rests both in Emerson's opinion that only better minds (those of his congregation?), not those of the "multitude," are able to intuit this lack and also in his suggestion that the very existence of such a lack implies that God's order is incomplete. Miracles are afterthoughts, additions to what God possibly should have done in the first place.

In the third section, almost a direct reversal of this argument, Emerson praises that very natural order which he has just implied is wanting. Here he decides that nature is in itself miraculous. "To an instructed eye the most common facts are the most wonderful." The "common facts" of nature are miraculous in general, but miraculous in particular are humankind's own physical and mental abilities. Emerson notes that it is a miracle to lift one's arm, to speak and be heard and understood, to remember: "Ourselves are the greatest wonder of all. Our own being is a far more astounding and inexplicable fact, than . . . could be the resurrection of a man from a tomb" (*YES*, p. 122). While one could argue that this focus on human ability is at the center of Unitarian thinking, one could conversely argue that Unitarians believed in miracles. Emerson is juxtaposing one of Unitarianism's uncomfortable inconsistencies: focusing on the religious and miraculous qualities of everyday experience in the context of a sermon about the value of belief in Scripture's miracles.

In the fourth section, he apparently realizes that he has related none of these "proofs" for the existence of the miraculous to the moral sphere. The section begins with a flat assertion that this connection exists and must be "proved." The law of compensation, as it operates in nature, becomes evidence that what is good for humankind "naturally" is good for them morally. "As you act so shall you receive" is a lesson taught on all levels of life. Once again, however, this argument becomes confused. Compensation, it is clear, provides a form of moral interrelation between people and nature that is not at all in need of verification by divine intervention. Beginning with the supposed subject of God's moral nature and the divine nature of acts like miracles, the section develops and ends as an argument about the already existent moral interrelation of people and their world. No miracle, Emerson comments in the following section (which seems uncomfortably tacked on to these comments), can be used to prove unnatural doctrines. Such an immoral act would cause the mind to revolt against it and the God who performed it. "To make a miracle of any effect as evidence, it must accompany the revelation of a truth which, when made known, is agreeable to the laws of the mind" (*YES*, p. 123). The compensation Emerson has just discussed is precisely such a law. The real subject of the entire passage has become not miracles in themselves, but a law discerned to operate naturally. Emerson uses one apparent subject to discuss yet another and uses one Unitarian mode of argument—the appeal to reason—to debunk another, the appeal to miracles. Unaware or unable to reconcile the possible contradictions in his argument, he concludes the first half of the sermon about the "circumstances" in which miracles could happen by noting that his "considerations" have proved "the credibility of a miracle."

According to Emerson's introduction, the second half of the discussion was to analyze the particular circumstances in the New Testament which had proved conducive to the performance of miracles. Liberal Unitarian as he was, however, Emerson begins this section not by considering these circumstances, but by warning that "a miracle is a lower species of evidence. It speaks to ignorance. It speaks to unbelief" (*YES*, p. 124). Given such a warning, how then is a Christian to view the New Testament? A belief in its history, its external events, including its miracles, would yield to an interest in the self-evident holiness of its principles, Emerson argues. Belief in the words of Christ or James or Paul must not rest on external proofs, but on an inner response to their goodness. Struggling in the webs of this argument, Emerson forces himself to add that even though the truths of the New Testament are self-evident, they are yet of such a quality that they "might be expected to be accompanied by miraculous power." Such power does not prove them, however; it merely accompanies a belief entirely based on response to an inner voice, not to outer evidence.

Emerson completes the sermon not by drawing his disparate and contradictory set of "considerations" together—how could he?—but by quoting a long paragraph from Coleridge. In its final lines this quotation also helps to undercut the ideas he has ostensibly been trying to analyze: the credibility of miracles and the circumstances in which they could occur.[10] In this passage, Coleridge argues that if outer signs and inner "laws" coincide in proving the existence of miracles, humankind must accept the fact that a true relation exists between God's outer power and his inner revelations. Coleridge warns that acknowledging this possibility, however, does not mean that humankind should limit the divinity to "the particular forms and circumstances of each manifestation." The miracle lies in the fact of the Spirit's intervention, not in the specific forms whereby it occurs.

If the passage from Coleridge contributes to the general confusion of Emerson's approach to his subject, it also indicates his equal desire to set up the terms of the relation of Spirit to its outer manifestations on entirely new grounds. If the standard Unitarian wish that intuition be balanced by a morally directed outer form is addressed in this sermon, Emerson pushes this wish beyond acceptable limits. His desire for an inner apprehension of Spirit slowly begins to supercede any concern with balance. For Emerson as for Coleridge, external forms become important only insofar as they manifest the working of an inner Spirit that continually discards them. This assumption is implicit throughout the sermon, and the concluding quotation from Coleridge is tantamount to an admission that such is the case.

THE QUOTATION from *The Friend* at the end of "Miracles" indicates Emerson's increasing interest in Coleridge's means of exploring the dilemmas he himself is confronting as a minister. Coleridge's general influence on

American Transcendentalists (and Unitarians and Trinitarians) has been widely studied.[11] Such work indicates that members of all sects were avidly reading Marsh's edition of the *Aids to Reflection* as well as *The Friend*. These texts presented, explained, and used (even plagiarized) the vocabulary and the philosophical categories of German idealism. Coleridge's theories, as well as the correspondential theories of men like Sampson Reed, Oegger, and Swedenborg, helped Emerson, in particular, to analyze the "true" relation which inner beliefs should bear to outer action.

Coleridge's ideas have largely been examined as they appear in the *Aids* and the *Biographia Literaria; The Friend* has not been so widely studied. Since it is *The Friend* which Emerson quotes at the end of "Miracles" and throughout journal entries from the early 1830s, and since Cabot particularly noted his interest in the concept of "method" developed in *The Friend*, let us examine in more detail how Coleridge's text could have helped Emerson not only in formulating a new concept of the Spirit/letter relationship, but also in reconceiving the part played by an audience/reader in completing this relation.

Midway through *The Friend* occurs an essay specifically attacking William Paley's system of moral and political philosophy. Like the Emerson of "Miracles," Coleridge here construes the problem of religious knowledge in terms of tensions with which we are familiar: the split between piety and morality. He argues that while religious truth should be self-evident, it has been defined by philosophers like Paley as a matter of moral expediency. As a result, religion's value has become totally subjective, gauged by its effect on an agent's actions, rather than a function of the divine principles which should underlie all moral action. True morality, argues Coleridge, must not be separated from inner principles; in their division of duty from an objective, self-evident belief, the false moralists have threatened the destruction of both religion and ethics.[12]

The specific connection which Coleridge draws between his concept of the relation of inner feeling to outer signs must have proved resonant for a young minister whose father had written a book on the Antinomian Controversy, and who himself was well-aware of debates over the issue between Trinitarians and Unitarians, and within Unitarianism itself. Furthermore, Coleridge intermingles this discussion of true principles versus outer moral expedience with a disquisition on the relation of faith to works that makes specific reference to the timeworn dispute over justification's relation to sanctification. Like Emerson in his own 1829 sermon "Faith and Works," Coleridge does not disavow the importance of works—men judge by what we do, God by what we are. However, again like Emerson, Coleridge is not interested in splitting the terms, but in relating them: "But faith is a total act of the soul; it is the whole state of the mind, or it is not at all; and in this consists its power as well as its exclusive worth."[13]

Faith, then, is one thing; it simply has two "bearings." Historically, continues Coleridge, these bearings have not been properly understood. He then proceeds to cast those who were responsible for dividing ethics from belief as Arminians, Latitudinarians, and even Sophists. In response to their stress on the importance of outer works, rational faith, and even a rhetoric which shapes and manipulates belief by using a series of external "techniques," other sects such as the Quakers and the Swedenborgians have arisen. These new sects claimed the overwhelming preeminence of Spirit over all outer forms and came close to denying that inner certainty could at all be manifested in outer actions or outer speech. Coleridge sympathizes with their reaction, but considers their position as unbalanced as those they have attacked. He argues that the true religious philosopher will show that Arminianism must be tempered by a sense of the grace that infuses works; Latitudinarian rationalism must be modified by a focus on intuition, and a mechanical effect-oriented, expressive theory like that of the Sophists must yield to a theory of organic form, or what Coleridge will later call "progressive transition" or "progressive arrangement." As suggested in the passage Emerson quotes at the end of "Miracles," Coleridge by no means denies that inner realities take outer shapes; he is simply searching for the best means of expressing their true relation.

Coleridge's plea for connection does not negate his belief in the overwhelming importance of Spirit; what it implies, however, is that this Spirit cannot be directly apprehended in a phenomenal world; it must infuse an outer form. This assumption pervades *The Friend* and becomes almost a general law. At the end of the discussion of faith and works, for example, Coleridge concludes, "Good works may exist without saving principles and therefore cannot contain in themselves the principles of salvation; but saving principles never did, never can exist without good works."[14] As the discussion proceeds, he will find analogies to this relation both in the faculties of mind and in nature.

The same realization that there is one Mind, just as there is one faith, which has been sundered into two faculties lies at the base of Coleridge's psychology. In the fifth essay of *The Friend*, he first quotes a text from James Harrington: "Man may rather be defined as a religious than a rational character, in this regard, that in other creatures there may be something of reason, but there is nothing of religion." Coleridge then suggests the following: "If the reader will substitute the word 'understanding' for 'reason' and the word 'reason' for 'religion' he has here completely expressed the truth for which The Friend is contending."[15] Faith becomes aligned with Reason, and works with the understanding. Like faith, which must be manifested through although not caused by good works, Reason, too, "cannot exist without understanding, nor does it or can it manifest itself but in and through the understanding, which in our elder writers is often called discourse, or the discursive faculty." Without reason, understanding can only "generalize and arrange the phaenomena of perception." Lacking the understanding, however, Reason lacks the shaping that makes it manifest.[16]

Coleridge thus transforms the older categories of faith and works into psychological capacities: Reason and understanding. In each case he denies that an outer manifestation (whether a "work" or an act of the "understanding") is either proof or cause of an inner state. Yet in each case, he also claims that "inner" states must express themselves through outer forms. In the quotation above, for example, he uses the term "discourse" to describe the working of the understanding, and then explains his concept of the function and limitations of this "discourse" by using an example from Scripture. If "we" can comprehend that Spirit speaks through the discourse of Scripture, but is not constituted or caused by it, then "we [can] reconcile the promise of revelation that the blessed will see God, with the declaration of St. John, God hath no man seen at any time."

The image of the mirror, a standard eighteenth-century analogy for the mind, provides yet another way of explaining the mind's double capacity. Coleridge establishes that the mirror, like scriptural language, is both an active and a passive instrument of Spirit: "In this piece of steel I acknowledge the properties of hardness, brittleness, high polish, and the capability of forming a mirror. I find all these likewise in the plate glass of a friend's carriage; but in addition to all these, I find the quality of transparency of the power of transmitting as well as of reflecting the rays of light."[17] The image makes his point: a double action is taking place, but there is a single mirror just as there is a single Mind in which and through which all action occurs.

Coleridge not only treats of faith and works and Reason and understanding, but dramatically broadens these relations to include an analogy between scientific law and its manifestations in outer phenomena. In making this analogy, he discovers not that each outer object, action, or agent in nature simply or statically corresponds to some inner truth, but that outer phenomena may exist in a tension. He speaks particularly of a "bi-polarity" between external phenomena which can only be reconciled by the fact that an inner law informs them both (his example is electricity). This insight leads him to argue that since the world of nature is perpetually changing, the law or Whole informing nature cannot inhere in solitary phenomena, but in the interrelation of different phenomena, even those that on the surface appear polarized.[18]

In *The Friend*, Coleridge sets up a complex series of analogies: a faith not constituted by works but manifested through them, when translated into "inner" terms becomes a Reason that is in no way caused by the understanding, yet again demands its "discourse" in order to be realized. In addition, human belief and human psychology are both found to act in ways analogous to scientific law, which like faith and Reason must also be deduced from its action within outer phenomena. Coleridge's consideration of scientific law adds to these analogies the new dimension of process and of change. "Self-evidence" in the natural world is revealed in a series of continually transforming relationships which are nonetheless integrated by virtue of their dependence on the Whole that infuses them.

Channing and Emerson were both fascinated with Coleridge's theories: "Likeness to God" demonstrated Channing's attempt to rework Unitarian theology in terms of inner and outer correspondences, while "Miracles" indicates Emerson's concern with the relation of inner truth to outer form. But the emphases of the two men come to differ greatly. Channing was interested at once in the power of inner law and in the retention of traditional outer forms. If at times he seemed to acknowledge that Spirit makes its own form, he more often turned to a conception of form as that which shapes and focuses Spirit rather than vitally expressing it. Inner Spirit must be balanced by outer form; spiritual growth is a function of balances that are slowly discarded and carefully reestablished. In contrast, Emerson's stress, as it is gradually formulated in the journals and sermons, falls on the shaping capacity of Spirit, not on the necessary balance of inner feeling with an imposed outer form. The Spirit expresses itself in forms whose boundaries it is continually bursting. At issue is not balance, but the vital and transforming expression of "self-evident" truth.

At this point, clearly, we are no longer simply speaking of Coleridge's analogies. In fact, such a discussion leads inevitably to a consideration of what shape the interplay between the universal and particular he has postulated will take. Emerson begins to part ways with Channing over the question of the Spirit's relation to form. In so doing, he also begins to reconceive his idea of the role played by an audience in the formulation of this relationship. Thus, while Emerson's reading of Coleridge will take him in different directions than that of Channing, he, too, like Channing, Colman, and Cotton before him, must confront the fact that the relation of Spirit to letter is never an isolated formal issue; it invariably reveals assumptions about the needs and capacities of an audience.

In this area, Coleridge again proved important to Emerson. For he not only provided the young preacher and his contemporaries with a theory that emphasized the centrality of inner self-evidence. He also offered a theory of "method" that dealt with how these varying interrelations of "inner" to "outer" were to be presented and with the important role played by an audience in this presentation.

IN THE CHAPTERS from *The Friend* on "method," Coleridge sets up Shakespeare's Mistress Quickly as an example of an unmethodical mind; Edmund Burke and Hamlet, on the other hand, provide examples of "true" method and of method carried to excess. The meandering of the unmethodical mind, like that of the garrulous innkeeper, argues Coleridge, "is occasioned by the habitual submission of the understanding to mere events and images as such, and independent of any power in the mind to classify and appropriate them."[19] Mistress Quickly operates in an "and then, and then" world in which information is simply accreted, not integrated. In Burke's speech, by contrast, Coleridge finds "the unpremeditated and evidently habitual arrangement of his words, grounded in the habit of seeing in each integral part, or more plainly, in every sentence, the whole that he intends to communicate. However irregular and desultory his talk, there is method in the fragments."[20] Coleridge also praises Hamlet's awareness of the source of method and his own individual use of it. Unlike those around him, Hamlet realizes "there's a divinity that shapes our ends / Rough hew them as we will." But Hamlet also shows the result of a reliance on human method run to excess. As he meditates on Yorick's skull and obsessively contemplates how Alexander's dust may stuff a hole, Horatio warns him, " 'Twere to consider too curiously." According to Coleridge, Hamlet's "method" here becomes too personal, unrelated to a larger, underlying design.

In his comments on method, as throughout *The Friend*, Coleridge attempts to distinguish between methods that are too reliant on individual understanding or passive sensual impression and that ideal "method or balance between our passive impressions and the mind's own reactions on the same."[21] But the issue is not simply to describe the necessity of establishing such a balance; the question also becomes how this balance can best manifest itself.

Coleridge uses Shakespeare as his consummate example of true method because his works evince that "just proportion, that union and interpenetration of the universal and particular which must ever pervade all works of decided genius and true science. For method implies progressive transition, and this is the meaning of the word in the original language, method means way of transition."[22] If somewhat abstractly, Coleridge offers an image of how such method works. It must present the transition between universals and particulars—that is, faith and works, Reason and understanding, law and phenomena—without losing the sense that the relations among them are "progressive," i.e., changing. An artist (Shakespeare), a philosopher (Socrates), and a scientist (Euclid) are each deemed "methodical" because each intuits how laws animate disparate phenomena and underly their relation and progression. For, as he warns, the term "method cannot otherwise than by abuse, be applied to a mere dead arrangement containing in itself no principle of progression."[23]

Theoretically, explains Coleridge, method can be discussed in terms of deduction. It is a function of that God whose "creative Idea not only appoints to each thing its position, and in consequence of that position gives it its qualities, yea gives it its very existence as that particular thing."[24] But method can also be approached inductively, using the findings of the understanding to help to grasp the common law which binds sensory phenomena. Plato and Bacon, says Coleridge, both search for law; they simply approach the problem from different poles, one from the "ideal" pole and one from the "material" pole. Finally, however, it is in the method of the fine arts, most particularly in poetry, that both these approaches to method can best be employed. Coleridge notes that the parts of any art, its materials, are drawn from the understanding, but in the experience of poetry, "in its most comprehensive sense. There is a necessary predominance of the Idea . . . and a comparative indifference of the materials."[25] Thus, poetry may be framed in the discourse of the understanding, but through this discourse it also speaks the revelations of the Spirit. Partaking of both worlds, poetry becomes the link that participates in both yet is constituted by neither. It displays the very enactment of "progressive transition."

In the essays on method, Coleridge establishes a more concrete theory of the link between the disparate terms considered in the philosophical essays. Faith and works, Reason and understanding, law and phenomena are related in a process of progressive transition that refuses to rest in static relations. Instead, each category is involved in a continual transformation and interpenetration with the other. Truly methodical minds, he notes, do not contemplate "things only or for their own sake alone, but likewise and chiefly the relation of things, either their relation to each other, to the observer, or to the state and apprehension of the hearers."[26]

At this point Coleridge has broadened from considering the related terms themselves to considering their equally important relation to the person who sees or to the hearers who hear them. One does not link these terms in a vacuum, but realizes their connection to those who respond to them. Like Hamlet, the overenthusiastic methodizer "in attending too exclusively to the relations which the past or passing events and objects bear to general truth and the moods of his own thought . . . is sometimes in danger of overlooking that other relation in which they are to be placed for the apprehension and sympathies of the hearers."[27] Certainly, the methodizer must seek out relations, but "the objects thus connected . . . are only proportionate to the connecting energy, relatively to the real, or at least to the desireable sympathies of mankind."[28] The act of interrelating cannot remain a solitary act; method must appeal to the "apprehension and sympathies" of an audience. Suddenly the fact that Coleridge has drawn his examples of "progressive arrangement" largely from Burke, Shakespeare, and Socrates takes on new resonance. The methodizing of each of these figures takes place in a dramatic situation in which a speaker speaks and is heard by an audience. Clearly, the connecting energy, the Spirit moving through forms, must become manifest in listeners as well as in speakers to be realized in all its complex relational fulness.

Qualifying this assertion in light of his previous comments, however, Coleridge pulls back to warn that important though it may be, even an enactment of "progressive transition" cannot of itself cause knowledge or belief in those who hear. In the end, Coleridge decides that the ability to respond to method does not at all lie in a response to external forms. The truest response is to the larger Being or "Idea" in which all people share, if they are open to its movement within them and within nature: "But as this principle [of Being] cannot be implanted by the discourse of logic, so neither can it be excited or evolved by the arts of rhetoric. For it is an immutable truth, that what comes from the heart, that alone goes to the heart; what proceeds from a divine impulse, that the godlike alone can awaken."[29] Here he has come full circle, back to the notion of "faith" as self-evidence with which this discussion of *The Friend* began. Even John Cotton might have approved of Coleridge's final phrasing. Establishing these analogies, developing a notion of "method" as a way of describing their working, then arguing the need for an audience's sympathies somehow to participate in this method, Coleridge, like Emerson, seems nonetheless determined to keep the forms by which they are expressed noncausal, and to make an audience's capacity for response more important than the forms through which that capacity is evoked. The Spirit still needs the letter, but the letter must not circumscribe and delimit the workings of the Spirit within it and within those who respond to it. In spite of the fact that Coleridge has expanded older notions of the faith/works, piety/morality relation by linking them to faculties of the mind and to the workings of nature itself, then, the dilemma of how to present self-evident knowledge to an audience remains. Moreover, Coleridge and (to an even greater degree) Emerson desired not simply to deal with the problem of connecting Spirit to language; they had also to deal with a natural revelation that called for its own translation into verbal terms. Clearly, the difficulties involved in relating Spirit to letter in a manner that expresses the needs and abilities of an audience have not grown simpler since the days of Cotton and Colman. As we remarked of Channing, in his desperate attempt to link Unitarian theology to the most effective forms, the task has become even more complicated.

IN HIS JOURNALS, Emerson reworks for himself both Coleridge's emphasis on the relation of law to phenomena and his stress on the role played by response in somehow participating in these relations. The journals provide a commentary on the ways in which his own ideas about the interrelation of speaker, composition, and audience evolved before and during the years of his ministry. They also demonstrate his shifting attitudes towards his Unitarian education and towards his reading, especially his reading in Coleridge. Coleridge must have proved attractive to the young preacher because he initially framed the issue within older religious categories and (what must have been more important to a man for whom preaching was the central fact of his ministerial experience) because Coleridge's notion of "method" stressed the importance of audience. What is merely hinted at in Coleridge, however, becomes Emerson's major concern.

Faith as self-evidence remains the central issue, but Emerson must also confront the question of how to include his hearers within this theory without falling into the formalism of which he first indirectly and then explicitly charged Trinitarians and Unitarians. Thus, if we see him considering the interrelation of "outer" to "inner" truth in "Miracles," "Action Based on Principles," "Love of God Innate," "Faith and Works," and other sermons, we also see him addressing a concern with eloquence, with preaching, and with the corresponding capacities and responsibilities of the preacher and his audience.

The "self-evidence" Emerson desires his audience to feel is not that of a solitary individual having a conversion experience, although this is, of course, involved. We need only think of his own mystical experience, reworked from the journals, in *Nature* (1836). But self-evidence, crucially, also includes a Spirit speaking though an orator to a Spirit in an audience. The idea of hearing—the speaker's hearing an inner voice, speaking this hearing in his sermon, and the audience both hearing the Spirit through his work and hearing the Spirit in themselves—also seems more in keeping with Coleridge's theory of "progressive transition." Somehow, Emerson must discern how a "self-evident" truth can be enacted in a "method" that neither coerces belief, nor manipulates listeners through the use of calculated, external, rhetorical techniques.

The Emerson of the first two journals started with the idea that the orator's words should provide a clear picture for his hearers that will persuade them to act morally; the picture can be rational, sentimental, or both, but it is still conceived of as a "picture." Here we are reminded not only of Colman's interest in verbal pictures judiciously placed in rational frameworks, but of Channing, whose greatest ability as a preacher, for young Emerson, lay in his talent for making listeners respond to a picture in their minds, not to his words.[30] By 1828, in his third journal, however, Emerson's ideas of what this picture is and what it does have both changed. He now desires to offer his audience analogies between moral and material nature, not pictures as verbal paintings of outer realities, or pictures as ornaments which merely clarify abstract thoughts, but "true" pictures of the relations between natural and spiritual facts. Such a notion of correspondences is derived, of course, from insights he gleaned from Reed, Swedenborg, Coleridge and others. Even though the initial correspondences Emerson notes are somewhat static, appealing more to the eye than the ear, his interest in simply "showing" them, rather than offering consciously didactic pictures, indicates his growing sense that the preacher should not, indeed cannot, create in his audience an awareness of self-evident truths by using traditional rhetorical means of persuasion. He comments, "I only tell how I have striven and climbed, and what I have seen that you may compare it with your own observations of the same object. It is important to have a formal observer, whether a keen-sighted one or not in order to furnish . . . some other point to negotiate thoughts by" (*JMN*, 3:171). He does not assert the need for control by the preacher or, by extension, by his doctrine. The minister's function is to offer a point of comparison, not rigidly to enforce a truth which he treats only because it is biblical, or because it has better external moral "effects" than another. The term "negotiate" is provocative, implying both "measuring," but also bargaining in order to reach a point of agreement. In using the term, Emerson suggests not only that the preacher provides such a point for the hearer, but also that his sense of his hearers provides such a point for the preacher. Thus he posits a more "dramatic" relation between them than he did when he conceived of ornamenting rational ideas with pictures. Observation alone is not enough; it must be spoken and then "negotiated."

By 1828 his sense of this more equal relationship with his audience led to Emerson's decision to dispense with set or conventional topics in his preaching. Setting a topic, whether biblical or otherwise, is bad both for the speaker and for his hearers. When the church calendar, a church committee, or even a lyceum predetermine his subject matter, he cannot transform his "inner" hearing into a speaking that will best evoke (not dictate) his audience's "inner" response. In his sermon "The Christian Minister"

(1829), Emerson warns his new congregation: "That man has very low and humble views of his office who satisfies his conscience with uttering the commonplaces of religion for twenty or thirty minutes, reciting a lazy miscellany of quotations from Scripture and then dismisses his unfed, unedified audience" (*YES*, p. 25). Even the freer topics introduced by Unitarian preachers may be too limiting; his notion of the minister/audience relationship will be even more daring. He "shall not be so much afraid of innovation as to scruple about introducing new forms of address, new modes of illustration, and varied allusions into the pulpit" (*YES*, p. 28). [31]

By 1830 Emerson has decided that true preaching is effective only if its subject evokes feelings latent in all people, not because it makes use of an external rhetoric. "Use powerful means to get access," he remarks, "but don't distrust the strength of truth" (*JMN*, 3:197). If the entry shows a more traditional awareness that "rhetoric" of some sort is still necessary, it also demonstrates his sense that a "self-evident" truth which is shared by all should not be violated by external means.

The solution to the problem of shaping self-evident truths, at least conceptually, is to align a notion of "self-evident" truth with a notion of "self-evident" composition, which "contains in itself the reason of its appearance." Emerson notes that when one speaks self-evidently, the audience will "stagger" not because of a false rhetoric that artificially stimulates them, but because the "Spirit" moving through the preacher's words awakens the voice latent in them: "It is God within you that responds to God without or affirms his own words trembling on the lips of another" (*JMN*, 3:302). Here, rather than discussing precisely what makes a form self-evident, Emerson moves full circle from the preacher's role to that of his audience. Indeed, throughout the fourth journal, he explores not only the issue of the preacher's responsibility to his audience, but also the audience's responsibility to the preacher. For example, he takes note of a Coleridge remark about four types of readers/listeners and then more seriously muses: "It were no bad topic for the preacher to urge the talent of hearing good sermons on their congregations. I can hear a good sermon where Surd shall hear none and Absurd shall hear worse than none." A good audience, composed of people infused with their own Spirit, "will inspire the preacher's words with a wisdom not their own" (*JMN*, 4:278).

Later, in 1835, Emerson will even comment, "The hearing man is good, unhappy is the speaking man. The alternation of speaking and hearing make our education" (*JMN*, 5:98). The quotation suggests that hearing offers room for more play of the mind than does the more concrete speaking. Hearing allows for expansion rather than compression of a speaker's meaning. In substantiation of this point, Emerson argues both in the third and fourth journals that "the best part of any discourse is that which is unspoken" but nevertheless heard. (*JMN*, 3:315; *JMN*, 4:278). Heard how? Heard via the Spirit which speaks to the hearer through the suggestiveness of the speaker's words. Listeners do not simply hear these words, however, as the remark on "alternation" suggests; they expand their "suggestiveness" through their own speaking.

Emerson resembles Channing speaking of Milton's suggestiveness, but differs from him as well. Channing speaks of a great mind's ability to be suggestive simply because it is great. Emerson, in contrast, acknowledges that any minister and any audience can speak and hear "suggestively." Channing, to be sure, initiates an emphasis on suggestiveness and certainly uses it in "Likeness to God," but, unlike Emerson, does not attempt to construct a conscious theory of belief and audience response around this concept. For Emerson, the idea of suggestiveness provides a bridge between his ideal of self-evidence and the need for form. If a form is "suggestive," it does not destroy the audience's freedom; it is the audience which completes a preacher's act both by hearing the "said" and the "unsaid" and by transforming their hearing into their own speaking. In Coleridge's terms, the Whole is sensed through a "progressive transition," the interrelations among parts, and such parts consist not only of the parts of a sermon, but also of the individuals in the listening audience who en masse suggest the presence of a Whole. One can never name this Wholeness directly, but its presence, or its voice, depending on the image used, can be felt/heard suggestively by those who remain open to it. Self-evidence does not consist in a belief caused by an external structure, then; it is the function of an interrelation created between the speaker and his hearers within the form of his speaking.

Just as nature is never completed, but always, as Emerson says, full of "tendency," so it seems that even apparently "set" outer forms are also always in motion because of their "suggestiveness" to hearers. The image that Emerson uses to describe his "process" of interrelating his own meanings and those intuited through his "forms" by his audience is thus not Coleridge's reflecting and transmitting mirror. Rather, says Emerson, "it is the property of the divine to be reproductive. The harvest is seed. The good sermon becomes a text in the hearer's mind. That is the good book which sets us at work. . . . Jesus is but the harbinger and announcer of the Comforter to come, and his continual office is to make himself less to us by making us demand more" (*JMN*, 4:180–81). Forms are not fruits themselves, but suggestive seeds; not absolute fulfillment, but the embodiments of "tendency" or "progressive transition." They are never completed, but transformed by an audience into its own progressive transition. The ideal of suggestiveness demands that more forms will spring from these seeds and also hints at a massive process immanent within all these transformations. Emerson has found a way to have his external forms while acknowledging that they speak more than they know, that their meanings are not only completed by an audience but in turn transformed by them, and, finally, that all these metamorphoses take place within the context of an infusing Whole.

Coleridge provided Emerson with a theory which linked universals to particulars, faith to works, Reason to understanding, and law to phenomena. His chapters on method outlined the shape such linkage should take and stressed that the audience was involved in this process. Emerson, more clearly, added the idea of method's "suggestiveness" and the necessary role played by the audience in "completing" it. The notion of "suggestiveness" could defend the ideal of "self-evidence" from entrapment in a set form and from entrapment by outer formal norms like those Unitarians had derived from Blair. Both Emerson's repudiation of "set" topics and his attraction for correspondences (rather than static pictures) are signs of his desire to avoid imposing formal rules on himself and his listeners. Heretofore we have discussed Emerson's general response to the problem of connecting notions about the interrelation of universal to particular truths with ideas about an audience's response. But even "suggestiveness" must take a shape. Faith needs works; Reason the understanding; and law, external phenomena in order to be revealed and in order to be completed within an audience. To understand fully Emerson's sense of his formal and theological differences with the "constable" religions, then, we turn to his more specific comments about composition and to his own experiments with the sermon form.

5. Emerson and the Shaping of Self-Evidence: Practice

How does Emerson's notion of "self-evidence" as suggestive, heard, and as somehow "completed" in the response of an audience take shape at the level of composition? Scholars have pointed out Emerson's initial enthusiasm about the possibility of seeing "true" one-to-one relationships between words and things, and his disappointing realization that the gap between the two would be closed, as Sampson Reed said, only in heaven.[1] But, if there is dissatisfaction, there is also a deepening recognition: self-evident truth is not static, but, as Coleridge suggested, a function of a Whole immanent in the interrelations of constantly metamorphosing particulars. Emerson was further becoming aware that his ideas of self-evidence as suggestiveness related the speaker to his audience in a different manner than ideas of simple correspondence could do. To relate fact to Spirit as Swedenborg had done, he was later to argue, was not only to limit meaning, it was to dictate an audience's response to meaning. Coleridge's concept of "progressive transition," then, not only involved correspondence theory; equally important for Emerson, it included suggestions about the role of an audience in shaping belief. The idea of progressive transition (as linked to suggestiveness) clearly distinguished the concept of a Whole that was attained in some mechanical way from a Whole that was implicit within the changing relationships of particular phenomena. Emerson may sound like a Platonist or Neoplatonist, and at times he certainly was, but one must also recall his increasing attraction to and use of the "organic metaphor."[2] The metaphor not only informed his metaphysic; it obviously influenced his ideas of composition and of audience. The parts of the sermon must be informed by "method" in a manner similar to the phenomena of nature. The audience is composed of individual hearers, but together they too suggest the presence of an infusing Whole. Emerson admitted there could be endless surface differences in these hearers but maintained that a response to universal meanings was latent in each of them. Ideally, a Christian congregation would provide the consummate image of the interrelation of individual parts sharing in a Whole; it displays the paradox of the "one Body" with "many members." The preacher must trust that individually and freely each of these members could transform himself or herself in accordance with individual freedom, but at the same time would also participate in an immanent universal.

His view of composition as a whole immanent in parts leads Emerson to attack the Unitarian idea of the universe as a Whole, the design of which is constituted by the sum of its accreted and classified fragments. It also contributed to his debunking of rhetorical criteria such as logical and rational (as opposed to intuitive) clarity, unity and consistency. Such criteria not only clash with the idea of "progressive transition"; they prohibit an audience's free response to the "self-evidence" suggested in the transformations of outer forms. Emerson repudiates the norms of Hugh Blair not simply on the well-known grounds that the individual self must express itself outward in forms that are not imposed from without, but out of a different sense of a responding audience's needs and rights. His theory of self-expression should not be divorced from his ideas about communication and reception. An audience does not merely acquiesce to and thereby confirm rationally structured analyses of belief or moral action which may or may not touch its members' feelings; for Emerson, the audience is present because they wish to enter into an experience which only their inner responses can complete and transform. The community comes together not to hear external knowledge about faith explained, to hear what external moral results such knowledge should have in their outer lives, but to bear witness to an experience of faith. An experience of "spiritual religion" results in a "new conviction of the mind" which is "God himself to the believer," not in a knowledge of external duties.

Desiring to preach a "new conviction" to an audience that meets its needs and abilities by conforming to an ideal of "suggestiveness," Emerson less abstractly had to face problems of composition and preaching.

The journals of this period reveal his reworking of the idea of method and his more concrete attitudes about a sermon's relation to its hearers.

Emerson, in addition to disliking "set" topics, also launches into varying attacks on the structure of sermons. In the journal, for example, he begins to debunk what he calls the "gingerbread distinctions" of sermons, their clear separation of argument from argument in the interest of promoting the most rational (i.e., logical) apprehension of the "meaning" of a subject. Instead, maintains Emerson, "Every form is the history of the thing." In other words, as in nature, so with arguments; they do not exist statically, nor do they add up to conclusions. A whole, whether in a sermon or in the life of a shell, is implicit in all its parts. These parts cannot be rigidly separated, but form a natural order, a "composition." To take them out of their places within this order is both to destroy their individual meanings and that of the entire composition. Emerson thus warns the student of science not merely to dissect individual phenomena, but to look for that "pure plastic Idea" within them. In concentrating on one subject, one "must not lose sight of the place and relation of the subject. Shun giving it a disproportionate importance, but speedily adjust yourself to see the thing tho' with added acquaintance of its intimate structure under the sun and landscape" (*JMN*, 4:288). His most famous example of his own experience of how things seem dead in isolation is that of the shell he takes home from the beach, only to find that it has lost its beauty because he has deprived it of its place in the system (*JMN*, 4:291).

This idea of composition as a system of interrelations carries over more specifically into Emerson's comments on a bad natural history lecture. The lecture has proved essentially worthless for him because it provided nothing more than an "enumeration of facts." He proceeds to attack it on grounds that repudiate rhetorical assumptions underlying both Unitarian preaching and Unitarian theology. Following Coleridge, Emerson comments, "A true method has no more need of firstly, secondly, etc. than a perfect sentence has of punctuation. It tells its own story, makes its own feet, creates its own form." For Emerson, it is the idea, the law, the unity infusing the parts of a lecture, just as it is the law immanent in the parts of nature (such as the shell) that a speaker should suggest. In his conclusion to this small diatribe he notes that "natural history is to be studied, not with any pretension that its theory is attained, that its classification is permanent, but merely as full of tendency" (*JMN*, 4:290). The same theory holds true, he is implying, for written composition. Far more than Channing, who began the process but did not complete it, Emerson thus translates unity and consistency into terms which make them at once internal to the phenomenon discussed, its form or its history, but also makes them a function of the phenomenon's relationships with other phenomena. As Coleridge points out in what becomes one of Emerson's own favorite arguments, such interrelations may even inhere between objects and arguments that seem on the surface in total opposition. The law of "bi-polarity," as Emerson adapts it, can be applied not only to the law of compensation, but also to composition.

In an 1829 journal comment, Emerson applies these remarks to actual preaching. He goes to hear sermons at the Swedenborgian chapel and at the seamen's church in Boston. The modes of the two preachers seem entirely opposite; but at the end of his description, Emerson praises both. The Swedenborgian sermon "was in its style severely simple in method and manner and had much the style of a problem in geometry wholly uncoloured and unimpassioned." Here we see Emerson's use of Coleridge's image of the mathematician, specifically the geometer, as methodizer. In working out theorems, a method that assumes the "immanence" of law is always used. Thus the Whole can invariably be intuited in the parts. Emerson notes with satisfaction that the manner of the sermon could have convinced any number of sects to claim it as one of their own. To this mathematical clarity he then juxtaposes the impassioned preaching of the well-known sailors' preacher, Father Taylor. In contrast to the Swedenborgian, Taylor's "whole discourse is a string of audacious felicities harmonized by a spirit of joyful love" (*JMN*, 5:4). His audience is unified, says Emerson, by this obvious and unegotistical pouring out of the self. What both preachers possess, although the one seems so reasonable and the other so emotional, is Coleridge's "method." The parts of their discourses are fused by a knowledge or a feeling immanent in each of them and in their interconnection. Both models evoke a feeling of "self-evidence" to which members of any sect, however different on the surface, can respond.

Almost immediately after these musings on preaching, Emerson describes his own image of the "Teacher" who is yet to come. This ideal preacher will speak "with more precision and universality, with piercing poetic insight, those beautiful, yet severe compensations that give to moral nature an aspect of mathematical science." As in Coleridge, "precision" and "universality", terms that apply both to "moral" and to "mathematical" science, become a function of inner qualities of the speaker and his hearers, not qualities applied to the speaker's subject matter. In his ending comment Emerson stresses this point, asserting that this teacher will dismiss historical formal religion and show his people "that God is, not was, and speaks, not spoke" (*JMN*, 5:6).

With "piercing poetic insight," this teacher will disregard Unitarian rhetorical assumptions. He will not use arguments that separate and encapsulate ideas, but conceive his arguments in light of their "vital" relationships. Nor will he be "clear." He will not bend his own ideas to meet a demand for external clarity when inner vision is needed: "The Unitarian preacher who sees that his orthodox hearer may with reason complain that the preaching is not serious, faithful, authoritative enough . . . is by that admission judged. It is not an excuse that he can with clearness see the speculative error of his neighbor" (*JMN*, 4:384). The teacher of "spiritual religion" will not make a fetish of an imposed clarity—even if it is rational; he will instead speak the truth of his own heart. His audience will not be lost should he do so because, argues Emerson, "Man's Universal nature is his inmost nature" (*JMN*, 5:53).

Those scholars who point out Emerson's increasing focus on the need of the "inner" self to speak its individual truths have overlooked the need to establish a link between "inner" and "universal" truth that is also a link between speaker and hearers. Emerson does acknowledge that "unto every mind is given one Word to say, and he should sacredly strive to utter that word, and not another man's without addition or abatement" (*JMN*, 4:348–49); but this comment occurs in the context of a larger meditation on preaching. If a preacher speaks his heart, he heart of his audience will respond to the universal truth suggested in his personal speaking. Emerson's point is clear: he does not separate preacher from audience; he reconnects them in a new way. Uttering personal truth will engender the best inner results, not only in the preacher, but in his congregation.

In Emerson's thought, Unitarian unity becomes internalized as a Whole implicit in parts; consistency becomes a function of a speaker and his hearers' intuition of connection, and universal clarity becomes a function of a very individual suggestiveness. All these criteria—traditionally considered only in light of Emerson's stress on self-reliance—must be reexamined in light of his desire to evoke an inner experience in an audience. Emerson never loses sight of the fact that it is the audience which completes his speaking. In the fourth journal, he again underscores the nature of this connection: "The maker of a sentence . . . launches out into chaos and Old Night and is followed by those who hear him with something of a wild creative delight" (*JMN*, 4:363). Their delight is not simply in him or his sentence. Although they "follow" him, the focus is on the "creative delight" that his sentence evokes, not causes, in them. The preacher's harvest is but seedtime for his listeners. Emerson's attempts to embody this developing theory of the interrelation of speaker, composition, and audience in his own sermonic practice remain, however, to be seen.

EMERSON'S SERMONS have been considered tepid attempts in the Channing vein, orthodox—insofar as Unitarianism had an orthodoxy—in their arguments and monolithic in their structure. A close reading of these sermons from 1826 to 1832 indicates, however, that Emerson's desire to find a new method of relating self-evident truth to an audience through an outer form led him to a number of important, if not entirely successful, experiments. Certainly, the sermons lack the complexity of many of the lectures and obviously of the essays; but they are of immense value for exploring Emerson's changing sense of composition and of audience and for indicating why he left the sermon for other forms of discourse.[3] Emerson's reading in Montaigne, in the classical essayists, in Johnson, in Addison and Steele, and in the numerous English and American reviews was, of course, a major factor in his changes. But what he learned from writing sermons, with their particular focus on the spoken word and the listening audience, remains to be explored. The young Emerson (and, one could argue, the older Emerson as well) wanted to be heard—not overheard. His message involved the hearing of the Spirit by the preacher, his speaking of this hearing to his audience, and their own responsive hearing and speaking.[4] Speaking and hearing provided the necessary link between the individual self and others, between personal and universal truth. The sermons provide his initial formal attempts to express this link.

An examination of Emerson's first sermon, two sermons from the middle period of his preaching, and the last sermon he preached before the Second Church as its minister demonstrate some of the range of his experimentation as a preacher. Trained in a Blair tradition that was considerably loosened by the teaching of Channing's brother Edward, Emerson moves in six years from a conventional use of the sermon form to a form similar to that of the later W. E. Channing. In spite of these similarities, however, his use of the form also suggests some important differences to come. By no means does Emerson reach the formal maturity he achieves after Ellen Emerson's death and after his return from Europe; the point to stress is that the sermons offer an important picture of his changing perceptions about the relation that self-evident faith should bear to a preacher's mode of presentation and to his audience.

The young Emerson wished to "put on eloquence as a robe," and this desire is certainly evident in his first effort as a preacher. For while "Pray Without Ceasing" provides a good example of Emerson's attempt to abide by a Blair structure (largely consisting of an introduction, narration, peroration, and conclusion), it is also an example of how his interest in an eloquence more aligned with intuition than reason and in a subject matter that stresses the inner dimension of prayer rather than the external proofs of religion begins to threaten that structure. Within a model that is based on "proof" and "inference"—terms he himself will use to describe his arguments—Emerson introduces rhetorical questions, dramatic examples, and an inflated language that divert attention from his arguments and seem geared, by and large, to move his audience and, parenthetically, to exhibit his own powers of eloquence. To be sure, Channing uses such strategies, and Blair in fact encouraged the use of emotional techniques within the argumentative sections of a discourse, but for both Channing and Blair the emotional strategies were to be closely related to the proposition at hand and used only to "color" it; they were never, except perhaps in the peroration, to draw attention to themselves as strategies. In his first sermon, Emerson displays a widening gap between the limits of the model and his desire to experiment with an imaginative expression that will move his hearers more than it rationally persuades them.

The sermon begins with a Blair-like introduction which acknowledges the audience's possible position on his subject even before Emerson offers his own. "It is the duty of men to judge men only by their actions," he begins. After admitting that they possess few other means of judgment than outer knowledge, he then qualifies his opening statement: "Because we are not able to discern the processes of thought, to see the soul—it were very ridiculous to doubt or deny that any beings can" (*YES*, p. 1). This comment leads to the conclusion that both outer and inner means of knowing exist and is followed by an appeal to his audience's own perhaps hidden belief that their thoughts can be read. Emerson then ornaments this whole series of thoughts, exhorting his audience to agreement through an extended use of rhetorical questions:

> I need not ask you . . . whether all this stir from day to day, from hour to hour of all this mighty multitude is to ascertain some question dear to the understanding concerning the nature of God, the true constitution and destination of the human soul, the proper balance of the faculties and the proper office of each . . . whether all men are eagerly intent to study the best systems of education for themselves and their children? Is it not rather the great wonder of all who think enough to wonder that almost all that sits near the heart, all that colours the countenance, and engrosses conversation at the family board are these humble things of mortal date, and in the history of the universe absolutely insignificant? Is it not outside shews, the pleasures of appetite, or at best of pride . . . that give the law to the great mass of actions and words? (*YES*, p. 2)

The introduction ends with a warning that a focus on the world leads to a disregard of the inner self, and Emerson is ready to propose his first argument. Before stating it, however, he returns to the language of rational proof: "The necessary inference from these reflections is the fact which gives them all their importance, and is the doctrine I am chiefly anxious to inculcate." He then proposes his doctrine: "We pray without ceasing."

Unlike Cotton, Colman, and even Channing, Emerson does not develop the "reasons" why his doctrine is true, but turns almost immediately to another series of rhetorical questions:

> And is it by paltry counterfeit of ignorance that you would disguise from yourselves the truth, and will you really endeavour to persuade yourself, that God is such as one as you yourself, and will be amused by professions, and may, by fraudulent language be kept out of faith? Is it possible that men of discretion in common affairs can think so grossly? Do you not know that the knowledge of God is perfect and immense; that it breaks down the fences of presumption, and the arts of hypocrisy; that right, and artifice, and time, and the grave, are naked before it; that the deep gives up its dead, that the gulfs of chaos are disembowelled before him? (*YES*, pp. 3–4)

This recourse to rhetorical questioning, used earlier in the introduction, seems employed to move the audience to an acquiesence in what it already knows: an emotional technique merely enforces the precepts of "common sense." Emerson concludes this introduction to his first proposition by pulling back from these questions. "Since, then, we are thus, by the inevitable law of our being, surrendered unreservedly to the unsleeping observation of the Divinity, we cannot shut our eyes to the conclusion that every desire of the human mind is a prayer uttered to God and registered in Heaven."

The second doctrine demonstrates his continuing expansion of a pattern of logical proposition, emotional proof, logical conclusion: "The next fact of sovereign importance in this connection is, that our prayers are granted. Upon the account I have given of prayer, this ulterior fact is a faithful consequence." Once again Emerson starts with a proposition that he does not develop through a series of rational proofs, but instead colors with rhetorical questions: "What then! If I pray that fire shall fall from heaven to consume mine enemies will the lightning come down? If I pray that the wealth of India may be piled in my coffers shall I straightway become rich?" Having asked these questions, however, rather than concluding his argument with another proposition, Emerson broadens it by using what Blair calls the "division" of his subject. He first offers a definition: "True Prayers are not forms or fleeting wishes; they are the daily, hourly, momentary desires that come without fear, without impediment into the soul . . . and these prayers are granted." He then expands his definition in the "narration" or development of the subject. Prayers are granted because humankind possess faculties that allow for fulfillment of their desires. At this point, however, the argument ceases to proceed through explanation, and Emerson turns to three dramatic examples of answered prayers: the rich man, the sensualist, and the good man. These examples serve a function similar to that of the rhetorical questions in the first section: he uses them to "move" his audience, not rationally to persuade it. Each view is presented in a parallel structure, and each uses inflated language. Following is the example of the sensualist:

> And will not the votary of other lusts, the lover of animal delight, who is profuse of the joys of sense, who loveth meats and drinks, soft raiment and the wine when it moveth itself aright and giveth its colour in the cup; or the more offensive libertine who has no relish left for any sweet in moral life, but only waits opportunity to surrender himself over to the last damning debauchery; will not these petitioners who have knocked so loudly at heaven's door, receive what they have so importunately desired? Assuredly they will. (*YES*, p. 6)

As he has done earlier, Emerson concludes his use of "moving" examples by returning to a more reasoned restatement of his proposition: "His prayers are granted; all prayers are granted. Unceasing endeavours always attend true prayers, and, by the law of the universe, unceasing endeavours do not fail of their end" (*YES*, p. 7).

At this point, in the seeming though unnecessary interest of clarity, Emerson draws back and offers a summary of what he has argued so far: "I have attempted to establish two simple positions, that, we are always praying, and that it is the order of Providence in the world, that our prayer should be granted" (*YES*, p. 7). He then appeals once more to his listeners' own experiences of this matter and particularly notes his lack of interest in any metaphysical questions surrounding the issue: "I shall content myself, at present, with having stated the general doctrine and with adverting to its value as a practical principle."

What follows is similar to the "uses" section of the older sermon form, which Blair calls the "peroration." In sermons, with their different doctrines, the peroration could be used after the discussion of each doctrine, as well as at the end of the whole sermon. Emerson notes that his ideas, if "distinctly apprehended," will elevate his congregation's conception of its relations and its duties. He does not offer a "practical" discussion of duties, however, but another rhetorical set piece similar to those used earlier: "Weep not for man's frailties, for if the might of Omnipotence has made the elements obedient to the fervency of his daily prayers, he is no puny suffered tottering, ill at ease in the universe, but a being of gigantic enterprises. . . . Weep not for the past; for this is duration over which the secret virtue of prayer is powerless. . . . Weep not for your wasted possession, for the immeasurable future is before you." The ending of this outpouring is especially notable; it has next to nothing to do with his subject, but a great deal to do with his desire to move his audience with his "eloquence." He warns his listeners not to compare themselves to other men for "they like you, are born to live when the sun has gone down in darkness, and the moon is turned to blood." Then, calmly for one who has just invoked the Book of Revelation, he concludes his observations: "My friends, in the remarks that I have just made I have already in part anticipated the third great branch of our subject, which is that our prayers are written in heaven" (*YES*, p. 8).

The final "branch" uses a mixture of techniques employed in the first two. Emerson states his proposition, follows with a brief number of rhetorical questions, and then offers examples. The issue at hand is whether the designs of Providence are complete in the examples he has provided of granted prayers. Using "division," he argues that such designs cannot be totally realized in a temporal world where all prayers, sinful or not, are granted. This idea leaves him in a logical quandary, compelled to offer a moral that can draw a larger generalization around his previous doctrines. To do so he constructs another lurid example, this time of a rich man who has grown fat on the wretchedness of the poor. Emerson demonstrates that while this man's prayers may be granted in life, in the end he, like all humankind, must go to the grave. The final reward or punishment is not meted out in life, but in death. In what is perhaps the most fanciful section of the sermon, he offers an extended image of the rich man gnawed on by his own desires: "Pampered appetites that grew in the soil of this world, find no aliment for them in heaven, no gaudy vanities of dress, no riotous excitement of songs and dances, no filling gluttony of meats and drinks, no unclean enjoyments, finding none of all this, it must happen, that these appetites will turn upon their masters in the shape of direst tormentors" (*YES*, p. 10). From his simple example of the fact that all must go to the grave, Emerson draws a broad conclusion about the workings of universal moral law: prayers are heard, prayers are granted, but the universe also operates according to a law of compensation through whose agency the good will surely be rewarded and the bad will be punished. Emerson does not align this law with God's revealed, scriptural judgment, but makes it analogous to a moral law continually operative in the world. Once again, although on a far larger scale, he has moved from a proposition to an emotional proof to a concluding proposition.

"Nothing remains but the obligation there is on each of us to make what use we can of this momentous doctrine," Emerson concludes. Rather than listing the concrete applications of his doctrine, however, he once again ornaments his statement with an exhortation and an oddly feeble rhetorical finale: "To you therefore it belongs, to every one who now hears me, to look anxiously to his ways; to look less at his outward demeanour, his general plausible action, but to cleanse his thought. The heart, the heart is pure or impure, and out of it, are the issues of life and DEATH" (*YES*, p. 12). Emerson's "uses," such as they are, have become inner- rather than outer-directed.

What conclusions can we draw from this description of this sermon's structural and conceptual movement? As Lawrence Buell has shown, Emerson, like many Unitarians, used the Blair model less to prove doctrines than to exhort hearers to a vague sense of moral uplift and moral responsibility.[5] What is patently obvious in the young Emerson's case is his attempt to cling to the rhetoric of "inference," "proof," and "conclusion" in spite of the fact that the sermon threatens to become an extended series of poorly linked moral exhortations couched largely in rhetorical questions, moving examples, and dramatic language. Each emotional outburst is surrounded by a rational proposition and conclusion with which it sometimes, but not always, has a logical connection. Given the stock nature of his rhetorical strategies, the language in which they are expressed and the response they seem to call for, one could argue that it is only the tenuous retention of the Blair framework that gives this sermon any substantive conceptual as well as structural weight.

Considered from another perspective, however, Emerson's structuring of the sermon could be understood in a different manner. If "Pray Without Ceasing" indicates Emerson's interest in an internal subject matter—continual prayer which is continually granted—his techniques, stock though they may be, are his means of suggesting a link between internal prayer and internal feeling. Thus his different strategies—his questions, his examples, his language—can be read in light of a need to overwhelm rational debate with appeals to inner feeling. At the end, he broadens outward to suggest that such feeling is not solitary, but connected to a general law of compensation that underlies the workings of the entire world. This law is not bounded by logic or the need for clear transitions among ideas; it is experienced intuitively, not rationally. The law of compensation to which Emerson tentatively turns at the end of the sermon would not only call for new subject matter, an immanent rather than a rationally explicable law, but for the breakdown of the old sermon form and the creation of a new one. By implication, it would also demand a new conception of the audience for whom one preached. Outer appeals to experience could yield to an enacting of an experience before this audience, not only in the peroration where Blair allowed rational arguments to put on a specifically emotional dress, but throughout the sermon. Such an enactment, in subject and expression, would encourage a participation in self-evident law rather than rhetorically moving hearers to rationally and then emotionally yield to logical "inferences." If "Pray Without Ceasing" thus demonstrates

Emerson's flexing of his oratorical muscles (as indeed in part it does), it also reveals his growing dismissal of rational proof in favor of intuitive feeling, his groping towards a means of expressing a self-evident truth unconstrained by doctrines or standard forms, and his desire to unify his audience through its felt rather than rational response to his preaching. Channing had introduced a sermon form that allowed for the alternation of reasonable explanation and rhapsody, but in his own preaching, at least, the two modes invariably converged. Emerson's sermon obviously strains against such convergence and threatens to become almost entirely a series of emotional appeals. Moreover, Emerson's sermon is not only close to becoming pure exhortation; as such, it is focused less on encouraging moral action than it is on encouraging a sense of the power and the pleasures of intuition. In other words, although it appears to be within the parameters of Unitarian respectability, "Pray Without Ceasing" offers an incipient awareness of how—structurally and conceptually—such respectability could be overthrown from within.

In "Summer," a sermon of 1829, Emerson seems to be moving towards a new apprehension of both his subject and his audience. His reading in Coleridge has clearly started to affect him. Again, however, he initially operates within what seems a standard Unitarian framework. As Buell has shown, the Unitarians' dearth of topics led them to turn to nature as a storehouse of images useful for moral exhortation.[6] Perry Miller has demonstrated that such a tendency is far older than the Unitarians; Benjamin Colman and Cotton Mather were both using Flavel's *Husbandry Spiritualized* at the end of the seventeenth century in order to meditate, sometimes almost as effusively as later ministers, on nature's emblematic lessons. As Miller is at pains to show, and as seems equally true for Unitarians, such a use of nature was not typological; making it emblematic did not necessarily mean tying its meanings to external history, as Edwards was to do, or to internal history, as Emerson was to do. Nature, like Scripture, as we saw in Colman, provided useful images and analogies, little more.[7] In fact, in the nineteenth century such meditations on nature's moral meanings could even become detached from their context and appear as properly moralized effusions in gift books.[8] Colman and Mather would probably have applauded.

Despite the fact that Emerson's "Summer" certainly flirts with this genre, however, scholars have noticed that its structure also bears a resemblance to that of *Nature* (1836).[9] Evidently, young Emerson views nature as more than a static source of analogies for moral dicta (although this is again partially true); he also perceives interlocking levels of divine meaning within nature, and such a perception affects the way he structures his sermon. His subject matter, far more than the dictates of an exterior oratorical form, begins to affect how this sermon "moves." His audience is increasingly asked to participate in an inner exploration of the subject, rather than to acquiesce to the outer imposition of a rhetorical framework—whether it be rational or emotional. In content and in structure Emerson is learning, as Coleridge had argued, that a Whole suggests its presence within parts; they do not "add up" to a Whole exterior to them. Indeed, the very subject of "Summer" turns out to be immanence, not separation. The sermon shows Emerson's interest in exploring how an outer form can be used to suggest an inner dynamism that can touch an audience from within. If Emerson does not totally succeed, "Summer" represents something new in his sermonic practice. Significantly, the sermon was written during the period in which issues of composition were becoming more important in his journals.

The introduction, like the beginning of the "Divinity School Address," woos the audience rather than immediately laying out his subject: "In this grateful season, the most careless eye is caught by the beauty of the external world" (*YES*, p. 39).[10] The introduction implies rather than states Emerson's point by referring to very common images of the city and country. Noticeably, he does not immediately turn to a series of rhetorical questions. Rather, he seems to have no predetermined argument to make as he gradually moves from a consideration of nature to the proper religious response to it: "Those who yield themselves to these pleasant influences behold in the activity of the vegetation a new expression from moment to moment of the Divine power and goodness." From here, Emerson turns unobtrusively to an analogy which blends natural imagery with references to an immanent God. Believers see him "in the small leaf, in the wide meadow, in the sea and the cloud." He is, Emerson implies, not separate from nature, but acting within it. Detailing impressions at this point in his introduction, Emerson refrains from stating his doctrine.

In the next section, he hearkens back to the word "goodness" that appeared in the first section. The transition between these sections is thus not made with distinct clarity as in "Pray Without Ceasing"; it is suggested through the use of the same term in a new setting: "We are confident children, confident of God's goodness." Finally, although at a leisurely pace, Emerson moves towards his doctrine. He admits that human beings do not doubt the fact of God's order, but argues that their sense of it is too abstract; they do not connect their knowledge to the actual substance of the concrete world. As a result, they fail to "derive from the changes of nature that lesson which to a pious, to a Christian mind they ought to convey" (*YES*, p. 40). Emerson still has not stated his doctrine; he both forestalls and continues his movement towards it by introducing another series of natural images from nature's "lesson book": "On the glorious sky it is writ in characters of fire; on the earth it is writ in the majesty of the green ocean; it is writ on the volcanoes of the south and the icebergs of the polar sea; on the storm, in winter; in summer on every trembling leaf; on man in the motion of the limbs, and the changing expression of the face, in all his dealings, in all his language is seen and may be read and pondered and practised in all" (*YES*, p. 40). Almost anticlimactically, he then announces his doctrine: "This lesson is the omnipresence of God—the presence of a love that is tender and boundless." Viewing nature in fragments, humankind has failed to sense the God within it. In his conclusion to this extended introduction, he therefore urges, "Let us lift up our eyes to a more generous and thankful view of the earth and the seasons."

Without qualification or distinction, without drawing attention to them, Emerson has introduced through his natural images the major topics he will discuss in the body of the sermon: nature is integrated; it is beauty, commodity, and language; it is the meeting of time and space, of the divine and the concrete. God is immanent in its smallest and largest phenomena. Emerson allows these images to resonate suggestively before introducing his doctrine.

When compared to *Nature*, 1836, the most traditionally structured of the major essays, "Summer" seems almost deliberately unstructured. It is for the most part a meditation more than an exhortation. Certainly it treats some of the same subjects as *Nature*, and in a similar order, but the transitions between these subjects are not drawn as rigidly as they are in the essay, and, as a result, the sermon's movement is less fragmented. Indeed, its first major summary occurs only after Emerson's first three topics—commodity, beauty, and language, the bulk of the sermon—have already been examined.

The individual sections of "Summer" are also far more complicated than scholars have heretofore noticed. Searching for parallels to the essays, they have neglected what actually occurs in the sermon's own movement. For example, in his initial discussion of "commodity," Emerson does not speak of commodity per se; he meditates on the process of seasonal change. The well-being which the seasons provide is not simply that of physical commodity, but of psychic well-being: "The faintness of despondence of a spring that never opened into summer; the languor of a constant summer, the satiety of an unceasing harvest, the torpor or the terror of a fourfold winter" are inner states alleviated by the fact of seasonal change (*YES*, p. 40). As the changing seasons meet inner needs, so at the same time their metamorphoses suggest God's inner presence within them. Emerson argues that it is through their transformations that "we may recognize our heavenly Father." God's "immanence" in natural process, not a static concept of nature's material commodity, is the idea shaping this section. Importantly, Emerson does not use the image of the seasons to "color" an outer argument; the image forms the subject and substance of the argument to which his audience responds.

The transition from the idea of "seasonal process" to the sermon's next topic is not made as clearly as it is in *Nature* or—more obviously—in "Pray Without Ceasing." The notion of commodity is structurally interwoven with the notion of nature's mystery as Emerson moves gradually from discussing the God present in the seasons to a God present in nature's smaller productions—the strawberry—to the God present in its smallest manifestation—the seed. From there he turns to a meditation on the mystery (beyond the ken of scientists) of natural growth:

> The frequency of occurrence makes it expected that the little kernel properly sowed, will become at harvest-time a good number of kernels. . . . But explain to me, man of learning! any part of this productiveness. There is no tale of metamorphosis in poetry, no fabulous transformation that children read in the Arabian tales more unaccountable, none so benevolent as this constant natural process which is going on at this moment in every garden, in every foot of vacant land in three zones in the globe. (*YES*, p. 42)

Once again, Emerson does not present a topic, then rationally prove it; rather, he explores the relation between outer appearances and the inner law that infuses them. In this first section, he has considered commodity as outer and as inner, and he has moved from a God present in the changing year to a God present in the growth of common gifts and finally to the fact that such growth is a mystery. The order here is not overtly logical, although Emerson has unobtrusively linked larger to smaller, general to more particular. These links are suggestive, not imposed. The gradual merging from subject to subject seems to make his point as much as an overt statement; through his manner as much as his matter, Emerson urges his audience freely to respond to a God who is not only immanent in the parts of the natural world, but immanent in their response to Emerson's interwoven form.

The comments on mystery, just as those on the seasons, are used to suggest the next topic: nature's beauty. Emerson begins the section with more discussion of the mystery of seeds, notes once again the seed's dependence on God's "present power," and then asks his congregation: "Needs there, my brethren, any other book than this returning summer that reminds us of the first creation to suggest the Presence of God? Shall we indulge our querulous temper in this earth when nature is fragrant with healthful odours and glowing with every pleasant colour?" While he then chides "men" for complaining when nature ignores their immediate needs, this remark on summer's colors has subtly implied the topic to which he almost immediately turns: "We have been looking at Nature as an exhibition of God's benevolence. It will be felt the more to be so when it is considered that the same result might have been brought about without this beauty" (*YES*, p. 43).

Having stated this topic, however, Emerson again fails to examine it directly but returns to the "little seed" of the previous section. Speaking of the seed leads him to meditate on the products of the different soils that nourish humankind, from New England to the Red Sea, from France to the West Indies. He concludes the section by returning to a version of his original topic that also prepares his hearers for his next: "But all this food might have been prepared as well without this glorious show. To what end this unmeasured magnificence? It is for the soul of man" (*YES*, p. 43).

Conceptually Emerson has spoken of the larger presence of God within seeds, the more particular inner powers of nourishment that seeds possess, how this nourishment goes on worldwide, and finally how it is a beautiful process. Each of these topics is not considered and then abandoned; each is carried over and structurally interwoven with the next. Thus, unobtrusively, Emerson moves his audience from nature's concrete to its more spiritual uses.

In the next sections, however, this process of interconnection stops. The focus is on the analogies nature provides for human life. Not only does nature exist for the human eye to take pleasure in "this profusion of design," but "there is the language of its everlasting analogies, by which it seems to be the prophet and monitor of man." Emerson uses the language of the psalmist: "Man is like the flower of the field. In the morning he is like the grass that groweth up; in the evening he is cut down and withereth. There is nothing in external nature, but is an emblem or hieroglyph of something in us. Youth is the spring, manhood the summer, and age the autumn, and death the winter" (*YES*, p. 44). It is as if the preacher needed to stop, define, take measure of the vital process so evident in the earlier sections, and fix set "meanings" for his listeners. Yet at the end of this section, these more static analogies give way to the image of an apple that draws attention anew to the themes of growth and process. Although life and time seem continually the same, they, like the seasons, are continually changing: "So is the harvest old, the apple that hangs on your tree 6,000 times has shown its white bloom, its green germ, and its ripening yellow since our period of the world began. And this day as the fruit is as fresh, so is its moral as fresh and significant to us as it was to Adam in the garden" (*YES*, p. 44).

At this point, Emerson again stops to summarize what he has done for his audience, circumscribing and forcing into explicit categories what has structurally been far less contained than his summary admits: "I have spoken of the great system of external nature as exciting in our minds the perception of the benevolence of God by the wonderful construction their fruits exhibit, by the food they furnish, and by the beauty that is added to them, and now of the admonition they seem intended to convey of our short life" (*YES*, p. 44). Surely admonition is not the main subject of the section on nature as language; the images he uses are more stock than monitory. Nonetheless, Emerson plucks up the term "monitory" from this section in order to link it to his final point about nature's highest, that is, its moral, function: "But there is yet a louder and more solemn admonition which they [the seasons] convey to my mind as they do from year to year their appointed work. They speak to man as a moral being, and reproach his lassitude by their brute fidelity." As before, nature hardens into an emblem. The section also returns to the rhetorical questions, so evident in "Pray Without Ceasing": "Are we as trustworthy as the weed at our feet? . . . Are ye not better than they? Shall we to whom the light of the Almighty has been given, shall we who have been raised in the scale of creation to the power of self-government, not govern ourselves? Shall the flower of the field reprove us and make it clear that it had been better for us to have wanted than to have received intelligence?" (*YES*, p. 45). Emerson here obviously falls back on the assumption that the structure of a sermon demands "uses" and a "peroration" in order to enforce its arguments. Yet, just as obviously, these questions have little to do with his real subject matter, the mysterious "immanence" of God in all the mysterious changes within nature and humankind alike.

In his final remarks, Emerson exhorts his listeners to compare nature's order to their own disorder, a standard classical (and Unitarian) analogy, but then adds a final "lesson" far more in keeping with the true tenor of the sermon: "Let us learn also the lesson they are appointed to teach of trust in God; that he will provide for us if we do his will; remembering the word of the Lord Jesus, who said—"If God so clothe the grass of the field, which today is and tomorrow is cast into the oven, will he not much more care for you, O ye of little faith" (*YES*, p. 45). Once again, the emphasis falls on the immanent God who infuses nature and to whom the response should be one of intuitive faith and trust.

In "Summer," Emerson proves he has learned much about structuring an address in terms of the demands of a subject, rather than the demands of a rhetorical model. The dual themes of growth and immanence pervade the sermon not only in its subject matter, but in its structure. Structurally, each section is interwoven, not separated from the last by distinct transitions, as conceptually the immanence operative in each outer part of nature becomes an immanence equally operative in humankind. The audience for "Summer" is not presented with an "argument," verified by proofs, which moves towards a completed statement that the orator may emotionally color. The listeners' response is to a subject they have all conceivably felt but have never participated in as it was articulated in speech. Their response implicitly verifies the connections that Emerson suggests, but does not impose on them. Obviously, this response is not assumed to be a function of an external rhetorical model—at least until the end—but a response based on an individual, but shared, sense of "Summer," that beautifully and dynamically integrated system whose parts, internal and external alike, are infused by an immanent God. The response is bound up with an apprehension of a Wholeness that is ideally not static but, as Emerson put it in the journals, "full of tendency."

This suggestive movement breaks down, however, in face of old assumptions about sermon form and about an audience's need for clarity. A minor battle between the demands of an outer structure and the demands of a more "progressive transition" seems fought because of Emerson's fear that in order to be convinced an audience needed more moral applications more distinctly offered than he has provided them in the body of his sermon. In spite of this conflict, however, "Summer" clearly represents an important development in Emerson's thinking about how to present self-evident truth to his hearers.

GIVEN HIS INTEREST in outer manifestations of inner law in "Summer," it is not surprising to find that in 1829 Emerson also wrote sermons specifically concerned with the relationship of faith to works. Some brief comments on his sermon of that title will serve as a bridge to a more detailed consideration of his last sermon as minister at the Second Church. In 1829, Emerson produced a number of compare/contrast sermons, not only "Faith and Works," but "Freedom and Dependence" and "Society and Solitude." Certainly he used this structure during earlier periods, but not in such a concentrated cluster. "Faith and Works" deserves attention not because it is structurally complex, but because it demonstrates his interest in experimenting with the possibilities of a different model, and thus in persuading his audience in a different way. In "Summer," an interwoven technique is used to express a movement from the outer world of phenomena to an inner law; in "Faith and Works," in contrast, each of these categories, inner and outer, is first considered in its own right, and then in relation. This structure obviously releases Emerson from a strict adherence to the Blair model; it is already "divided," allowing him, as Richard Adams has remarked of a later technique in the essays, to push a subject as far as possible in one direction, and then to return to push it in another—only to find that the two are similar expressions, or, as Coleridge maintained, are two "bearings" on one law.[11] In other words, the structure allows for an extended treatment of concepts that appear at variance with each other, then turns full circle to express these concepts' underlying interdependence. This sense of structure as including both difference and relation is also analogous to Emerson's maturing idea of compensation and to his use of Coleridge's concept of "bi-polarity."

Emerson begins with a lengthy discussion of the historical conflict between faith and works, in which he appears to come down securely on the side of those who support the necessity of works for salvation: "By their fruits, by their fruits, said the Savior, ye shall know them." This is emphasized by an appeal to the common sense of "enlightened minds," and finally by an appeal to the precepts of Christianity as a system. The comments on faith that follow are far more brief; faith is necessary, he remarks, because the "subject is imperfect when all has been said for Virtue; the human heart yet demands its author, its source; yet gropes for the Great Intelligence whereon the affections may rest." There is a "longing that is in the soul of man to love and adore."[12] At this point, the differences between the two having been considered, the discussion takes a new turn.

Instead of reintroducing or summarizing the historical or moral division between the two concepts, Emerson considers how the two modes of knowing correspond to the nature of human psychology. The comments on faith have hinted that such is the case: faith is necessary because the human heart needs to "love and adore." At this point, however, he views both categories as equally internal. What was earlier set up as mutually exclusive is now tightly linked as Emerson concludes that both faith and works are functions of the whole Mind. Like Coleridge, he argues that while they may be "distinguished," they cannot be "divided": "Man is made of two parts, Reason and Affection. The Reason dictates works: Affection teaches faith. Reason proscribes duty, Affection makes it pleasant. Works prepare the mind to receive the idea of God . . . but Faith must come in to perfect the man, by connecting him and his works to God."[13] While faith is, in part, still subservient to works in this comment—making duty "pleasant," for example—Emerson also acknowledges that faith alone can connect virtuous action to God. The two ways of knowing are interdependent, not separate; both must live "blended in one character to exhibit the perfection of man."[14] What he had hinted in his discussion of faith here becomes applicable to works. From a discussion of an historical conflict between ways of believing, to a separate consideration of each of these ways, Emerson has moved to a mode of thought that views both of them as functions of a unified human character. The audience, initially asked to view each term as an external, historical phenomenon, are now encouraged to experience both faith and works as functions of their own inner lives.

"The Genuine Man" (1832), the final sermon Emerson preached as minister of the Second Church, uses both the strategy of interweaving employed in "Summer" and the strategy of separation and relation through internalization found in "Faith and Works," but it also hints at new strategies that Emerson will perfect in the lectures and essays.

"The Genuine Man" has recently been read as an "inspirational oration" which, moving to "increasingly higher levels of spirituality," reinforces in its broad structure Emerson's need for "self-culture."[15] Viewed from this perspective, Emerson's structure becomes a function of his use and transformation of a well-known Unitarian preoccupation. I, too, am concerned with this move to "higher levels," but with a different, though related, end in mind. The subject of the sermon is "genuineness," and the movement of the sermon is directed towards the evocation of an experience of "genuineness" in an audience. The subject matter does not exist in isolation, but becomes a function of a relationship created between a speaker and his hearers within a form. At issue in such an approach is not only the sermon's "broader movement," but the movement in and between its individual sections, as Emerson attempts (both successfully and unsuccessfully) to meet his criteria for "suggestiveness" and "progressive transition." As he proceeds through the sermon, he develops a notion of audience far closer to that of John Cotton than that of most Unitarians; as the Spirit supercedes the letter, piety (or, in his terms, "self-evident" truth) becomes far more important than duties, and community becomes increasingly based on an intuitive intersubjectivity rather than on an objective sharing of fixed external knowledge. As we shall see, hearing, perhaps even more than seeing, becomes central to the experience Emerson attempts at once to describe and enact.

Presented with a series of "circumstances," "parts," and "fragments" which are both external facts and internal qualities, hearers are asked either to discard or to reconceptualize them as expressions of an immanent Whole at work in themselves as well as in the preacher. At the sermon's beginning, Emerson presents these circumstances as detachable from "true" unity; by its end the whole notion of the relation of outer to inner circumstances has been redefined in line with the Coleridgean notion that the Reason expresses itself through the "discourse" of the understanding, just as the Spirit manifests itself through the letter. This strategy of relating parts to infusing wholes clearly anticipates Emerson's discussion of the fragmented man who becomes the "One Man" during the course of "The American Scholar."

The introduction, unwinding in a series of five statements of almost equal length, sets up a sense of expectancy. It is far from leisurely or diffuse: the structure is tightly knit, focused, yet suggestive, evincing the almost mathematical certainty Emerson remarked in the Swedenborgian sermon: "We hear the opinion often expressed that men are in a state of rapid improvement. It is thought that juster views of human nature are gaining ground than have yet prevailed. Men are beginning to see with more distinctness what they ought to be, that is, what true greatness is. What was called greatness they have discovered to be imposture. We stand on tiptoe looking for a brighter age, whose signs and forerunners have already appeared" (YES, p. 180). As in "Summer," Emerson does not reveal what the sermon's precise subject will be, but prolongs his hearers' expectation, noting only that "it seems to be left to us to commence the best of all works." This comment is followed by a discussion of what other periods in history have attained, all "partial" attainments, until finally he asserts, "To us has been committed by Providence the higher and holier work of forming men, true and entire men" (YES, p. 180).

Almost immediately, however, rather than defining what a "genuine man" is or even that such is to be his subject, he launches into the problem of finding an "entire" man. Here he employs a structural pattern he learned from sermons as early as "Pray Without Ceasing," but developed in sermons like "Summer." He makes a proposition, follows with an image which expands or clarifies it, then repeats his proposition only to have it serve as the introduction to a new repetition of the pattern. In "The Genuine Man," the pattern is used with a control lacking in the earlier sermons. The argument does not move by the precise proof or dismissal of propositions; the audience hears repeated patterns that are juxtaposed, not analyzed.

He begins the first section, for example, by asking, "A finished man— who has seen?" He then expands into an image: "Men are everywhere, on land and sea, in mountains and mines, cities and fields. . . . They are reckoned by thousands and myriads and millions," and then concludes, "There is a man in us, we have not seen executed out of us" (*YES*, p. 181). The expansion outward to millions of men is reduced in its restatement to the one man who is "in," not outside of, "us." This conclusion becomes the opening proposition of his next remark, which again broadens outward, this time not by a focus on "everywhere" and "millions" but by an appeal to his listeners' own experience in their own town and among their own acquaintances. He asks them if they have encountered "one" man who is "independent of his circumstances"—"one whom you venerate as a man, whose value to your eye consists entirely in the richness of his own nature, in the ability and disposition you suppose him to possess and not because he belongs to a particular family, or fills a certain office or possesses a huge estate, or is preceded by a great reputation." As in "Summer," Emerson, through this almost randon listing, has suggestively introduced the major themes discussed throughout the sermon: partials or "circumstances" as contrasted to the richness of the genuine man's nature. He concludes the section with a variation of his initial question: "There is nothing for the most part less considered than the essential man" (*YES*, p. 181). This statement looks two ways, back to the appeals just made, and forward to an expansion of a topic already implied: "The circumstances are much more attended to" than seeking to become genuine.

The section ends with an enumeration of the more concrete "circumstances" that surround a man and is followed in the next section by a listing of those more abstract. In both cases Emerson uses a strategy of separation, naming only the "parts" of the man. In the first series of examples, he notes that "the man is the least part of himself. We hear the wheels of his carriage. We feel the company that walk with him. We read his name in the newspapers . . . but him, the soul of him, the praised, the blamed, the enriched and accompanied we know not; what matter and quality and color of character he has by which he is that particular person and no other" (*YES*, p. 181). In the next section Emerson argues that his fame, his prosperity, his "fine plausible manners and polished speech" are equally partial. The movement of the section concludes with the revelation of the man behind all these "screens": "Behind all the barricades of circumstances is often found a poor, shrunken, distorted almost imperceptible object who, when exposed, is found helpless and unhappy" (*YES*, p. 182). The greatest of outer "circumstances" is shown up as partial; all the screens conceal a neglected soul. With this, the first movement—from millions to "one," from screens to what they conceal—is completed.

In the next movement of the sermon, Emerson does not continue the outer search conducted in the first movement. Instead, he begins a new line of enquiry that follows a similar structural pattern. Again, he starts with a question and uses a pattern of proposition, expansion through analogy, and subtle repetition in a new context. Just as he had begun the first section ("A finished man—who has seen?"), this section begins, "Is it not true to your experience brethren that thus the man is the least part of himself?" (YES, p. 182). As before, he does not directly answer his question, but reframes it through expansion and repetition; this time, however, the object of his quest has become inner rather than outer. Hearkening back to the preceding section, he remarks, "Arts and professions, wealth and office, manners and religion are screens which conceal lameness and imperfection of character." In this section they serve not only to hide the self from others, but from the self. The initial movement of the section concludes with another question that serves as a lead-in to a series of questions. "Is it not true that men do not think highly, reverently of their own natures?" Emerson asks. At this point he falls into the rhetorical questions of "Pray Without Ceasing" but uses them quite differently. This time they expand rather than color his subject matter, and serve to set up the contrast he next wishes to discuss: "Is it not true that men do not think highly, reverently of their own natures? . . . Does not the Apostle Paul, they say, teach that a man ought not to think highly of himself? Do we not say of a trifler that he thinks too much of himself?" (YES, p. 182). The issues set up in these different questions obviously lead to the necessity of drawing a distinction "between a right and wrong" estimate of the self. Using division, Emerson distinguishes between a selfishness that shows no knowledge of self and is thus only another "partial," and true self-knowledge, "that which comprehends a man's whole being, of that self which Jesus said, What can a man give in exchange for his soul?" This whole self is distinct from its circumstances, whereas the partial man, defining his self by means of outer phenomena, not only lacks real self-knowledge, but is not "man enough" to seek it. He has lived so long on the "outside" of his own inner world that even he "does not yet believe in its existence" (YES, p. 183). Having moved inside to the hidden self in the first section, Emerson now shows how this self lives outside itself in the second.

He ends this carefully constructed discussion of partial "circumstances" and the partial soul with an intrusive peroration. As in "Summer," the interwoven movement stops as Emerson exhorts his hearers to learn to distinguish between what in their lives is genuine and what is imitated. Then, as if he conceived it necessary to further clarify what he has been speaking about, he notes that his "object in the present discourse is to draw the picture of the Genuine Man." This summary, following an already detailed analysis, obviously interrupts the complex, interlocking progress of the sermon.

In the next section, however, almost as if this summary had never occurred, Emerson continues where he had left off—with the self that is living outside itself. He calls upon this man to "believe in himself" and urges that a "counterbalance" be set up to all that has impeded his self-understanding. At this point, he briefly abandons the sermon's initial pattern of question, expansion, and restatement, and begins to employ a structural variety of this "counterbalance." He notes that the "object" in view is

> to raise up a great counterbalance to the engrossing of riches, of popularity, of the love of life in the man and make him feel that all these ought to be his servants and not his masters, that he is as great, nay much greater, than any of these: to make him feel that whereas the consequence of most men now depends on their wealth or their popularity, he is capable of being sought to become a man so rich and so commanding by the simple force of his character, that wealth or poverty would be an unnoticed accident, that his solitary opinion and his support to any cause whatever would be like the acclamation of the world in its behalf. (*YES*, pp. 183–84)

The varying clauses play off against one another structurally: He sets up the circumstances, then notes they should be servants and the man greater than they. He sets up wealth and popularity against a rich character, then, leaving the language of opposition, blends what has been divided: "His solitary opinion and his support to any cause whatever would be like the acclamation of the world in its behalf" (*YES*, pp. 183–84).

Emerson concludes by remarking that this raising of the self against its circumstances (which are no longer the simple screens of the earlier sections, but have become the very "laws and customs of mankind") can only be accomplished by linking the soul's nature to religion: "It can only prefer this self because it esteems it to speak with the voice of God" (*YES*, p. 184).

At this point, turning from his example of the public man, Emerson once again exhorts his audience in a manner that breaks the sermon's movement. He asks "you and I" to attach what he has said to "our" own private realms. In another use of the "counterbalance" strategy, he argues that what could seem failures in the outer world—bankruptcy, death, lack of marriage (for women)—may prove inestimably valuable for inner growth. He calls upon all his listeners, particularly the young ones, to offer criticism of his view of genuineness.

As before, however, having "clarified" his meaning, Emerson returns to his real argument. Continuing his earlier discussion of the "voice of God," he now argues that a man "should follow the leading of his own mind like a little child" (*YES*, p. 184). The question of a divine voice is then expanded, but not through the use of logical transition. Emerson simply sets the genuine man in contrast to "vulgar people" who do not act "in character." Punning, Emerson changes the meaning of the phrase: the whole man acts "in" character, because he always acts "from" character, and this is no more evident than in his speaking. "Vulgar people . . . are always plotting. They always have one meaning on their lips and another in their hearts." This discussion is then interwoven with the one preceding it: "This duplicity shows that there is no sufficient power of reason within the mind that practises it to counterbalance the temptations of external motives" (*YES*, p. 185).

Abandoning the notion of counterbalancing (both structurally and conceptually), Emerson returns to the issue of genuine speech. The genuine man, having counterbalanced his internal and external "motives," ideally becomes "transparent," wearing no "veils," practicing no "dissimulation." David Robinson has noted the similarity of this language to that of *Nature* (1836), and the observation bears repeating. What is particularly noteworthy in this passage, however, is that unlike the later essay, Emerson here specifically relates "transparency" to hearing. He quotes both Fox ("That which I am in word, I am the same in life") and Swedenborg, who called his words "another self."

The importance of such hearing is reinforced in the expansion of the section that follows. Coming "closer" to his point, Emerson exults that when a truth speaker speaks, "it is not he who speaks, so much as reason that speaks through him. You are not dealing with a mere man but with something higher and better than any man, with the voice of Reason common to him and you and all men. It is as if you conversed with Truth and Justice" (*YES*, p. 186). Earlier, of course, he had prepared his audience for this "revelation" when he noted that the self should esteem the self because it "speaks with the voice of God" (*YES*, p. 184).

As the strategy of counterbalance, so briefly used, is abandoned, Emerson involves his audience in his preaching in a new way, echoing ideas and images expressed earlier in different contexts. For example, as he had earlier urged that the mind esteem its inner instincts as the "voice of God," and later, that the mind follow this voice like a little child, here he expands the notion by claiming that a man not only speaks with God's voice, but, in so doing, "he parts with his individuality, leaves all thought of private stake, personal feeling, and in compensation he has in some sort the strength of the whole, as each limb of the human system is able to draw to its aid the whole weight of the body. His heart beats pulse for pulse with the heart of the Universe" (*YES*, p. 186). Emerson has reached the high point of his sermon as all that is partial and separate yields to a vital image of intimate participation in, even identity with, a universal Whole.

Sounding like his later Unitarian critics, he then describes how this "vague expression" should be understood. Unlike Channing, however, who immediately applied his rhapsodies to duties, Emerson remains in the realm of Spirit, arguing that the literal truth which a genuine man speaks is not as important as the "Spirit" in which he speaks. It is this "Spirit," not the subject or contents of his speaking, that indicates his participation in the divine Whole. The "Spirit of truth" cannot be constituted by externals, although it moves through them; it springs from the man's perpetual hearing and speaking forth of internal truth. When this man speaks, he speaks from the "whole" heart, not simply from rational knowledge: "And so the effect upon the hearer is that you have his whole being a warrant for every word" (*YES*, p. 188).

In the next section, Emerson considers the importance of what he has said not only as it refers to speech, but to action. First, he returns to the notion of "partials." The subject, obviously pertinent for one who is leaving the ministry, is the "genuine" vocation. The problem echoes those considered throughout the sermon. Men, he decides, feel unhappy in their work because their approach to it is partial: "They do not give themselves to the affairs they undertake, they only half act, they speak much, and do much, and yet do not embark themselves fairly and frankly, for better for worse, in the cause, but are ever looking around to see, what chance there is for their advantage." They have split causes from effects, means from ends. To the genuine man, means become ends and causes effects because "it is his own cause and his life is in it" (*YES*, p. 188). This whole man is fitted to his work by spirit and this spirit expresses itself outward in his vocation. The actions of the genuine man in the end "have nothing to do with consequences; he is above them; he has nothing to do with the effect of his example; he is following God's finger and cannot go astray" (*YES*, p. 188).

In his conclusion, Emerson uses a Channing-like acknowledgement of an objection from those who may comment that "this quality is good but is there not something better." To meet this objection, he returns to a notion established at the end of the first section, where he had asserted that the genuine self "can only be founded in religion." Now, after a series of unifications, he repeats "that the convictions must be produced in our minds that this truth of character is identical with a religious life; that they are one and the same thing; that this voice of your own mind is the voice of God" (*YES*, pp. 188–89). This connection is not constituted by externals, like the knowledge of circumstances, or the hearing of hypocritical words or the doing of false actions, but "written . . . in the flesh and blood, in the faculties and emotions of your constitution" (*YES*, p. 189). There is nothing "better," because there is nothing more vital. Hearing God's voice and, by extension, speaking it has become an organic given, part of the self's very life.

Having unified this self, Emerson follows with an image of the effect of this unification: "This alone can teach him how to blend his religion with his daily labor so that every act shall be done with the full consent of his head and his heart and he shall not regard his business as so much interruption or so much injury to his religious life and leave his faith at home when he goes to his store" (*YES*, p. 189). The happy man who acts from his internal desires blends his love of God and his work until his life "reveals a new heaven and a new earth to his purer eyes." In a reversal of the genuine man's own transparency, the world becomes transparent to him and reveals the inner meanings which are also his own. How different is Emerson's use of the Book of Revelation here than in "Pray Without Ceasing"; there the language was used to "color" his ideas; here it has become a function of an earned vision in which his audience is encouraged to share.

In his final remarks Emerson makes an unforeseen nod to the virtues of the poor—genuineness can be found in all classes—but then turns to a "use" of his doctrine more integrated with the sermon just delivered. He repeats the texts that serve as the sermon's epigraph: "Be genuine—Be girt with truth." But he makes his own addition: "Aim in all things at all times to be that within that you would be without." Once again, his scriptural texts are not applied from without, but made integral to his own meanings. He does not "open" Christ's meanings; he incorporates them, with the full weight of the organic metaphor, into his own—and urges the audience (which has just experienced his preaching) to do likewise. In concluding, Emerson exhorts his congregation to look for inner, not outer, gains and returns to the theme of "progressive" movement alluded to in the sermon's introduction. He has now demonstrated that this progression is at once individual and universal. Turning inward to God's voice, Emerson's hearers "will be watching the wonderful opening and growth of a human character, . . . who was designed by his Maker to be a growing benefit to the world and to find his own happiness in forever enlarging the knowledge, multiplying the powers and exalting the pleasures of others!" (YES, p. 190). Listening to the inner voice leads not to selfishness but to a universal sense of the needs of others. These needs, however, are not external: they are not to be met by performing set duties. Rather, the genuine man expresses a sense of "method," not of doctrine. He enlarges knowledge, powers, and pleasure, by exhibiting the movement of the Spirit, not by performing externally demanded moral actions.

"THE GENUINE MAN" shows an Emerson whose ideas about shaping self-evident faith have become increasingly aligned to his interest in an audience's free response to "suggestiveness." What had been standard devices in the demonstrative oration—summaries and particular appeals to experience—here break into the complex overall patterning and movement of the sermon. They seem more like momentary lapses into an older sense of audience (as needing explicit explanation and rational control) than functions of Emerson's overall intention. For the most part, the sermon uses strategies that attempt to be consistent with Coleridge's notion of "progressive transition." These structuring devices are not imposed on his listeners; they instead seem to ask an audience to complete their meanings as structures.

Emerson begins with a pattern of proposition, expansion, and repeated proposition that is dovetailed to similar patterns through structure and diction. He does not call attention to these similarities; he simply suggests them. This pattern allows him—through juxtaposition—to imply a relation between outer "circumstances" and inner states, between partial phenomena and infusing universals. Since he does not directly state these relationships, the audience is left free either to intuit their connection or to deny it. As in "Faith and Works," Emerson also briefly uses a strategy of counterbalancing that once again depends on the audience to blend the categories it opposes. And, by the time he reaches the middle of the sermon, it has also become clear that he has employed an imagistic echoing similar to that used in "Summer," but which is here less distinctly interwoven from section to section and thus far more dependent on the audience's ability to complete his suggested connections. An early mention of religion as "God's voice," for instance, is later transformed into the image of the "little child" following an inner voice and finally becomes the man who speaks with the "voice" of reason and whose heart beats "pulse for pulse" with the universe. Finally, of course, there is the imagery of sight and particularly of hearing that pervades the sermon. This imagery moves from outer to inner sight to the inner hearing of a voice that is translated into outer speech and outer action. Both "sight" and "hearing" are necessary conditions of "transparency," Emerson's most complete image of a self-evident "genuineness." Once again, however, it is the audience which must complete these images by hearing and responding to them throughout the sermon. In other words, Emerson desires not simply to talk about this genuineness; he enacts the process of becoming "transparent" in a manner that encourages (but does not force) his hearers' participation in it as well.

While the older Channing may have aspired to such a structure, especially in "Likeness to God," it is clear that, far more than Emerson, he clung to an external frame. Particularly evident in Emerson's sermon is the almost total absence of the clear "divisions" of an argument and the use of the objection/answer strategy so important to the Blair model. Emerson also dismisses the pattern of explanation followed by rhapsody—so evident in Channing's sermons and in his own earlier efforts. Instead, he attempts to speak with the mathematical certainty he ascribed to the Swedenborgian preacher. There is very little separation of statement from emotional restatement in this sermon; the feelings he wishes to engender are already suggested in the propositions he makes. These propositions are left to resonate, without complete explanation or ornamental "coloring," in the minds (and ears) of his listeners.

The "uses," "applications," or, in Blair's term, the "peroration"—the section used to exhort the audience to action on issues raised by the orator (and the section that was becoming nearly the whole sermon for the Unitarians)—also fades out in Emerson. He is not presenting the moral "uses" of a doctrine in the sense of directing his hearers to outer action; he is rather expressing a transforming revelation that in its suggestiveness attempts to evoke within them an experience of a "genuineness" that is at once personal and universal.

To focus on suggestiveness rather than the importance of external effects means, in the context of this study, to return to the "reasons" section of the old sermon form. Emerson offers a series of propositions connected thematically, structurally, and imagistically that grow or expand in their range of application to a central subject—"immanence" in growth ("Summer") or sight/hearing of "genuineness" ("The Genuine Man"). Whether the structure expands from a core subject outward through a series of developing repetitions or is structured around a comparison/contrast model, what invariably occurs is the relating of particulars to a whole, of abstractions to concrete phenomena, of internals to externals, faith to works, Reason to understanding, and, of course, Spirit to letter. Emerson is clearly attempting to encourage a sense of "method" or "progressive transition" in his listeners.

These listeners play an engaged, not a static, part in this demonstration. Indeed, it is their free response alone that can make Emerson's "method" a method. Like Coleridge, Emerson could not remain content with devising a theory that was merely formal. Far more than Coleridge did he argue that self-evident truths must be spoken forth to others and, in turn, transformed by them. Such an attitude locates "faith" neither in a form, in a speaker, nor in an audience, but in their complex interrelation. Without an audience's participation in an act of speaking, no "progressive transition" can occur—only a dead formal performance with significance only to the performer. In contrast, when an audience truly hears his words, the Spirit within them is ideally reshaped into their own hearing and speaking, which, in turn, can help to reshape the understanding of their preacher.

The assumption grounding this belief is that no matter how different the forms through which a preacher and his congregation manifest their hearing of the Spirit, the impulse immanent in each and all of them is both universal and moral.

In his attempt to develop a new sense of the interplay between faith, form, and audience, it becomes clear, Emerson has unwittingly travelled full circle, back to assumptions about religious knowledge shared by John Calvin and John Cotton. Like that of his precursors, Emerson's main focus becomes a "self-evident" knowledge distinct from external obligations; like them (and like Coleridge), he too acknowledges the necessity for external forms—verbal or moral—but emphasizes that the Spirit grants power "above and beyond" any letter. Finally, and most importantly, Emerson comes to share their belief that those who truly "hear" the word preached (and, for Emerson, all people, not simply the elect, can so hear) do not passively receive objective knowledge, but themselves participate in a dynamic shaping, renewing, and sharing of religious experience.

To assert these connections is not to argue that Emerson succeeds in meeting these exalted ends either in his sermons or elsewhere. Indeed, whether such a possibility ever exists is, of course, dubious. What remains important is the fact that Emerson desires to express a particular vision of this interplay, that he continually experiments with different ways of expressing it, and that his return to a conception of the relation of faith to its believers, so allied to that of earlier preachers, suggests not only the personal importance which expressing this relation held for him, but its continuing social and cultural importance to New England and to New England letters.

Coda

E MERSON'S "real" audience at the Second Church was generally pleased with its young minister, in spite of some complaints to the senior pastor, Henry Ware, about his Quaker "tendencies" and Ware's own warnings about his use of secular references in his sermons.[1] Gay Wilson Allen notes that when the church met to take a final vote on Emerson's request to be allowed not to dispense the "Lord's Supper," many church members stayed home—unable to vote for him, unwilling to vote against him. Good Unitarians as they were, however, who believed not only in the theological but in the traditional importance of the "Supper" for defining a church community, they had very little choice but to let him go. Even his willingness to administer the sacrament privately to those who wished it was simply not tenable; the "ordinance" was public and demanded public expression. As Allen remarks, Emerson was not only flying in the face of convention, he was opening the church to the possibility of severe economic difficulties if the conservative bankers and merchants who provided its main support departed because of his unorthodox views.[2] Like Channing, Emerson found that his portrait of the self-making capacities of the "genuine" individual was tenable, even laudable, as long as it did not interfere with the subtle hierarchy implied in conventional practice. Emerson, of course, did not share his hearers' fears about the moral or practical repercussions of his preaching; with increasing frequency he preached against the need for external forms of authority in favor of a self-reliance that was at base universal. Shaped in the context of orthodox Unitarian thought, his precepts and even the vision of audience implied in them were permissible as long as they did not entirely repudiate the need for some adherence to Christian convention. After his return

176

from Europe, however, when he began to preach outside the church's stabilizing boundaries, Emerson's ideas were attacked as the "latest form of
infidelity." Paradoxically, the criticism of Unitarians like Andrews Norton
and Ware himself (particularly after Emerson delivered the "Divinity
School Address") served only to create an enthusiastic new audience for
the unchurched preacher.

To present the process of a "self" becoming a universal self through an
experience of "self-evident" truths was of course a desideratum of Channing's preaching as well as that of Emerson. Such preaching at once included and aroused an audience's piety before its own capacity for divinity.
Indeed, it is clear that the older Unitarian's concern with the "moral
sense" set the stage for the younger man's preoccupation with the affective
nature of "self-evident" truth. But Channing was unwilling to give up
either the clarity of framework offered by the demonstrative oration or the
belief that individual intuition and feeling somehow demanded the balance
provided by external forms of authority.[3] Emerson increasingly sought the
overthrow of both. Their preaching manifests both their similarities and
their growing differences. While each projects an image of a free audience,
for example, Channing (with some notable exceptions) does so more by
talking about this freedom, Emerson by attempting to enact it in his
forms. And it is precisely for his manner of presentation (and its dangers to
an audience) that Emerson is later criticized in the Unitarian magazine, the
Christian Examiner. The editors not only question the "unintelligible notions" he presented in the "Divinity School Address"; they link this unin-
telligibility to his style. For example, they note with approbation the manner in which Henry Ware responds to the address. Unlike those of
Emerson, both Ware's topic and his manner of presenting it are "clear":

> There is a personal God or there is none. . . .
>
> This is sense; this is truth; and this good writing. Here is important doc-
> trine clearly and plainly announced, so that there is no mistaking it, and so
> that it approves itself equally to the most and the least instructed minds. Here
> is a style which becomes the subject, simple, manly, straight forward. Give us
> such writing and such preaching as this and defend us from the wordiness and
> mysticism, which are pretending to be a better literature, a higher theology,
> and almost a new revelation.[4]

The fear that is demonstrated here is obviously not simply of a new theology, but of the effects of its "mystical" presentation on an audience that

is not carefully divided into "the most and the least instructed minds." The quotation could be an attack on Trinitarian preaching, or rephrased in seventeenth-century terms as an attack on the preaching of "enthusiasts." For if Emerson's preaching reveals a debt to Unitarian thought and rhetoric, he expanded both in directions they could not follow. His preaching reveals his gradual return—in his own context—to questions and to paradoxes about the interplay of belief and its presentation to an audience that arise in the preaching of John Cotton.

Cotton's belief in the special capacity for "faith" that was granted to the elect led him in his theology to stress the importance of justification over sanctification, of "faith" over "works," and of Spirit over letter. In his preaching, such a belief led him to use the Perkins sermon model in a manner that stressed suggestive "reasons" rather than the "uses" of a text and its doctrines. Cotton realized that his audience consisted of those who possessed election (whether they were "assured" of it or not) and those who did not, but his preoccupation with allowing the Word freely to resonate in elect hearers encouraged Thomas Shepard to accuse him of "darkly" delivering his truths, and of thereby confusing and dividing his audience. At issue was not simply the clarity with which a text was "opened"; more subtly the question involved choosing the basis whereby the community formed itself: was it to be pious or was it to be moral? The shaping of belief was thus construed not only to "inform" a community; it also helped to define this community.

Before and during the Antinomian Controversy, Cotton upheld the position that certainty of faith and morality of act were generally inseparable. He simply insisted that the former must precede the latter. In accordance with Calvinist orthodoxy, the elect community would thus be a function of an inner Spirit that manifested its presence in outer behavior. In the course of the Antinomian Controversy, however, the concepts of "justifying faith" and "sanctification" became increasingly sundered and finally twisted into a new relation not only by the preparationists, but also by Cotton. In the 1640s, seeking to defend the "Congregational way" against the attacks of Roger Williams, Cotton departed from the intellectual and spiritual openness he had demonstrated about religious debate (and "elect" hearing) before the controversy. Turning to notions of religious "truth" that were at once medieval and Calvinist, he argued that since "visible" sainthood was a reality in Massachusetts, the so-called intolerant treatment levied by the "saints" against those who believed differently was perfectly justifiable. Such miscreants sinned not against the virtue and security of the commonwealth alone, but against the dictates of their own consciences.[5] They thus fully deserved the punishment levied against them by an elect community. Thus, ironically, could a theology initially so concerned with individual, "free" response be translated into its own particular form of social control.

In returning to notions of faith and its presentation to an audience that are similar to those of Cotton (and which were attacked on similar grounds), Emerson reopened the broader question of the relation which individual faith should bear to a larger social world. In so doing, he expressed subtle tensions at the heart of his own culture's response to this question.

On the surface, at least, Emerson acknowledged the connection between his attitudes towards form and the social and political activities of Jacksonian Democrats. While the journals manifest his Brahmin distaste for the Jacksonians ("in the woods," at least, he finds "no Jackson placards"), still Emerson admitted in 1834 that the Jacksonians were involved in the same enterprise as he—the destruction of reliance on older forms of authority and the concomitant shaping of a different sense of community:

> We all lean on England, scarce a verse, a page, a newspaper but is writ in imitation of English forms, our very manner and conversation are traditional and sometimes the life seems to be dying out of all literature and this enormous paper currency of Words is accepted instead. I suppose the evil may be cured by this rank rabble party, the Jacksonism of the country heedless of English and of all literature—a stone cut out of the ground without hands—they may root out the hollow dilettantism of our cultivation in the coarsest way and the new-born may begin again to frame their own world with greater advantage. (*JMN*, 4:297)

In the expression of such feelings Emerson not only departs from Unitarian thinking, but also from that of Coleridge. After setting up the relationship of the understanding to the Reason in *The Friend*, Coleridge warns that by no means must his philosophical and aesthetic theories be applied to the necessarily "expedient" realms of politics and government. Arguing from the Reason, he particularly notes, does not involve "a necessary preference for the democratic or even the representative form of government."[6] Emerson, in spite of his reservations, could not agree. While he expressed a decided preference for political uninvolvement, Emerson remained a problematic Democrat who believed that the universal Spirit could and did manifest itself in the workings of the restless and expanding system of mid–nineteenth century democracy.[7]

It was for Alexis de Tocqueville, another European, to open up the possibly darker implications about democracy suggested in Emerson's belief that self-evident truth could find both individual and universal acceptance if presented in the proper "method." When Tocqueville's comments about the relation of the democratic Whole to its individual members are carefully examined, they suggest how Emerson could unconsciously become embroiled in a paradox analogous to that of Cotton. As Marvin Meyers has argued, the French Catholic aristocrat found a doubleness at the center of Protestant democratic America. On the one hand, American democracy seemed composed of separate yet equal individuals, each involved in an unceasing and continually transforming quest for personal betterment.[8] On the other hand, side by side with this individual quest for self-aggrandizement, Tocqueville also found what Coleridge feared: an astounding group dependence among these individuals who, when they failed, could turn only to the authority which was "themselves en masse," the *volonté generale* of the "ignorant multitude."[9]

As Tocqueville explored America, argues Meyers, he discovered that his "pure" theory was not entirely borne out; rather than a tendency to fall completely towards one of these poles or the other, he perceived a continual tipping and tilting between them, a "bi-polarity" that expressed the paradox of change coupled with stability. "Two things are surprising in the United States: the mutability of the greater part of human actions, and the singular stability of certain principles. Men are in constant motion, the mind of man appears almost unmoved."[10] Yet, if democracy thus seemed the ideal political image of "progressive transition," Tocqueville had also inadvertently suggested that such a system could pose new questions about the expression and shaping of an audience in an "organic" form.

The "latest form of infidelity" that split Emerson from the Unitarians— and which was viewed as socially (and aesthetically) radical by Trinitarians and Unitarians alike—could, in its extreme emphasis on the universal law active within individual intuition, express a new constraint as well as a new freedom for an audience. Historians have argued that Emerson's stress on an individual power embedded in universal principles offered both an analogy to and a possible justification for the unchecked laissez-faire activity of the Jacksonian period.[11] But this equation could also be reversed. If Emerson's thought (and his structures) justified individual action, could not his equal reliance on the universal law that permeated mind and form also restrict and focus individual action precisely because this law was conceived as "natural" and "organic"? Could not a sense of this organic Whole come, in a far more subtle way than visible constraints, to dictate as much as to express the needs and desires of its individual "parts"? Viewed from this angle, Emerson could become not only his culture's spokesman for a renewed vision of individual freedom coupled with communal stability, but also its prophet of a new means of power, a new foundation for control.

To suggest such possible reversals is not to argue stringently that Emerson's sermons, even his later ones, directly confront this paradox. Emerson's richest conscious and unconscious rendering of the relation between individual desire and universal law is shaped in the essays. Nor is even suggesting this possibility to engage perversely in debunking the belief towards which we have moved throughout this discussion: that Cotton's and Emerson's beliefs and, to a degree, their practices, seem to offer a listening audience a different, freer participation in a process of making meanings (without imposing set moral interpretations) than the preaching of Colman and early Channing. This is not to deny further that both Cotton and Emerson in the eyes of "real" audiences posed threats to conservative notions of the "proper" relation of piety to morals. Rather, it is to conclude with the assertion that talking about sermon structures and the way they help to express and form a culture's needs proves far more complicated than simply ascribing to these models one meaning, one intention, and one effect. For if the possibility of an individual and a community "freedom" is posited anew in the theory and preaching of all these preachers, each, in his own unique context, also projects the possibility of a new kind of control. Thus, even an Emerson, who seems in some respects so opposed to certain tendencies of his age, can come unwittingly both to conform to and to aid in shaping these tendencies.

Clearly, the knowledge which New England sermons as cultural constructions can offer about social assumptions and social structuring demands more investigation. What is offered here is only a sample, a beginning that suggests some of the ways in which theories about sermon form, changes in these theories, preaching that conforms to them, and preaching that does not, embody complex feelings about the nature of faith, of authority, and of community.

IN *The Scarlet Letter*, Hawthorne offers his own meditation on the difficulties involved in presenting "self-evident" truths in an external form to an audience. He seems to warn his readers that sermons of whatever form demand closer analysis by their hearers than they have generally been willing to give them.

Himself a man of faith, the Reverend Arthur Dimmesdale's "works" are hypocritical, bearing no relation to his internal state; his sanctification is no evidence of his justification. His inner and outer realities are split. Yet, says Hawthorne, he preaches with the "voice of an angel," and in spite of his own inner division his preaching at least suggests the possibility of individuals sharing a unified response: "What was it? The complaint of a human heart, sorrow-laden, perchance guilty, telling its secret, whether of guilt or sorrow to the great heart of mankind. . . . It was this profound and continual undertone that gave the clergyman his most appropriate power."[12] While he is unable to link his own faith to his works, Dimmesdale is still paradoxically capable of unifying parts with a whole or, more specifically, individuals with their community, at least within the "method" of his speaking.

But what is this speaking? Hawthorne compares his preaching to music, which appeals totally to the ear of the listener: "The vocal organ was in itself a rich endowment, inasmuch that a listener, comprehending nothing of the language in which the preacher spoke, might still have been swayed to and fro by the mere tone and cadence."[13] The audience responds to a pure composition, a pure form, in which the words, "if more distinctly heard, might have been only a grosser medium, and have clogged the spiritual sense."[14] Such a speaking and such a response are, in the terms we have just analyzed, the preacher's ideal: the emotions of the single elect "instrument" of the Spirit are shared with his audience. All are united in a common feeling and a common response, as the Spirit moves through and apparently dissolves the letter.

As if to corroborate this idea, Hawthorne uses another musical analogy to describe the congregation's response to Dimmesdale's preaching. Their "symphonious" feelings, says Hawthorne, produced a "more impressive sound than the organ tones of the blast, or the thunder, or the roar of the sea; even that mighty swell of many voices blended into one great voice by the universal impulse which makes likewise one vast heart out of the many."[15]

A subtle irony runs through this whole chapter. Not content with simply showing that the underpinnings of this unity, this response to a "suggestive," "self-evident" truth is in part a function of the preacher's inner division, his lack of genuineness, Hawthorne casts further doubts on Dimmesdale's motives and ends in so speaking. In the beginning of the chapter Hawthorne slyly notes that the "election" speech is a means ministers could use of gaining political as well as religious power in the colony; by its end, he comments that "the admirable preacher was looking down from the sacred pulpit upon an audience whose very inmost spirits had yielded to his control."[16] Dimmesdale, for all his apparent sanctity, has the power not simply to express the feelings shared by the entire community, but like a despot to control and focus such feelings for his own ends, be they sexual or political. The minister offers a momentary image of how a democracy can subtly transform itself into a "soft totalitarianism" feared by Coleridge and suggested by Tocqueville.[17]

But Hawthorne does not stop here. Immediately after his discussion of the unifying power of the sermon, he turns to the scene of confusion on the scaffold, "The Revelation of the Scarlet Letter." In this chapter, the crowd which was so unified during Dimmesdale's sermon breaks up in confusion. What is the dying minister's final revelation? How is it to be understood? Was there a letter etched over his heart or not? There is confusion of both sight and hearing. The difficulties of interpretation reflect back on the sermon just heard. They underscore the fact that there may have also been differences in this apparently unified hearing, and that the experience of shared understanding felt in the church was false. Was the sermon a universal allegory, a personal confession, both, or neither? Hawthorne characteristically offers a variety of reactions to the scene, commenting "there was more than one account of what had been witnessed on the scaffold," and then leaves "the reader [to] choose among these theories."[18] What was unified, community response, is once again fragmented, and given the source of that unity—unspoken sin and inner division on the one hand, and the possibility of a subtle yet powerful social control on the other—Hawthorne suggests that its loss is rather to be celebrated than lamented.

Thus does Hawthorne, like Roger Williams before him, point up the ironies in a formal theory which had insisted from the beginning that it was the Spirit moving through the form, not form itself, that was important; that form could and must be used to manifest self-evident truth; and that the truly elect would not only freely and individually recognize the truth immanent in this form, but also be unified in their response to it. Form, Hawthorne suggests, is the product of both a conscious and unconscious interplay between the artist and the community. An expression of personal and group needs and ambivalences, it does not necessarily embody the movement of any spirit, and the unity it creates, when actually tested, may prove to be illusory. Neither a written nor a heard composition necessarily demonstrates the presence of inner or outer unity; form conceals as much as it reveals its meanings, multiplies and divides its audiences as much as it unites them.

But the issue for Hawthorne in the nineteenth century and certainly for an audience in the twentieth is not, finally, whether Cotton, Colman, Channing, or Emerson's theories are actually borne out in their practice, but what ideals, what illusions about the relation of self-evident faith communicated through a form to an audience their attempts make manifest. Hawthorne himself cannot be exempted from this question. The problem of seeing and of "hearing" self-evident truths lies at the heart not only of his subject matter, but of his own form of presenting it to an audience. The issues confronted by the preachers, of finding a form commensurate with faith, a form which suggests rather than imposes, unifies rather than divides, supports a notion of social order while allowing for free and individual response, are translated into the problems of the romancer, who, as Melville so presciently saw in his essay "Hawthorne and His Mosses," was replacing the clergyman as the central moral spokesman of his culture.[19]

Notes

Introduction

1. John Calvin, *Institutes of the Christian Religion*, vol. 1, chap. 7, par. 5, quoted in H. Jackson Forstman, *Word and Spirit: Calvin's Doctrine of Biblical Authority* (Stanford: Stanford University Press, 1962), p. 17.

2. See Edmond Morgan, *Visible Saints: The History of a Puritan Idea* (Ithaca, N.Y.: Cornell University Press, 1963). Of course neither Calvin nor many of the so-called "Puritan" sects read the notion of the "visibility" of sainthood in the same manner. I overstate the case to make the distinction.

3. Calvin, *Commentary on the Psalms*, 78:3, quoted in Forstman *Word and Spirit*, p. 56. The phrase "objective and informational" (p. 102) is Forstman's, not Calvin's.

4. John Cotton, *Some Treasure Fetched out of Rubbish* (London, 1660), p. 40.

5. See Patricia Caldwell, "The Antinomian Language Controversy," *Harvard Theological Review* 69 (1979): 345–67. For differing discussions of preparation, see also Norman Pettit, *The Heart Prepared* (New Haven: Yale University Press, 1966) and R. T. Kendall, *Calvin and English Calvinism to 1649* (Oxford: Oxford University Press, 1979).

6. See David Hall, ed., *The Antinomian Controversy, 1636–1638: A Documentary History* (Middletown, Conn.: Wesleyan University Press, 1968), pp. 336–37.

7. Cotton quoted in Hall, *The Antinomian Controversy*, p. 370.

8. Cotton quoted in Hall, *The Antinomian Controversy*, p. 373. "And soe your opinions frett like a Gangrene and spread like a leprosie, and infect farr and near, and will eate out the very Bowells of Religion, and hath soe infected the Churches that God knowes whan they will be cured."

9. Perry Miller, *The New England Mind: The Seventeenth Century* (Boston: Beacon Press, 1961), p. 362.

10. The phrase is Alan Simpson's in *Puritanism in Old and New England* (Chicago: University of Chicago Press, 1955), p. 21.

11. See, for example, Charles Feidelson, *Symbolism and American Literature* (Chicago: University of Chicago Press, 1953); Larzer Ziff, *Puritanism in America* (New York: Viking Press, 1972) and his important essay, "The Literary Consequences of Puritanism," *English Literary History* 30 (1963), 292–305, rpted. in *The American Puritan Imagination: Essays in Revaluation* ed. Sacvan Bercovitch, (Cambridge: Cambridge University Press, 1974), pp. 34–44. In the same collection see also Norman Grabo, " 'The Veiled Vision': The Role of Aesthetics in Early American Intellectual History," pp. 19–33; Sacvan Bercovitch, *The Puritan Origins of the American Self* (New Haven: Yale University Press, 1975); and Sacvan Bercovitch, *The American Jeremiad* (Madison: University of Wisconsin Press, 1978). For a recent discussion of the aesthetic underlying Puritan writing see Patricia Caldwell, *The Puritan Conversion Narrative* (Cambridge: Cambridge University Press, 1983).

12. Feidelson, *Symbolism and American Literature*, pp. 77–118.

13. Bercovitch, *Puritan Origins*, p. ix, and *American Jeremiad*, pp. xiv–xv.

14. Ziff, "Literary Consequences of Puritanism." See note 11 above.

15. Ziff, "Literary Consequences of Puritanism," p. 298.

16. See Stephen Greenblatt, *Renaissance Self-Fashioning: From More to Shakespeare* (Chicago: University of Chicago Press, 1980), introd.; see also Clifford Geertz, *The Interpretation of Cultures* (New York: Basic Books, Inc., 1973), especially the first essay, " 'Thick Description': Towards an Interpretive Theory of Culture," pp. 3–30.

17. Geertz as quoted in Greenblatt, *Renaissance Self-Fashioning*, p. 3.

1. John Cotton and the Shaping of Election

1. See, for example, John Norton, *Abel Being Dead yet Speaketh* (London, 1658), pp. 13–14; Cotton Mather, *Magnalia Christi Americana* (Boston, 1702), 3:256; Thomas Allen, preface to *An Exposition upon the Thirteenth Chapter of Revelation*, by John Cotton (London, 1655). Quoted in Everett Emerson, *John Cotton*, (New York: Twayne Publishers Inc., 1965), p. 34. See also Miller, *The New England Mind: The Seventeenth Century*, p. 331; Larzer Ziff, *The Career of John Cotton* (Princeton: Princeton University Press, 1962), p. 32; Jesper Rosenmeier, " 'Clearing the Medium': A Reevaluation of the Puritan Plain Style in Light of John Cotton's *A Practicall Commentary Upon the First Epistle Generall of John*," *William and Mary Quarterly*, 3d ser., vol. 37 (1980): 555–91.

2. John Wilson as quoted by Cotton Mather in the *Magnalia* (1702), 3:25–26. Also quoted in Emerson, *John Cotton*, p. 18.

3. John Winthrop, *Journal*, ed. James K. Hosmer, 2 vols. (New York: C.

Scribner's Sons, 1908), 1:116. Also quoted in Emerson, *John Cotton*, p. 104; Ziff, *The Career of John Cotton*, p. 106.

4. Alfred Habegger, "Preparing the Soul for Christ: The Contrasting Sermon Forms of John Cotton and Thomas Hooker," *American Literature* 41 (1969): 342–45; see also Emerson, *John Cotton*, pp. 104–5, for a discussion of Cotton's stylistic lacks when compared to Hooker.

5. Everett Emerson, introduction to *God's Mercie Mixed with His Justice*, by John Cotton (Gainesville, Fla.: Scholars' Facsimiles and Reprints, 1958), pp. v–xiii.

6. For specific criticism other than that of Emerson, Habegger, and Ziff see Stanley Fish, *Self-Consuming Artifacts* (Berkeley: University of California Press, 1972), pp. 70–77. Relying on Cotton as his chief example, Fish attacks the Perkins form as "methodical," "self-sufficient," lacking in "surprise," and "self-glorifying" when compared to the "self-consuming" sermons of John Donne. See also Babette Levy, *Preaching in the First Half-Century of New England History* (Hartford: The American Society of Church HIstory, 1945), p. 41.

7. William Perkins, *The Arte of Prophesying* (London, 1607). The 1607 version is a translation by Thomas Tuke of a Latin version published in 1592. I am using the *Arte* found in the *Works* (London, 1612–13), 2:646–73. Whereas Habegger and others draw on Richard Bernard, *The Faithful Shepheard* (London, 1607), I rely on Perkins because his manual was used while Cotton was a student at Cambridge. Also, as Habegger notes, Bernard "recommends essentially the same sermon form as Perkins" (p. 343). See also Larzer Ziff, *The Career of John Cotton*, pp. 149–69. While Ziff discusses Cotton's style, he does not relate it to Perkins's sermon model. See also Ziff's "Literary Consequences of Puritanism," pp. 292–305, which does indeed consider certain premises underlying the Puritan sermon structure, but not in terms of Cotton's use of it. For an excellent discussion of Perkins, see Barbara Lewalski, *Protestant Poetics and the Seventeenth Century Religious Lyric* (Princeton: Princeton University Press, 1979), esp. pp. 214–20. The standard source for discussions of seventeenth-century sermon form is W. F. Mitchell, *English Pulpit Oratory from Andrewes to Tillotson* (New York: Macmillan Co., 1932). See also Phyllis Jones, "Biblical Rhetoric and the Pulpit in Early New England," *Early American Literature* 11 (1976–77): 245–58. Jones mentions structure, but is more concerned with locating general patterns of biblical imagery, often Pauline, used by Puritan preachers. See also Michael Clark, "'The Crucified Phrase': Sign and Desire in Puritan Semiology," *Early American Literature* 12 (1978–79); Robert Daly, *Puritan Poetics: The Word and the Flesh in Puritan Poetry* (Berkeley: University of California Press, 1978); Mason Lowance, *The Language of Canaan: Metaphor and Symbol in New England from the Puritans to the Transcendentalists* (Cambridge: Har-

vard University Press, 1980). Lowance makes disparate comments about Cotton and other Puritans' "eschatological and prophetic symbolism," approaching Cotton as a typologist. He, too, does not concern himself with how Cotton's metaphoric fragmentation is related to his use of the Perkins sermon form. David Leverenz, *The Language of Puritan Feeling* (New Brunswick, New Jersey: Rutgers University Press, 1980) offers very useful close readings of Puritan sermons but, again, is not interested in viewing them in terms of the Perkins model. More generally, see David D. Hall's important study, *The Faithful Shepherd: A History of the New England Ministry in the Seventeenth Century* (Chapel Hill, N.C.: University of North Carolina Press, 1972).

8. Perkins argues, "The supreme and absolute meanes of interpretation is the Scripture itself" (*Arte*, p. 651). He is paraphrasing Calvin's commentary on 2 Peter 1:20: "The Spirit who spoke by the Prophets is the only true interpreter of himself." Calvin is quoted in Forstman, *Word and Spirit*, p. 77. John Cotton, Perkins's erstwhile follower, takes the question of interpretation to its next logical conclusion. If Scripture offers its own interpretation of itself, then "ye shall not add unto the Word (or things) which I commanded unto you . . . we are forbidden to add ought to the word written." *Some Treasure Fetched out of Rubbish* (London, 1660), composed 1618, p. 11.

9. While Puritans would never argue that preaching could cause grace, they emphatically stressed its importance as the divinely prescribed occasion for the recognition of one's justification. As Everett Emerson notes, they frequently quoted 2 Tim. 4:2: "Preach the word"; and Rom. 10:17: "Faith cometh by hearing." But while Cotton himself argues "there is a mighty power in the holy scriptures to supply the faith of God's people" (*Christ the Fountaine* [London, 1651], preached 1624–32, pp. 198–99), he also believes that the Spirit moves through the elect preacher as well as through the Word: "Such an one believeth what he teacheth, not by an human credulity from his author, but by a divine faith from the Word, and because he believeth, he therefore speaketh, and speaking from faith in his own heart, he speaketh more powerfully unto the begetting of strength and faith in the hearer" (prefatory epistle to John Hildersham, *Lectures upon the Fourth of John* [London, 1629]. The Spirit moves through the elect preacher, through the words he speaks (from Scripture) and from thence into the hearts of elect hearers. Calvin, too, notes that "the Spirit uses the ministry of men whom he employs as his delegates," but he does so "not to transfer his right and honour to them, but only that he may himself do his work by their lips" (*Institutes*, vol. 4, chap. 3, par. 1, quoted in Forstman, *Word and Spirit*, p. 78). Neither minister nor Scripture can cause grace, but in combination they can provide the occasion of its coming. Assured hearers somehow receive the Spirit which speaks through the "letter" of Scripture. While unassured people do not receive the Spirit, both they and the

chosen can still be guided to knowledge about the Bible's history and its laws for moral conduct. Whether listeners are elect or non-elect, they are equally commanded to participate in the sharing of the "milke" of elect preaching.

10. Perkins, *Arte*, pp. 665–68.

11. Perkins, *Arte*, p. 649.

12. I am, of course, not arguing that Perkins's or any English Puritan's polemic on behalf of the "literal" or "natural" sense in any way overthrew figural interpretation. Perkins's (and Calvin's) adherence to the "analogie of faith" puts him right back into the realm of allegorical, moral, and anagogical readings. Bercovitch, Lowance, Daly, and others have shown the Puritans' own distinctive ways of reading figures and types, biblical and natural. In fact, a large section of Perkins's *Arte* is given over to how to interpret and to use the "figures." What is interesting here, however, is that Perkins advocates a method—finding the circumstances, collating them, and applying the results to the "analogie"—which conceals its own status as an interpretive theory.

13. Perkins, *Arte*, p. 651.

14. Perkins, *Arte*, p. 651.

15. Perkins, *Arte*, p. 654.

16. Perkins, *Arte*, pp. 656–57.

17. R. T. Kendall, *Calvin and English Calvinism to 1649* (Oxford and New York: Oxford University Press, 1979), pp. 61–62.

18. Kendall, *Calvin and English Calvinism*, p. 5.

19. Perkins, *Arte*, p. 673. See also Emerson, *John Cotton*, pp. 36–37 (Emerson argues elsewhere that the "uses" section was added by John Udall, although it, too, is implicit in Perkins's form); Habegger, "Preparing the Soul for Christ," pp. 342–45; Levy, *Preaching*, pp. 81–97; Miller, *The New England Mind: The Seventeenth Century*, esp. chapters 10, 11, and 12 dealing with Puritan rhetoric. See also William Haller, *The Rise of Puritanism* (New York: Harper and Brothers, 1957), pp. 128–72; Mitchell, *English Pulpit Oratory;* and Wilbur Samuel Howell, *Logic and Rhetoric in England, 1500–1700* (Princeton: Princeton University Press, 1956).

20. Norton, *Abel Being Dead*, p. 12. Also quoted in Kendall, p. 111.

21. Ziff, *Career of John Cotton*, pp. 48–49. As Ziff notes, Cotton saw the difference between the "lilies" and "thornes," but did not separate them entirely. Still, his church was composed of a congregation within a congregation.

22. Although it is not the focus of this essay to consider the Cotton/Williams debate, it is interesting to point out that here we find yet another doubleness in Cotton. On the one hand, Cotton could preach in a manner that seemed to many to be overly directed towards elect experience. On the other hand, even in sermons he was preaching at the onset of the Antinomian Controversy, he seeks to distinguish

between the varying types of listeners within a congregation (sheep and goats, tares and wheat). Finally, in the end, he will repudiate Roger Williams precisely because Williams believed that the tares and wheat should be entirely separated on this earth. Williams's approach, as Emerson points out, was too pure even for Cotton. (See *The New Covenant; or, A Treatise unfolding the order and manner of the giving and receiving of the covenant of Grace to the Elect* [London, 1654], pp. 44–47, 64–69.) These sermons were apparently preached in 1636. See the selections from this series in *The Puritans*, ed. Perry Miller and Thomas Johnson, 2 vols. (New York: Harper and Row, 1963), 1:314–16.

For Cotton, a recognition of the unassured or even the hypocritical souls within a congregation did not mean that the whole attempt to found "pure" congregational churches should be abandoned. He was not a "seeker" who by default would encourage religious toleration. His sermons about the sheep and the goats were his effort to suggest that one can—as far as is humanly possible—distinguish between the "saints" and those who are not elect. Scripture itself, he argues, provides the grounds and the means for making covenants and forming churches composed of the professed elect. In these cases we see him using Scripture for what it offers as historical and legal information about the covenant with Abraham. This is information which all reasonable people—even if they are unassured—should be able to understand. As such, a certain kind of orthodoxy in the founding and upholding of churches could be determined even in a mixed and fallen word. The churches would therefore be justified in casting out members who refused to accept clear scriptural truths "on fundamental points of religious doctrine and worship" (Emerson, *John Cotton*, p. 138). See Emerson's entire discussion, pp. 133–40; see also Ziff, *Career of John Cotton*, pp. 85–95, 211–23.

For the analyst of Cotton's sermon style, what becomes interesting is how he attempts to allow for the elect individual's experience of the mysterious and the transcendent within the frame of an "orthodox" theology, an "orthodox" (in his terms) church polity, and the orthodox sermon structure laid out by William Perkins. Cotton's disagreements with Williams were occurring at about the same time he was preaching some of his own more problematic sermons, in 1635 and 1636. Cotton, as the champion of Congregational orthodoxy against Williams, clearly did not see the implications of some of the truths the other ministers accused him of "darkly" delivering.

23. See, for example, Lewalski, p. 16.

24. See Hall, *The Antinomian Controversy*, p. 52.

25. *Encyclopedia of Religion and Ethics*, ed. James Hastings (New York: Charles Scribner's Sons, 1981), 7:615.

26. John Cotton, *A Briefe Exposition . . . of Ecclesiastes* (London, 1654), p. 16.

27. Hastings, *Encyclopedia of Religion and Ethics*, 11:182–83. The quote is from the *Westminster Confession* of 1647. See also Cotton's own response to the elders'

request for his definition of sanctification: "I meane by Christian sanctification the fruit of the Spirit of Christ dwelling in true Beleevers, working and acting in us, both infused Habits, and actions of Holinesse, contrary to all vitious Habits and actions of corrupt Nature. And yet I doe not (therefore) meane, that the Image of God in Adam renewed in us (and no more then so) is our Sanctification: our Sanctification in Christ hath in it this more; Faith in the righteousness of Christ and Repentance from dead works (& that which is the Root of (both) The indwelling Power of the Spirit to act and keep Holinesse in us all, which Adam wanted" (Hall, *The Antinomian Controversy*, p. 51).

28. John Cotton, *A Treatise of the Covenant of Grace* (London, 1659), quoted in Kendall, *English Calvinism*, p. 172.

29. Cotton by no means saw the moment of justification as ever reaching a set completion; he argues that "justification is a Perennius actus, a perpetual act of God" which is never interrupted. Saints keep coming to "drink" of Christ, who is their justification, yet they do not see such "coming" in any way involving steps which will earn them grace. Their very ability to come to him paradoxically assures them that they already have him. A comment which Cotton makes to the elders regarding justification sounds very much like—although more logically explained than—a famous earlier passage from *The Way of Life* (London, 1641), preached 1624, in which the saint "wades" in grace. Kendall would argue that sermons written prior to Cotton's coming to America demonstrate Cotton's clear voluntarist leanings. But here in America in 1636, Cotton uses the same scriptural example to explain his ideas of justification. Cotton was clearly preaching similar views in England before he came to America—and these views do not always display a clear-cut, unequivocal voluntarism. In both the English sermon and in the explanation offered to the elders, Cotton does not argue that the saint who has the ability to wade or to renew himself is performing set steps which gain him grace; he is, rather, enacting his perpetual justification. In America Cotton uses the same passage from John 7:37–39 to explain his notion of the real relation of justification to sanctification: "Out of his belly shall flow rivers"—i.e., spirit. "He doth not send men that are thirsty to consider of their thirst, what a gracious disposition it is; and to drink well of their thirsting till they be filled with it, and such satisfaction out of it: No, no but let them come (saith he) to me, (even unto me) and drink; not drink their consolation out of their thirst, but out of Christ. And the same word that calleth them to Christ giveth them in a reserved measure the Spirit of faith, by which they do come to Christ, and do drink to the satisfying of their souls in the full Assurance of his grace and righteousness freely given to them of God. So that when men come to be first thus qualified (as poor and mourning and hungry) it is from the revelation of free grace in Christ, and when they come to be first satisfied with Christ and with the assurance of his love; it is not from their good conditions or qualifications but from the same free promise of Grace, bringing them again to

come to Christ and to drink again of him and of his free grace more abundantly"
Hall, p. 90.

The similarity between this passage and the passage from *The Way of Life* led me
to use the latter as a good example of Cotton's preaching practice, not only in
England, but in America, too. Anne Hutchinson makes the same claim about the
similarities between his preaching in both places, and Cotton himself argues that
he has preached the same "publickly" in both Bostons. Thus, while earlier sermon
series may include more voluntarist language, they are also often qualified.

30. See Hall, *The Antinomian Controversy*, chap. 5.

31. Patricia Caldwell, "The Antinomian Language Controversy," *Harvard Theological Review* 69 (1979), p. 354. While Caldwell does not explicitly address the
issue of structure, her discussion of the struggle between Cotton and the elders to
define the proper order of the salvation process has structural implications.

32. Hall, *The Antinomian Controversy*, p. 26.

33. Hall, *The Antinomian Controversy*, p. 30.

34. Calvin, *Institutes*, vol. 1, chap. 9, par. 3, quoted in Forstman, *Word and
Spirit*, p. 18.

35. Calvin, *Institutes*, vol. 3, chap. 2, par. 14, quoted in Forstman, *Word and
Spirit*, p. 101.

36. Habegger, "Preparing the Soul for Christ," p. 350.

37. In his bibliography to *John Cotton*, Everett Emerson attempts to date both
the composition/delivery date and the publication date of Cotton's works. His findings largely concur with those of Ziff. *God's Mercie Mix'd with His Justice* was
probably composed in 1622. It was published in London, 1641. When applicable,
other dates are noted in the body of the essay as date of publication followed by
date of composition.

38. See Cotton, *God's Mercie*, pp. 3, 6, 20.

39. See, for example, Emerson, *John Cotton*, p. 36 and Habegger, "Preparing
the Soul for Christ," pp. 352–53.

40. Cotton, *God's Mercie*, p. 1.

41. Cotton, *God's Mercie*, p. 3.

42. Cotton, *God's Mercie*, p. 4.

43. Cotton, *God's Mercie*, pp. 7–8.

44. Cotton, *God's Mercie*, pp. 8–9. See also Emerson, *John Cotton*, p. 36.

45. Cotton, *God's Mercie*, p. 13.

46. John Cotton, *The Way of Life* (London, 1641), composed 1624–32, p. 96.

47. Cotton, *Way of Life*, p. 97.

48. Cotton, *Way of Life*, pp. 97–98.

49. Cotton, *Way of Life*, pp. 102–3.

50. See Perry Miller and Thomas Johnson, *The Puritans*, 1:318.

51. Cotton, *Way of Life*, pp. 104–5, repr. in *The Puritans*, 1:318.

52. Ezek. 47:3–5 and passim.

53. Cotton, *Way of Life*, p. 107.

54. Cotton, *Way of Life*, p. 107.

55. Norman Grabo, "John Cotton's Aesthetic: A Sketch," *Early American Literature* 1–3 (1968): 4–10. Cotton's interest and distrust in imagery is also explored in the early treatise, *Some Treasure Fetched out of Rubbish* (London, 1660), composed 1618. Here, like most Puritans, Cotton rejects the use of man-made signs, verbal or visual, yet also appears very interested in the possibility of using "signs" found in Scripture. They are God-given and therefore permissible. See Grabo, "John Cotton's Aesthetic," pp. 8–10.

56. John Cotton, *Singing of Psalms a Gospel Ordinance* (London, 1647), p. 5.

57. Cotton, *Singing of Psalms*, p. 56.

58. Habegger is particularly interested in tracing the differences between Hooker's focus on his preparational system and Cotton's focus on his texts ("Preparing the Soul for Christ," p. 345). Hooker's interest, as Cotton Mather early noted, "lay in the Points of the most Practical Religion." Not surprisingly, then, Mather reports his greatness with a "use," for the "uses" exhort believers to conduct. In the "uses" Hooker threatens his listeners with heaven's terrors, but comforts them with the possibility that they may prepare themselves to escape such a fate. Cotton, while retaining the "uses" in his sermon structure, does not implement them in the same way as Hooker. Scholars have noted not Cotton's threats or contentiousness, but his "gentleness." Habegger argues that Hooker breaks down the Perkins sermon form because he makes it conform to a preparational system; I am arguing that the possibility for doing just that is implicit in the form itself, with its movement from the doctrines to their application in the world of conduct. I argue that Cotton also undermined the form, although in a far subtler way and for different ends.

59. Paul Alpers, *The Poetry of the Faerie Queene* (Princeton: Princeton University Press, 1967). Alpers has argued that partial readings of *The Faerie Queene* have occurred because critics have failed to take account of the different kinds of response Spenser wishes to evoke in his reader. Response has been limited to the reader's understanding of and engagement in the overall narrative of the poem rather than in the actual experience of the poetry of the individual stanzas. Alpers argues that there are techniques Spenser uses within the lines of the stanzas which call for a very different response than one which simply translates the characters of the overarching narrative into their allegorical equivalents. Alpers' account becomes useful in discussing Cotton's own digressive or "diffuse" characteristics. Within the particular sections of the Perkins sermon model, Cotton is calling for a response different in kind from that which the overall structure of the sermon

seems to demand. Alpers maintains that "an episode in *The Faerie Queene* . . . is best described as a developing psychological experience within the reader, rather than as an action to be observed by him" (p. 14). Thus Spenser's visual effects are not to be understood as literal descriptions of persons or landscapes. They have a "psychological" rather than a "real visual" impact (p. 10). John Cotton, I would argue, comes close to using "collation" and "circumstances" within the doctrine and reasons sections of the sermon in a manner which likewise encourages a psychological response to a particular kind of descriptive language.

60. Grabo, "John Cotton's Aesthetic," p. 7.

61. Sharon Cameron, *Lyric Time* (Baltimore: John Hopkins Press, 1979), p. 15.

62. Hall, *The Antinomian Controversy*, p. 247.

63. See especially Miller, *The New England Mind, The Seventeenth Century,* pp. 365–462, on the nature of the three interrelated covenants—individual, social, and church; see also Ziff, *The Career of John Cotton*, pp. 106–48. What is so curious about the situation with the Antinomians, of course, is that Cotton was such a strong supporter of the Congregational Church system and of the Massachusetts social/political theocracy, but at the same time could preach doctrine in a manner that, to the ministers and Winthrop, undermined the delicate balance among the covenants in favor of the "covenant of grace."

64. Kai Erikson, *Wayward Puritans: A Study in the Sociology of Deviance* (New York: John Wiley and Sons, Inc., 1966), pp. 67–107. Erikson argues persuasively that the polarization took place primarily because the goals of the community had changed; as the spirit of Puritan piety died down in the New World, the practical issue became how to form an ongoing community which would abide by certain rules for conduct. Edmund Morgan notes how John Winthrop wished the colony's laws to grow up situationally; he saw dangers involved in encoding them. It was the colonists themselves who demanded a codification of both their own and their rulers' "rights." See *The Puritan Dilemma: The Story of John Winthrop* (Boston: Little, Brown, 1958), esp. pp. 155–73.

65. Hall, *The Antinomian Controversy*, p. 119. The ministers, in turn, respond defensively to Cotton's first response to their questions to him: "Nor see wee, why you should conceive it needless to answer sith you say nothing privately, which you have not publickly preached, as neither Christ had. For though you speak nothing, yet others might publickly conceive you to be of this or that Opinion, which they father on you. And sundry things which you have publickly uttered, were darkly and doubtfully delivered; whereof as we have privately besought you to consider, so we desire to see them interpreted" (Hall, p. 62).

66. Erikson also points up both the ritual nature of the Hutchinson trials—her expulsion from the "tribe" and the fact that the trial itself manifested the search for a language by which the community could define itself and, in the process, define

its "deviants." He concludes that "in many ways the magistrate's decision to banish Mrs. Hutchinson was a substitute for the words they could not find. The verdict against her was a public statement about the new boundaries of Puritanism in Massachusetts Bay. For in passing sentence on Mrs. Hutchinson the magistrates were declaring in the only way they could that the historical stage she had come to represent was now past. No simpler language was available for the purpose" (Erikson, *Wayward Puritans*, p. 107).

67. Robert Middlekauf, "Piety and Intellect in Puritanism," *William and Mary Quarterly*, 3rd ser., vol. 22 (1965): 458.

2. Benjamin Colman and the Shaping of Balance

1. For varying discussions and interpretations of these changes and conflicts, see Perry Miller, *The New England Mind: From Colony to Province* (Cambridge: Harvard University Press, 1953) and Ziff, *Puritanism in America*. See also Christopher Reaske's excellent biographical and historical introduction in the facsimile of Ebenezer Turrell, *The Life and Character of the Reverend Benjamin Colman, D.D.* (Boston, 1749; reprint, Delmar, N.Y.: Scholars' Facsimiles and Reprints, 1972), pp. v–xxiii; Clayton H. Chapman, "Life and Influence of Reverend Benjamin Colman, D.D., 1673–1747" (Ph.D. diss., Boston University, 1948); Norman Fiering, "The First American Enlightenment: Tillotson, Leverett and Philosophical Anglicanism," *New England Quarterly* 54 (September 1981): 301–43. See also Fiering, *Moral Philosophy at Seventeenth-Century Harvard* (Chapel Hill, N.C.: University of North Carolina Press, 1980). For a more general study of the generation preceding Colman's and the similar though altered conflicts—cultural, psychological, and intellectual—undergone by it, see Emory Elliott's important study *Power and the Pulpit in Puritan New England* (Princeton: Princeton University Press, 1975).

2. See Fiering, "The First American Enlightenment," pp. 301–43.

3. See, for example, Robert Daly, *God's Altar: The World and the Flesh in Puritan Poetry* (Berkeley and Los Angeles: University of California Press, 1978). In contrast to past criticism, Daly argues that Puritans never totally "scorned" the use of language that appealed to the senses. After all, God had made the sensible world. On the other hand, the pleasure of sensuous imagery was never viewed as an end to be sought in itself. Such images expressed the "harmony" of the world or "figured forth, albeit imperfectly, the mind of its Creator" (p. 21) by shadowing forth correspondences between "worldly and divine things." Jonathan Edwards, as Alan Heimert points out, saw using images solely for pleasure, whether it was a visual or a rhythmic pleasure, as "false imaginations" that ran counter to the duty of a Christian to interpret his or her experience in the light of the "history of Redemp-

tion." See *Religion and the American Mind* (Cambridge: Harvard University Press, 1963), p. 145.

4. W. F. Mitchell, *English Pulpit Oratory*, p. 278.

5. Fiering, "The First American Enlightenment," p. 324.

6. Theodore Hornberger, "Colman and the Enlightenment," *New England Quarterly* 12 (June 1939): 227–40; see also James Jones, *The Shattered Synthesis* (New Haven: Yale University Press, 1973), pp. 90–103.

7. Perry Miller, *The New England Mind: From Colony to Province*, p. 270 and passim.

8. Miller, *From Colony to Province*, p. 270.

9. Benjamin Colman, "To the Reader," in *Practical Discourses on the Parable of the Ten Virgins* (London, 1707). Also quoted in Miller, *From Colony to Province*, p. 273.

10. Leverett as quoted in Miller, *From Colony to Province*, p. 269.

11. Benjamin Colman, *Practical Discourses on the Parable of the Ten Virgins*, 2d ed. (Boston, 1747), p. 1.

12. Colman, *Practical Discourses*, p. 55.

13. Colman, *Practical Discourses*, p. 61.

14. Colman, *Practical Discourses*, p. 57.

15. Colman, *Practical Discourses*, p. 71.

16. See Samuel Lothrop, *A History of the Church in Brattle Street* (Boston, 1851), pp. 21–28, in which the entire Manifesto of 1700 is reprinted.

17. Colman, *Practical Discourses*, p. 68.

18. Colman, *Practical Discourses*, p. 81.

19. Colman, *Practical Discourses*, p. 99.

20. Colman, *Practical Discourses*, pp. 86–93. Note the number of excuses Colman offers his hypocrite.

21. Colman, *Practical Discourses*, p. 94.

22. Colman, *Practical Discourses*, p. 106.

23. Colman, *Practical Discourses*, p. 115.

24. See Lothrop, *A History of the Church in Brattle Street*, pp. 21–28.

25. Increase Mather, *The Order of the Gospel* (Boston, 1700), pp. 47, 131, 117–36.

26. See Henry Stecher, *Elizabeth Singer Rowe, The Poetess of Frome* (Bern: Herbert Lang, 1973), pp. 72–79.

27. Samuel Johnson quoted in Stecher, *Elizabeth Singer Rowe*, p. 103. Also quoted in James Boswell, *The Life of Dr. Johnson* (London, 1946), 1:208. Discussed also in Ziff, *Puritanism in America*, p. 274 and passim.

28. Rowe as quoted in Stecher, *Elizabeth Singer Rowe*, p. 43.

29. Stecher, *Elizabeth Singer Rowe*, p. 100.

30. Isaac Watts, preface to *Elizabeth Singer Rowe, Devout Exercises of the Heart* (Norwich, 1808), pp. 47–48. First edition, Coventry, 1737.

31. Isaac Watts, preface to *Horae Lyricae* (London, 1854), p. lxxxiv. First edition, London, 1706.

32. Watts, *Horae Lyricae*, p. xc.

33. Watts, *Horae Lyricae*, p. xcviii.

34. Watts, *Horae Lyricae*, p. xcviii.

35. Benjamin Colman, *Some of the glories of our Lord and Savior Jesus Christ exhibited in Twenty Sacramental Discourses* (Boston, 1728), p. 235.

36. Benjamin Colman, *Souls Flying to Jesus Christ pleasant and admirable to behold* (Boston, 1740), p. 11.

37. Colman, *Practical Discourses*, (London, 1707), p. 301.

38. See Colman, *Practical Discourses*, p. 2.

39. Benjamin Colman, *The Government and Improvement of Mirth* (Boston, 1707), p. 33.

40. Ebenezer Turrell, *Life and Character of the Reverend Benjamin Colman*, p. 169. See also Heimert, *Religion and the American Mind*, p. 225. Heimert notes that Colman used the Bible as "a source of metaphors with which to adorn his sermons."

41. Benjamin Colman, *Practical Discourses*, p. 327.

42. Daly, *God's Altar*, p. 21.

43. Heimert, *Religion and the American Mind*, p. 145.

44. Benjamin Colman and Samuel Cooper, preface to *The Character of Mr. Whitefield*, by Josiah Smith (Boston, 1740).

45. Benjamin Colman, "Introductory Letter," in *The Divining Marks of a Work of the Spirit of God*, by Jonathan Edwards (Boston, 1742).

46. See the Colman/Watts exchange on Whitefield in *Massachusetts Historical Society Proceedings* 29, 2d ser. (1895), pp. 314, 387. See also Benjamin Colman, "A Letter from the Reverend Dr. Colman of Boston to the Reverend Mr. —— of Lebanon upon Reading the Confession and Retraction of J. D.," (Boston, 1744).

47. Colman, *Practical Discourses*, pp. 70–71.

48. Colman, *Twenty Sacramental Discourses*, p. 50.

49. Colman, *Practical Discourses*, p. 11.

50. Colman, *Practical Discourses*, p. 290.

51. C. S. Lewis, *An Experiment in Criticism* (Cambridge: Cambridge University Press, 1961), chap. 3.

52. Mitchell, *English Pulpit Oratory*, p. 337.

53. Ziff, *Puritanism in America*, pp. 272–79.

54. Colman, *The Government and Improvement of Mirth*, p. 142.

55. Gary Nash, *The Urban Crucible: Social Change, Political Consciousness, and*

the Origins of the American Revolution (Cambridge: Harvard University Press, 1979).

56. [Benjamin Colman et al.?], *The Gospel Order Revived* (New York, 1700), pp. 5–7. The ascription of this work to Colman is explored by Thomas Holmes in *Increase Mather: A Bibliography* (Cambridge, Mass., 1931), 2:395.

57. Colman et al., *The Gospel Order Revived*, p. 12.

58. Miller, *From Colony to Province*, pp. 270–71.

59. Raymond Williams, *Keywords: A Vocabulary of Culture and Society* (New York and Oxford: Oxford University Press, 1976), pp. 235–38.

60. Miller, *From Colony to Province*, p. 270 and passim.

3. William Ellery Channing and the Shaping of Unity

1. Conrad Wright, *The Beginnings of Unitarianism in America* (Boston: Starr King Press, 1955), chap. 1.

2. Wright, *Beginnings of Unitarianism*. Wright also importantly notes the social bases of these religious cleavages. See p. 31 and passim.

3. For discussions of Unitarian scriptural exegesis, see especially Daniel Howe, *The Unitarian Conscience: Harvard Moral Philosophy, 1817–1837* (Cambridge: Harvard University Press, 1970); Lawrence Buell, *Literary Transcendentalism* (Ithaca: Cornell University Press, 1972); Philip Gura, *The Wisdom of Words* (Middletown, Conn.: Wesleyan University Press, 1981); Robinson, *Apostle of Culture*. For a more general study of exegetical arguments within and among varying denominations, see Jerry Wayne Brown, *The Rise of Biblical Criticism in America, 1800–1870: The New England Scholars* (Middletown, Conn.: Wesleyan University Press, 1969).

4. Howe, *The Unitarian Conscience*, p. 108.

5. William Henry Channing, *The Life of William Ellery Channing* (Boston: John Wilson and Son for the American Unitarian Association, 1904), pp. 222–23.

6. William Ellery Channing, *The Works of William Ellery Channing*, 8th ed., (Boston, 1848), 1:243.

7. See Howe, *The Unitarian Conscience*, chaps. 1 and 2; see also William Charvat, *The Origins of American Critical Thought 1810–1835* (Philadelphia: University of Pennsylvania Press, 1936), p. 35 and passim; Frederick Copleston, S. J., *A History of Philosophy* (Garden City, N.Y.: Image Books, 1964), vol. 5, *The British Philosophers*.

8. William Ellery Channing, *Remarks on the Reverend Dr. Worcester's Second Letter to Mr. Channing on American Unitarianism* (Boston, 1815), p. 23.

9. Channing, *Works*, 3:73.

10. It is interesting to note that the sense of a major division between listeners still exists, although Channing's division is more like that of Colman than that of Cotton.

11. Channing, *Works*, 4:189.

12. Channing, *Works*, 3:174.

13. Channing, *Works*, 3:176.

14. W. E. Channing, *Remarks on the Reverend Dr. Worcester's Second Letter*, p. 22. "I have stated once and again that the differences between Unitarians and Trinitarians lie more in sounds than in ideas; that a barbarous phraseology is the chief wall of partition among these classes of Christianity; and that would the Trinitarians tell us what they mean, their system would generally be found little else than an obscure form of Unitarian doctrine." See Andrew Delbanco's cogent analysis of this language controversy in *William Ellery Channing: An Essay on the Liberal Spirit in America* (Cambridge: Harvard University Press, 1981).

15. Channing, *Works*, 4:159.

16. Channing, *Works*, 4:197.

17. Channing, *Remarks on Dr. Worcester's Second Letter*, pp. 38–39.

18. Channing, *Works*, 4:48. The quotation is from "Christianity is a Rational Religion," but Channing is obviously referring to Unitarian Christianity.

19. Channing, *Works*, 3:171.

20. Channing, *Works*, 3:84.

21. Channing, *Works*, 4:36.

22. See Charvat, *Origins of American Critical Thought*, p. 44. Charvat notes that Blair's was "a textbook which half the educated English speaking world studied in its day and its day was astonishingly long. . . . By 1812 the volume had gone through twelve editions."

23. Hugh Blair, *Lectures on Rhetoric and Belles Lettres*, 4th ed. (London, 1790), 2:172.

24. Blair, *Lectures*, 2:304: "At the same time, it must be remembered, that all the Preacher's instructions are to be of the practical kind; and that persuasion must ever be his ultimate object. It is not to discuss some abstract point, that he ascends the Pulpit. It is not to illustrate some metaphysical truth, or to inform men of something which they never heard before; but it is to make them better men; it is to give them, at once, clear views, and persuasive impressions of religious truth."

25. Blair, *Lectures*, 2:308: "What I mean by Unity is, that there should be some one main point to which the whole strain of the sermon should refer."

26. Blair, *Lectures*, 2:370.

27. Blair, *Lectures*, 1:361: "Figures give us the pleasure of enjoying two objects presented together to our view without confusion, the principal idea which is the subject of the discourse, along with its accessory which gives it the figurative dress." See also 1:363: "An image that presents so much congruity between a moral and a sensible idea, serves like an argument from analogy, to enforce what the author asserts, and to induce belief."

28. W. H. Channing, *Life*, p. 307.

29. W. H. Channing, *Life*, p. 105.

30. W. H. Channing, *Life*, p. 106.

31. Mary Worden Edrich, "The Channing Rhetoric and 'Splendid Confusion,'" *Emerson Society Quarterly* 57 (1969): 5–12.

32. Channing, *Works*, 3:68–69.

33. Channing, *Works*, 3:69.

34. See Buell, *Literary Transcendentalism*, pp. 102–39.

35. I am not maintaining that Unitarians possessed doctrinal principles in an "orthodox" sense of the word, but that they did have tenets which involved notions of God's "unity," "consistency," and "harmony." Not only did such conceptions of Godhead call for a certain ethical response on the part of believers; I am arguing that they also called for a particular rhetoric and manner of structuring Unitarian sermons.

36. Blair, *Lectures*, 2:300.

37. William Ellery Channing, *Letter to the Rev. Samuel C. Thacher* (Boston, 1815), p. 15.

38. W. H. Channing, *Life*, p. 304.

39. W. H. Channing, *Life*, p. 186.

40. W. H. Channing, *Life*, p. 308.

41. W. H. Channing, *Life*, p. 140.

42. Blair, *Lectures*, 2:370.

43. Channing, *Works*, 3:7–8. The rest of the quotations from the sermons will be noted in the text as *W* (*Works*) followed by volume number and page.

44. Channing, *Works*, 3:140. In this ordination sermon, "The Demands of the Age on the Ministry," Channing not only calls for more eloquent preaching, he also speaks directly of the techniques and effects of poetry and prose fiction. He speaks against the "artificial" rhetoric and the "measured sentences" of past preaching, and praises the poet's ability to show the soul's "mysterious workings, borrowing from the whole outward creation fresh images and correspondences with which to illuminate the secrets of the world within us." The comment on the "heart-withering" philosophy is quoted in the *Life*, p. 276.

45. Delbanco, *William Ellery Channing*, pp. 161–62.

46. Delbanco, *William Ellery Channing*, p. 128 and passim.

4. Emerson, Coleridge, and the Shaping of Self-Evidence: Theory

1. See Buell, *Literary Transcendentalism*, pp. 23–54, and Robinson, *Apostle of Culture*, pp. 2–5, 7–68, for discussions of this "unfolding" of ideas implicit in Unitarian thinking. For a discussion of those Transcendentalists who remained within

the ministry, see William R. Hutchinson, *The Transcendentalist Ministers: Church Reform in the New England Renaissance* (New Haven: Yale University Press, 1959).

2. Ralph Waldo Emerson, *The Journals and Miscellaneous Notebooks of Ralph Waldo Emerson*, ed. Wm. Gilman et al. (Cambridge: Harvard University Press, 1960–), 4:363–64. Henceforth cited parenthetically in the text as *JMN* by volume and page.

3. Howe, *The Unitarian Conscience*. See especially chaps. 1 and 2.

4. Discussions of Unitarian pietism include Howe, *Unitarian Conscience*, pp. 151–66; Lawrence Buell, "The Unitarian Movement and the Art of Preaching in Nineteenth-Century America," *American Quarterly* 24 (1972): 178 and passim. See also Robinson, *Apostle of Culture*, pp. 7–29.

5. Cotton's response is in Hall, *The Antinomian Controversy*, p. 30.

6. For standard discussions see Jonathan Bishop, *Emerson on the Soul* (Cambridge: Harvard University Press, 1964); Sherman Paul, *Emerson's Angle of Vision* (Cambridge: Harvard University Press, 1952); Stephen Whicher, *Freedom and Fate* (Philadelphia: University of Pennsylvania Press, 1953). For more recent discussions see Quentin Anderson, *The Imperial Self* (New York: Knopf, 1971) and Joel Porte, *Representative Man* (Oxford and New York: Oxford University Press, 1979).

7. Vivian Hopkins, *Spires of Form: A Study of Emerson's Aesthetic Theory* (Cambridge: Harvard University Press, 1951), p. 166.

8. Michael J. Colacurcio, "A Better Mode of Evidence—The Transcendental Problem of Faith and Spirit," *ESQ* 54 (1969): 12–22.

9. Arthur McGiffert, ed., *Young Emerson Speaks* (Boston: Houghton Mifflin Co., 1938), p. 120. Hereafter cited parenthetically in the text as *YES* followed by page number.

10. See *Young Emerson Speaks*, p. 126. Following is the full quotation from Coleridge: "Was it an appropriate mean to a necessary end? Has it been attested by lovers of truth? Has it been believed by lovers of wisdom? Do we see throughout all nature the occasional intervention of particular agencies in countercheck of universal laws? (And of what other definition is a miracle susceptible?) These are the questions and if to these our answers must be affirmative, then we too will acquiesce in the traditions of humanity, and yielding as to a high interest of our own being, will discipline ourselves to the reverential and kindly faith that the guides and teachers of mankind were the hands of power no less than the voices of inspiration; and little anxious concerning the particular forms and circumstances of each manifestation, we will give an historic credence to the historic fact that men sent by God have come with signs and wonders on the earth."

11. The relationship of both Unitarians and Trinitarians to Coleridge has been recently treated by Gura, *The Wisdom of Words*. Gura also places this interest in the context of religious disputes over the nature of biblical exegesis. See also John J.

Duffy, ed., *Coleridge's American Disciples: The Selected Correspondence of James Marsh* (Amherst: University of Massachusetts Press, 1973); for a theoretical discussion of Marsh in context, see Peter Carafiol, *Transcendent Reason: James Marsh and the Forms of Romantic Thought* (Tallahassee: University Presses of Florida, 1982). For a related, but very different, approach to the Emerson/Coleridge relationship, see Barry Wood, "The Growth of the Soul: Coleridge's Dialectical Method and the Strategy of Emerson's Nature," *PMLA*, 91, no. 3 (1976): 385–97.

12. Samuel Taylor Coleridge, *The Collected Works of Samuel Taylor Coleridge*, ed. Barbara Rooke et al. (Princeton: Princeton University Press, 1969), 1:314 and passim.

13. Coleridge, *Collected Works*, 1:315.

14. Coleridge, *Collected Works*, 1:317.

15. Coleridge, *Collected Works*, 1:154.

16. Coleridge, *Collected Works*, 1:156.

17. Coleridge, *Collected Works*, 1:157.

18. Coleridge, *Collected Works*, 1:478–81. See also his analogous discussion of botany, 1:470–71.

19. Coleridge, *Collected Works*, 1:451.

20. Coleridge, *Collected Works*, 1:449.

21. Coleridge, *Collected Works*, 1:453.

22. Coleridge, *Collected Works*, 1:457.

23. Coleridge, *Collected Works*, 1:457.

24. Coleridge, *Collected Works*, 1:459.

25. Coleridge, *Collected Works*, 1:464.

26. Coleridge, *Collected Works*, 1:451.

27. Coleridge, *Collected Works*, 1:454.

28. Coleridge, *Collected Works*, 1:455.

29. Coleridge, *Collected Works*, 1:524.

30. Emerson, *Journals and Miscellaneous Notebooks*, pp. 160–61. Emerson calls Channing's language "a transparent medium conveying with the utmost distinctness, the pictures in his mind, to the minds of his hearers."

31. For a fine discussion of "The Christian Minister" that also deals with Emerson's obsession with eloquence, see Robinson, *Apostle of Culture*, pp. 40–44. Robinson, too, is concerned with Emerson's desire to make what is most personal most universal. While I am interested in Emerson's paeons to the experience of preaching for speaker and hearers—"It is like the breath of the Almighty moving on the deep"—I am more directly concerned with his ideas about the shape this "breath" should take and with how this "shape" is related to a notion of audience. See also Gay Wilson Allen's discussion of this sermon in *Waldo Emerson* (New York: Penguin Books, 1982) pp. 133–37.

5. Emerson and the Shaping of Self-Evidence: Practice

1. See Emerson, *Journals and Miscellaneous Notebooks* 5:51. Hereafter cited parenthetically in the text as *JMN* followed by volume number and page.

2. See especially Richard P. Adams, "Emerson and the Organic Metaphor," *PMLA* 59 (1954): 117–30.

3. For varying discussions of Emerson's conceptual and stylistic debts to the Unitarians, see Howe, *The Unitarian Conscience;* Gura, *The Wisdom of Words;* and Robinson, *Apostel of Culture.* See especially Buell, *Literary Transcendentalism* and "The Unitarian Movement and the Art of Preaching in Nineteenth-Century America." Let me take the opportunity here to note wherein my discussion is related to or differs from that of these scholars and others. In *Literary Transcendentalism* and "The Unitarian Movement," Buell traces the history and development of the Unitarian sermon as an increasingly "literary" genre. As I do, but in a slightly different context, he argues that the Unitarians' dearth of doctrine led them not simply to focus more on exhortation than on doctrine, but also to put a far greater degree of emphasis on their manner of preaching. He also notes the changes in subject, in form, and in scriptural usage occurring generally in Unitarian preaching. Buell is not as concerned as I am, however, with relating these changes to the particular conflation of rhetoric and theology that I find taking place in Channing and which I then see both used and challenged by Emerson. Furthermore, although he notes the Unitarians' desire to please their "real" audiences (in order, at times, to retain them), Buell is not directly concerned with the image of audience projected in their sermon structure. More specifically, my focus in the Emerson chapters of this study is not on the Unitarian background alone. I also deal with Emerson's use of Coleridge (among others) as a means of helping to reconcile questions about the relation of "self-evident" faith, preaching form, and audience to which his Unitarian training could not (according to him) adequately respond. Buell has also written an earlier essay, "Reading Emerson for the Structure: The Coherence of the Essays," *Quarterly Journal of Speech* 58 (1972): 58–69. Although offering very useful close readings of the essays, he does not relate them to the Unitarian background in the way he does in the later book and essay on Unitarian preaching. In this article he also notes in passing that Emerson's sermons are "plain . . . sometimes to the point of formula." David Robinson deals more specifically with Emerson as preacher. He does so, however, with a specific eye to Emerson's desire to express the Unitarian-derived notion of "self-culture" rather than with a concern for Emerson's specifically rhetorical/theological notions as they are expressed in his sermon structures. He shares my focus on Emerson's desire to include his audience in his preaching. As my analysis of "The Genuine Man" demonstrates, however, our means of discussing this inclusion are somewhat different. Sheldon Liebman, in "The Development of

Emerson's Theory of Rhetoric, 1821–1836," *American Literature* 41 (1969): 178–206, has been more directly concerned with Emerson's rhetoric, particularly in the Harvard essays and lectures, but he, too, has overlooked the sermons. Unlike Buell, he has neglected to relate Emerson's development and transformation to his Unitarianism. Liebman treats Emerson's use and repudiation of Blair, but not in the religious and critical context analyzed here. Wesley Mott considers the Puritan underpinnings of Emerson's sermons in "Emerson and Antinomianism: The Legacy of the Sermons," *American Literature* 50 (1978): 369–97: "In all matters except literal church polity Transcendentalism reconstructed the Puritan worldview as it was concerned with the nature of the Spirit, human faculties and affections, moral conduct and national mission" (p. 396). Mott is not interested in seeing how these issues are played out in Emerson's theories and practice of preaching, however. One could also argue with his tendency to align Emerson so neatly with the "preparationist" camp. I would argue, as this chapter indeed suggests, that Emerson is in many ways closer to John Cotton than he is to Thomas Hooker. Important as it is, Mott's essay also loses some of the richness of the studies of Buell and Robinson because he fails to consider these "Puritan" issues within Emerson's specifically Unitarian context. More satisfactory, because directed more broadly to the issue of "conversion" itself, and to the changes Emerson undergoes in relation to this concept is J. A. Ward's " 'The Educated Will': Notes on the Conversion Process," *English Literary History* 34 (1967): 495–517. Slightly closer to my approach—philosophically and theoretically, if not historically—are David M. Wyatt's "Spelling Time: The Reader in Emerson's 'Circles,' " *American Literature* 48, no. 2 (1976): 140–51 and Roland F. Lee's "Emerson through Kierkegaard: Toward a Definition of Emerson's Theory of Communication," *English Literary History* 24, no. 3 (1957): 229–40. Using contemporary theorists Michel Foucault and Harold Bloom, Wyatt argues that "Circles" enacts a patterning of "spiralling and staying" which both discusses and enacts a desire for stability and continuity coupled with a need for freedom and expansion. It thus rests only to "de-center" or "re-center" itself. Wyatt also argues for the central position played by the reader in helping the writer to "complete" this complex and continuous act of destabilization and recentering. Clearly, however, he does not view Emerson's use of such strategies within a larger religious and cultural matrix. Likewise, Lee argues for Emerson's interest in communicating the experience of "faith" to his readers, rather than imposing it on them. He, too, however, does not place his considerations within Emerson's context as a preacher. His comments on the means by which Emerson includes his readers within the experience of faith are also vague and need expansion and clarification particularly with reference to strategies used by Emerson in the sermons. For an excellent discussion of general romantic attitudes towards the problem of acknowledging and incorporating an audience into the work of art, see Morris Eaves, "Romantic Expressive Theory and Blake's Idea of the Audience," *PMLA* 95 (1980): 784–801.

4. See F. O. Matthiessen, *American Renaissance* (Oxford and New York: Oxford University Press, 1972), pp. 17–24. Matthiessen connects Emerson more broadly to an American oratorical tradition and specifically notes his attitudes towards oratory occurring after 1836. I am instead more interested in Emerson's comments and his own practice (in the sermon) before 1836.

5. See Buell, *Literary Transcendentalism*, chaps. 1 and 4; and see "The Unitarian Movement," p. 167 and passim.

6. Buell, "The Unitarian Movement," p. 181.

7. Miller, *From Colony to Province*, p. 404.

8. Buell, "The Unitarian Movement," p. 185.

9. Adams, "Emerson and the Organic Metaphor," p. 121.

10. Compare this beginning to that of the address: "In this refulgent summer, it has been a luxury to draw the breath of life. The grass grows, the buds burst, the meadow is spotted with fire and gold in the tint of flowers." See *Nature, Addresses, and Lectures*, ed. Robert Spiller and Alfred Ferguson (Cambridge: Harvard University Press, 1971), 1:76.

11. Adams, "Emerson and the Organic Metaphor," p. 126.

12. Ralph Waldo Emerson, "Faith and Works," bMs Am 1280.215 (48), Houghton Library, Harvard University.

13. Emerson, "Faith and Works."

14. Emerson, "Faith and Works."

15. See Robinson, *Apostle of Culture*, pp. 60–68.

Coda

1. See Allen, *Waldo Emerson*, p. 177, and David Robinson, *Apostle of Culture*, p. 8.

2. Allen, *Waldo Emerson*, p. 192.

3. I am not discounting Channing's obvious turn (in the 1830s) against the varying forms of authority that upheld the slave interests. I *am* arguing that this turn does not belie his intellectual, emotional, and rhetorical commitment to the need for stabilizing external forms.

4. Quoted in Perry Miller, *The Transcendentalists: An Anthology* (Cambridge: Harvard University Press, 1950), pp. 197–98.

5. See note 22 to chapter 1. See also Irwin Polishook, "Roger Williams, John Cotton, and Religious Freedom," in *Roger Williams, John Cotton, and Religious Freedom: A Controversy in New and Old England* (Englewood Cliffs, New Jersey:

Prentice-Hall, Inc., 1967), pp. 1–35, and Larzer Ziff, ed., *John Cotton on the Churches of New England* (Cambridge: Harvard University Press, 1968).

6. See S. T. Coleridge, *Collected Works*, 1:196.

7. See especially Perry Miller, "Emersonian Genius and the American Democracy," in *Nature's Nation* (Cambridge: Harvard University Press, 1967), pp. 163–74. Miller traces the early inner debate in Emerson between his Brahmin Federalism and his scorn for the Jacksonians, and his transcendental interest in the free non-class-bound expression of the individual genius. Miller finds these strands reconciled only by the time Emerson writes *Representative Men*.

8. See Alexis de Tocqueville, *Democracy in America*, 2 vols. (New York: Vintage Books, 1945), 1:105–6.

9. See Tocqueville, *Democracy in America*, 1:259 and passim, for his discussion of democratic "mediocrity." See also Marvin Meyers, *The Jacksonian Persuasion* (Stanford: Stanford University Press, 1968), p. 39 for a discussion of Tocqueville's views of the "double potentiality of the democratic situation: toward radical independence: toward submergence in the brotherhood."

10. Tocqueville, *Democracy in America*, 2:271. Quoted in Meyers, *Jacksonian Persuasion*, p. 43.

11. For a recent discussion of Emerson's relation to Jacksonian America, see Amy S. Lang, "'The Age of the First Person Singular': Emerson and Antinomianism," *ESQ* 29 (1983): 171–83. Lang, too, is interested in the cultural implications of Emerson's theories, but approaches them from a conceptual rather than a formal angle.

12. Nathaniel Hawthorne, *The Centenary Edition of the Works of Nathaniel Hawthorne*, ed. William Charvat et al. (Columbus: Ohio State University Press, 1962–80), 1:243–44.

13. Hawthorne, *Works*, 1:243.

14. Hawthorne, *Works*, 1:243.

15. Hawthorne, *Works*, 1:250. "Each felt the impulse in himself, and, in the same breath, caught it from his neighbour."

16. Hawthorne, *Works*, 1:246–7. See also *Works*, 1:238: "His was the profession [the ministry], at that era, in which intellectual ability displayed itself far more than in political life; for—leaving a higher motive out of the question—it offered inducements powerful enough, in the almost worshipping respect of the community, to win the most aspiring ambition to its service. Even political power—as in the case of Increase Mather—was within the grasp of the successful priest."

17. The phrase is from Meyers in *The Jacksonian Persuasion*, p. 39.

18. Hawthorne, *Works*, 1:259.

19. See Herman Melville, "Hawthorne and His Mosses," in *The Norton Anthology of American Literature* (New York: Norton, 1979), 1:2056–70.

Index